The Corinthian War
395–387 BC

The Corinthian War 395–387 BC

The Twilight of Sparta's Empire

Jeffrey A. Smith

Pen & Sword
MILITARY

First published in Great Britain in 2024 by
Pen & Sword Military
An imprint of Pen & Sword Books Limited
Yorkshire – Philadelphia

Copyright © Jeffrey A. Smith 2024

ISBN 978 1 39907 219 9

The right of Jeffrey A. Smith to be identified as
Author of this Work has been asserted by him in accordance
with the Copyright, Designs and Patents Act 1988.

A CIP catalogue record for this book is
available from the British Library

All rights reserved. No part of this book may be reproduced or
transmitted in any form or by any means, electronic or mechanical
including photocopying, recording or by any information storage and
retrieval system, without permission from the Publisher in writing.

Typeset by Mac Style
Printed in the UK by CPI Group (UK) Ltd, Croydon, CR0 4YY.

Pen & Sword Books Limited incorporates the imprints of After
the Battle, Atlas, Archaeology, Aviation, Discovery, Family History,
Fiction, History, Maritime, Military, Military Classics, Politics,
Select, Transport, True Crime, Air World, Frontline Publishing, Leo
Cooper, Remember When, Seaforth Publishing, The Praetorian Press,
Wharncliffe Local History, Wharncliffe Transport, Wharncliffe True
Crime and White Owl.

For a complete list of Pen & Sword titles please contact

PEN & SWORD BOOKS LIMITED
47 Church Street, Barnsley, South Yorkshire, S70 2AS, England
E-mail: enquiries@pen-and-sword.co.uk
Website: www.pen-and-sword.co.uk
or
PEN AND SWORD BOOKS
1950 Lawrence Rd, Havertown, PA 19083, USA
E-mail: uspen-and-sword@casematepublishers.com
Website: www.penandswordbooks.com

For Carole Marr

Contents

Chronology		vii
Glossary		xiv
Introduction		xvi
Chapter 1	Inheritance of Empire	1
Chapter 2	Thirty Reasons to Despise Sparta	16
Chapter 3	The Anti-Spartan Confederacy	29
Chapter 4	Dawn of War: The Battle of Haliartus	43
Chapter 5	The Bloody Year 394	56
Chapter 6	Disaster at Cnidus	67
Chapter 7	A Costly Victory at Coronea	77
Chapter 8	The Reconstruction of Athens	86
Chapter 9	Lechaeum: A Final Athenian Victory	102
Chapter 10	Piraeus Burning	118
Chapter 11	The King's Peace or the Peace of Antalcidas?	129
Conclusion		137
Character List		144
Notes		147
Bibliography		160
Index		163

Chronology

404	Sparta and its Peloponnesian League defeat Athens in the Peloponnesian War. Lysander begins to install decarchies and harmosts across Asia Minor. Lysander and the Spartans install the Thirty Tyrants in Athens.
403	Thrasybulus overthrows the Thirty Tyrants and restores Athenian democracy.
401	Sparta's War on Elis. The Persian governor Cyrus the Younger leads an unsuccessful coup against his brother, Artaxerxes II.
399	Agesilaus II becomes the Spartan king. The Conspiracy of Cinadon.
396	Agesilaus' invasion of Asia Minor begins. Agesilaus and Lysander compete for influence.
395	The Corinthian War formally begins. Sparta surprisingly loses the Battle of Haliartus. Lysander is killed in combat and the Spartan king Pausanias is exiled.
394	Sparta wins the Battle of Nemea outside of Corinth. The Battle of Cnidus and the destruction of the Spartan navy. Agesilaus II and the Spartans win a costly victory in the Battle of Coronea.
393	Conon triumphantly returns to Athens and begins to rebuild Athenian naval power.
392	Antalcidas and the Spartans hold unsuccessful peace talks with the Persians.
391	*Assemblywomen* by Aristophanes debuts in the Dionysia in Athens.
390	Iphicrates and the Athenians destroy a Spartan regiment at the Battle of Lechaeum.
388	*Plutus* by Aristophanes debuts in Athens. Teleutias and the Spartan navy raid the Piraeus harbour in Athens. Thrasybulus leads a successful naval campaign for Athens, but is soon assassinated.

387 The King's Peace is brokered by Antalcidas. The Corinthian War ends.
378 The Theban–Spartan War begins.
362 Sparta is defeated at the Battle of Leuctra.
     The Spartan Empire ends.

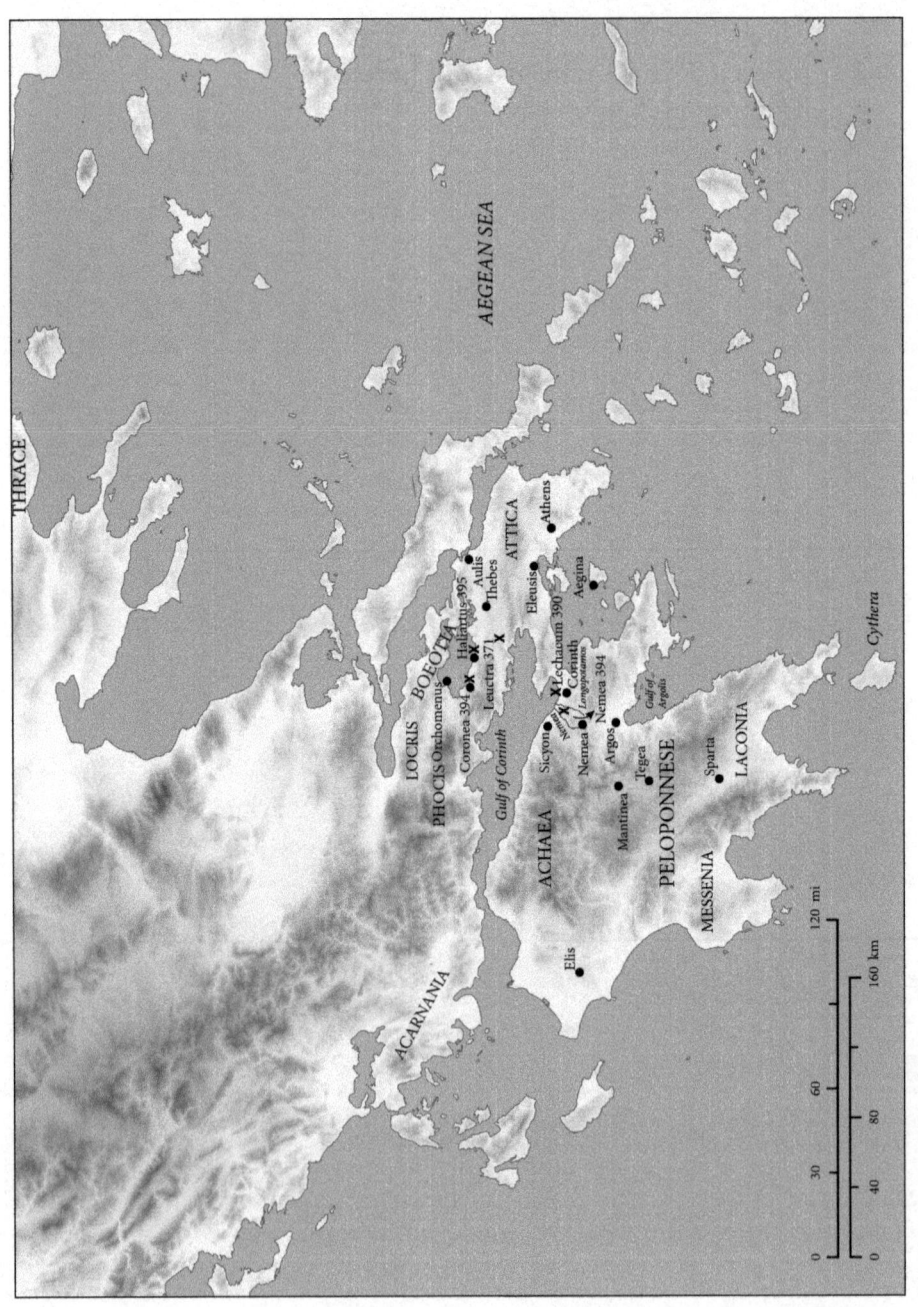

The Greek Mainland, 395 BC.

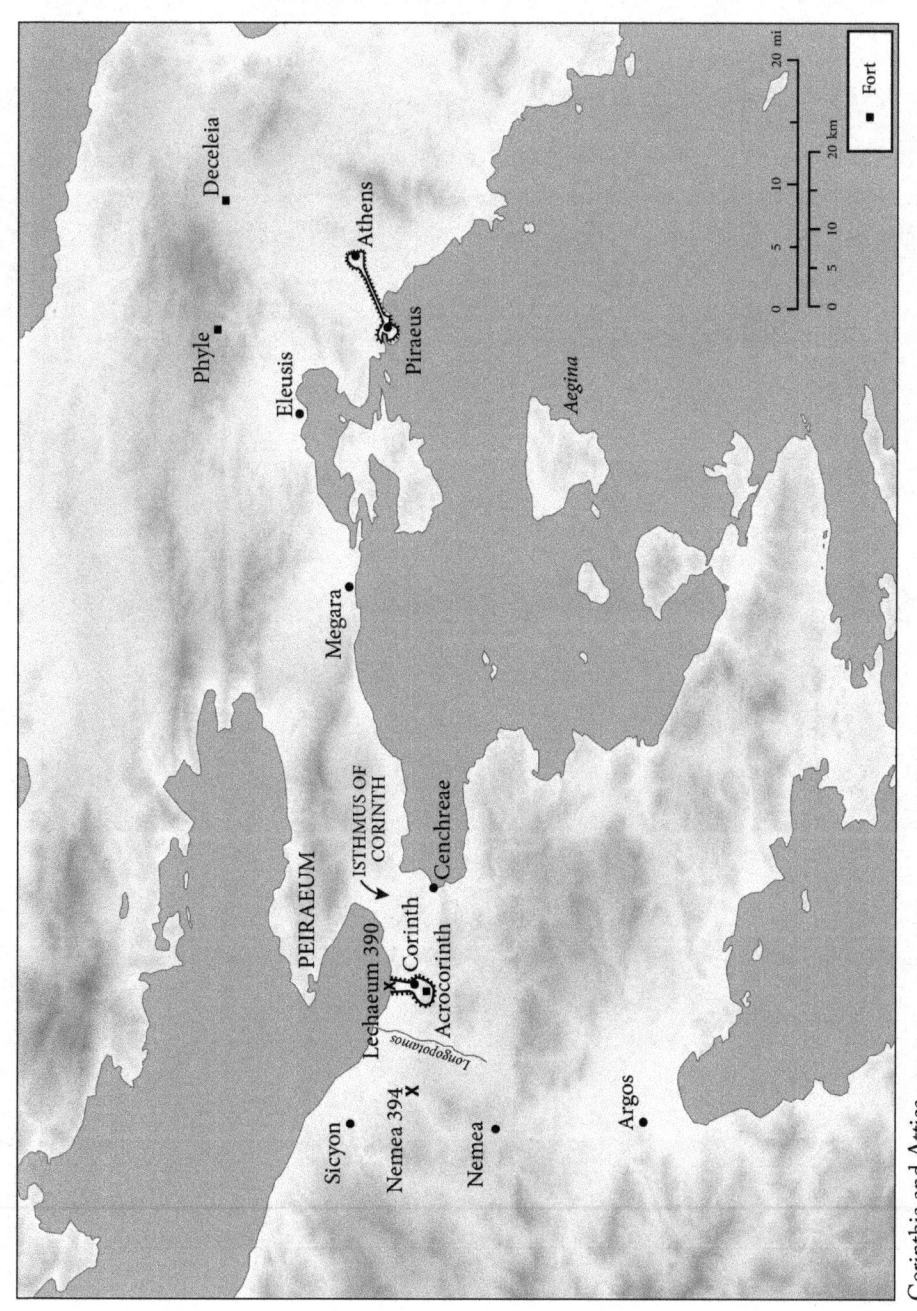

Corinthia and Attica.

Central Greece.

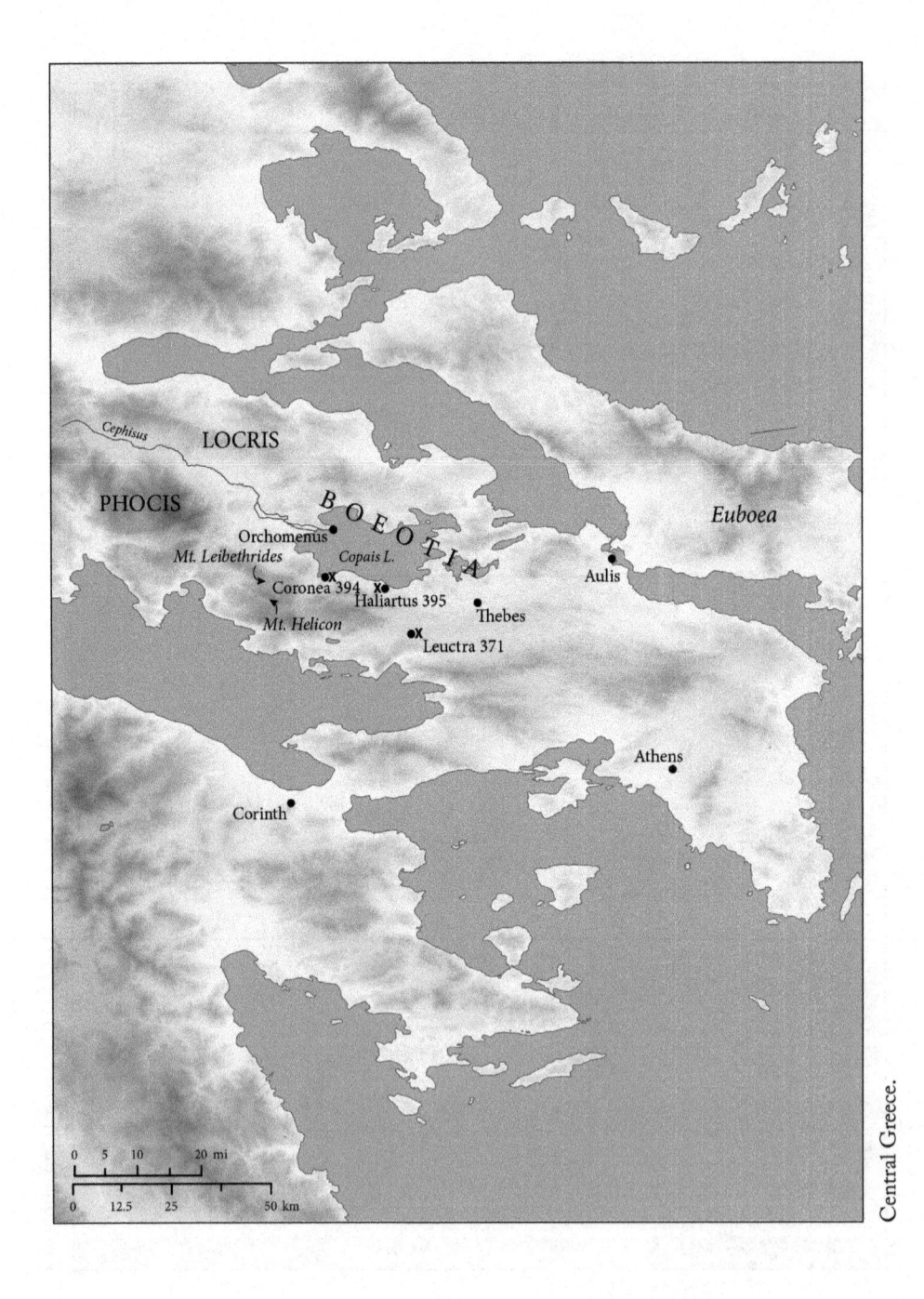

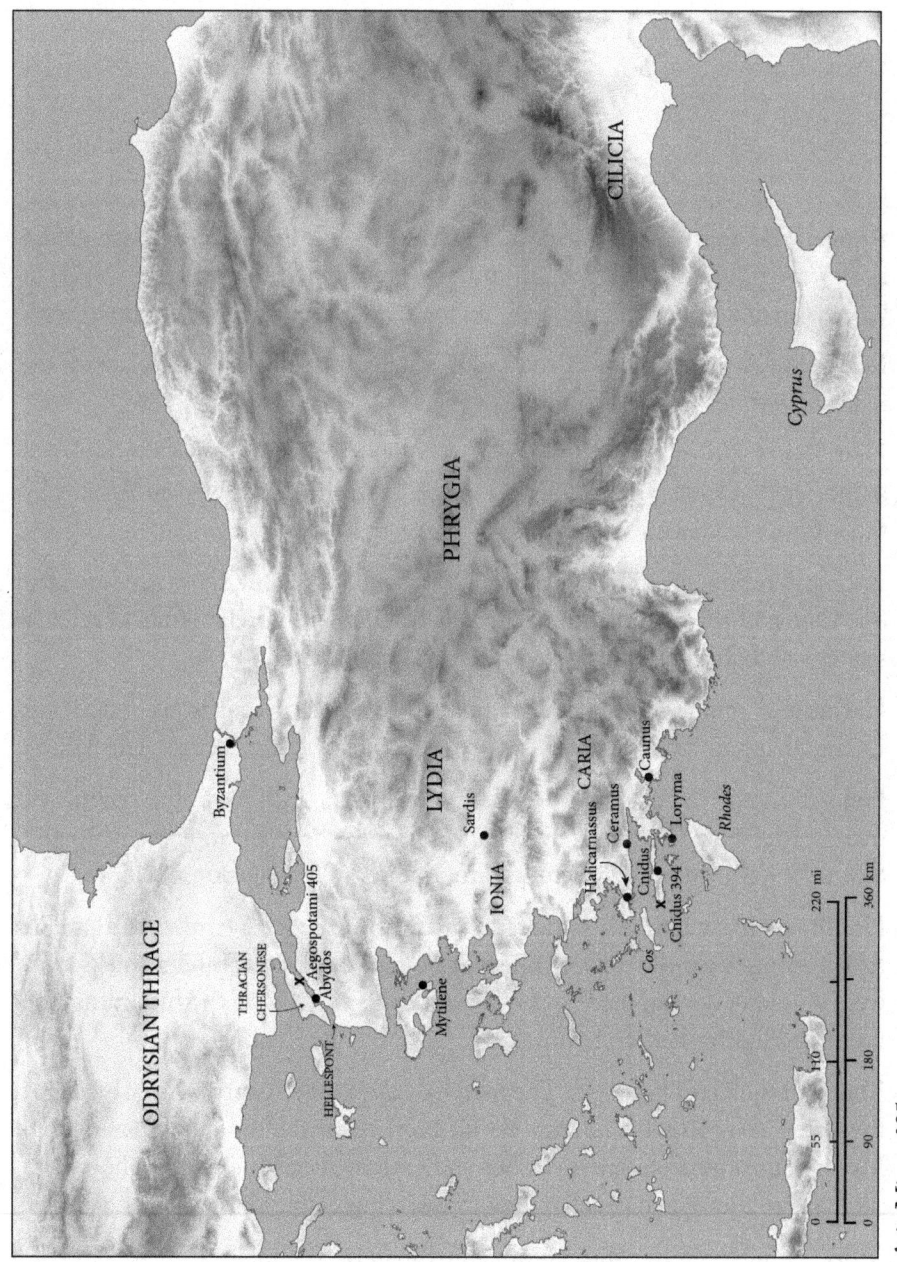

Asia Minor, 395 BC.

Glossary

Agoge: The Spartan 'rearing' of its warrior-citizens. From an early age young boys were rigorously educated in military tactics, fighting skills and Spartan virtue. Graduates became the Spartan hoplites and full citizens, the Spartiates.

Decarchy: A government of ten oligarchs appointed by Lysander across his many city-states in Asia Minor.

Democracy: A government system in which the people have the political authority to decide policy and hold office. It was first invented in Athens by the reforms of Cleisthenes in 508 BC.

Ephor: A ruling oligarch in Sparta, elected by the assembly. Only five served at one time and their primary purpose was dealing with foreign affairs, military strategy and checking the power of the two monarchs.

Harmost: A military commander appointed governor of a garrison or city-state. Lysander appointed many of these, personally loyal to him, across Asia Minor.

Helot: One of the enslaved population of Sparta and her home territories, mainly Messenia. They massively outnumbered the Spartan citizenship and Sparta brutally oppressed them in turn, leading to many helot rebellions.

Hoplites: Heavy infantry soldiers from Classical Greece. Armed with an 8ft to 10ft-long spear, 40–50lb of heavy armour, a short sword and a shield, they were a unique development in Greece and were highly successful against the faster and lighter Persian infantry.

March of the Ten Thousand: The march of Greek mercenaries, hired by Cyrus the Younger in his rebellion against his brother for the throne of Persia, from Mesopotamia north to the Black Sea and back to Asia Minor. Xenophon was a surviving soldier who recounted their tortuous but heroic journey in his *Anabasis*.

Mora: A full Spartan regiment of approximately 600 hoplites.

Navarch: A Spartan naval commander appointed by the ephors for a campaign and serving a one-year term; one of the few elite positions available in Sparta to sub-elites like Lysander.

Neodamodes: The 'new citizens' of Sparta composed of freed helots who served in the Spartan army.

Oligarchy: Rule by a few elite individuals. Oligarchy was a common form of government in ancient Greece, and Athenian democracy emerged from a long struggle in Athens against tyranny and oligarchy.

Peltast: A light infantry fighter of Greece. Armed with javelins and focusing on mobility and flexibility in lieu of close combat, the peltast became the primary fighter in the fourth century in Greece, supplanting the heavy infantry hoplite.

Perioeci: Free non-citizens of the Spartan state.

Phalanx: A military formation of hoplites in close arrangement with interlocking shields to guard their allies. The phalanx formed a shield wall and could attack an opponent with its 8ft to 10ft-long spears strategically arranged to complement the shields.

Satrap: A regional governor and military commander of the Persian Empire.

Spartiate: A full citizen of Sparta with legal and political rights earned by birth, graduation from the *agoge* and service as a hoplite.

Stasis: Meaning a 'standing still', stasis described the constant political struggle between the pro-democracy forces (often aligned with Athens) and the pro-oligarchic factions (often aligned with Sparta).

Symmachy: An alliance of Greek city-states banded together to fight against a common enemy.

Thete: A rower on a Greek trireme, typically from the lower or middle classes. They held a stable wage and respect in Athenian society, and with 180 rowers on each ship the thetes became an influential political group courted by democrats.

Thirty Tyrants: The thirty oligarchs appointed to rule Athens by Sparta after the Peloponnesian War. They were ferociously unpopular and massacred much of the Athenian population during their brief reign of terror.

Trireme: A three-decked warship in the ancient world built for fast travel and ramming opponents. Triremes had about 180 rowers and were the gold standard on both sides for naval warfare during the Persian and Peloponnesian Wars.

Introduction

The Athenian-styled Spartan Empire

In a little less than a century, Sparta had become quite Athenian.

It was not intentional, of course, as the Spartans detested the Athenian imperial model, their insufferable emphasis on the arts and sciences, and their profligate commercial and financial system. The Spartans far preferred the martial hegemony over their Peloponnesian League allies that had, slowly but surely, drained the coffers and resources of the Athenian Empire and delivered victory in the decades-long Peloponnesian War. However, with that victory came the inheritance of governing Athens and its many territories and colonies, and Sparta desperately lacked the resources and unified political determination to administer the vast Athenian Empire they had conquered.

Compounding matters, the Spartan allies in the Peloponnesian League lacked the capital, the manpower and the ambition necessary to run an empire. The Peloponnesian League had been the alliance of anti-Athenian city-states in Greece that supported Sparta in the toppling of Athens. The majority of its members, such as Pylos, Epidaurus, Elis and Mantinea, were far too agrarian to concern themselves with anything more than seasonal warfare. Their hoplites spent much of the year farming, and so they lacked standing armies due to their hoplites' need to return for the harvest season. Consequently, their financial and political systems could contribute little to the empire-building projects now faced by Sparta.

Meanwhile, the major city-states allied with Sparta – Corinth and Thebes – were livid with Sparta for not destroying Athens outright and burning it to the ground when the Peloponnesian War ended in 404. Corinth and Thebes were eyeing rebellion against the Peloponnesian League, and only the traditional military might of Sparta could hold them in check.

In the wake of the Peloponnesian League's victory over Athens, Sparta was celebrated across Greece as the liberators from the oppressive regime of Athens. However, in just a few short years, Sparta began to employ the iron-fisted political and diplomatic practices deployed by Athens to subdue Greek city-states under the banner of democracy. It was now not much more than a rebranded Athenian Empire. Known as the Spartan hegemony, their imperial experiment lasted from their victory over Athens in 404 until their defeat by Thebes in 371.

The Spartan hegemony was, however, an exercise in cognitive dissonance from its inception. This is because it was no longer truly a hegemony: an unofficial Spartan dominance over its inferiors. Instead, Sparta had functionally transitioned to a centrally-governed, constantly-expanding empire like Athens beforehand. They had played the role of populist insurgent against an unpopular and oppressive regime, but were now equated with the corrupt and heavy-handed policies of Athens. Sparta's core distinction, however, was that they lacked the essential economic and trade infrastructure – and internal political unity – to survive in the role.

The Spartan king Archidamus II identified this problematic paradigm very early on in the war between Athens and Sparta. At the outset of the war in 431, he delivered a speech encouraging the Spartans to outwit Athens by depleting their naval assets. Archidamus diagnosed the core distinction between the Athenian and Spartan approaches to war: 'war is a matter not so much of arms as of money, which makes arms of use.'[1]

Early in his treatment of the war between Athens and Sparta, the historian Thucydides famously pinpointed the original cause of the conflict: 'It was the growth of the power of Athens and the alarm that this inspired in Sparta that made war inevitable.'[2] In pursuing the resources needed for their newfound empire and their own survival, the Spartans had reconfigured this formula: it was now the growth of the power of Sparta and the alarm this inspired across Greece that made war inevitable. The Corinthian War was the devastating civil war that ensued.

Why the Corinthian War?

The Corinthian War was a fascinating entanglement of clashing empires, complex diplomatic alliances and betrayals, and political fissures erupting after centuries of tension. Situated between the great Peloponnesian War and the advent of the Theban hegemony and later the Macedonians, the Corinthian War is often overlooked or understood as a simple aftershock of the civil war just endured by Greece or as a prelude to the coming conflicts.

Most historical writing focuses on the post-Peloponnesian War era and is fixated on the rise of Thebes and Thebes' crushing defeat of Sparta at the hands of Epaminondas and the Sacred Band. Also while Sparta's formal decline had begun on the battlefield of Leuctra in 371, the roots of their failed empire were exposed two decades earlier in the military and diplomatic proceedings of the Corinthian War.

At the same time, the Corinthian War was much more than a kind of imperial birth pang or the dark underbelly of Spartan supremacy at its pinnacle. It was a violent reconfiguration of the fickle political make-up of Greek city-states and a grim demonstration of the limitations of Spartan, Athenian and Persian diplomatic and military power. It was an eight-year engagement between the Spartans and the previously inconceivable confederacy of Athens, Corinth, Thebes and Persia. In short, the entire Aegean world abandoned past alliances and united against Sparta.

As a case study, it unveils some of the essential questions with which the ancient Mediterranean wrestled. What makes an empire? How should it effectively absorb new populations and governments? How can an empire satisfy the home front and past alliances while focusing on expansion? To what extent can strategic alliances replace an empire's weaknesses? Can the decay of an empire truly be stopped, even after its causes have been identified? Most critically, why does the state want an ever-expanding empire and what do they intend to *do* with it? Athens, Sparta and Persia each confronted these questions in the early fourth century BC, with varying degrees of failure.

There was betrayal: Sparta's longtime allies Corinth and Argos partnered in a conspiracy to overthrow Spartan rule, and Sparta betrayed their Persian patrons in pursuit of more power. There was rebellion: Sparta's new colonies across the Aegean systematically abandoned their overlords for enticing offers from Persia or Athens. There were astonishing new alliances: Athens forgave Persia for burning their city-state to the ground a century earlier and accepted Persian funds to rebuild their navy. There was civil war: in Corinth the friction between political factions erupted into outright war, and in Sparta the power struggle for the empire's direction led to corruption, sabotage and assassination. Then there was devastation: both in the ruins of the destroyed powers like Corinth and in Sparta's pyrrhic victory in the Corinthian War which propped up a brittle empire.

The Corinthian War was also an outpouring of many of the common tensions and developments that did not make it into the historical or archaeological record: palace intrigue, familial jealousy, romantic betrayals and those many other human peculiarities that truly shape statecraft which Edward Gibbon described as 'those trifling but decisive causes which so often influence the fate of empires.'[3]

These malignancies were not just unique to Sparta, although the Corinthian War's spotlight shines most brightly over them. Persian *satrapies* in Asia Minor faced major economic limitations, stemming from their funding of the Spartan navy at the end of the Peloponnesian War. The meritocracy of the Persian military and bureaucracy, historically an imperial benefit that fostered growth and talent, became a source of dissension and corruption, particularly in the Mediterranean coastal territories of the empire. The Spartans invaded Persian territory across Asia Minor, burning farmlands, taking bribes and exploiting the competitive relationships between regional governors. Conquered territories sensed opportunity and Egypt successfully rebelled, opening diplomatic talks with Sparta immediately.

Most importantly, the Persians faced their own crisis of empire after the death of their strongest king in decades, Darius II. A series of infighting and *coup d'états* quickly followed among governors and royal family members, plaguing internal politics and limiting foreign affairs. Few jobs were as risky as a Persian *satrap* in the Mediterranean arena during the early fourth century; a bloody churning-through of Persian governors in Asia Minor even resulting in hiring Spartans to fight for them in civil conflicts against fellow Persian governors. Such practices culminated in the failed rebellion of the prince Cyrus the Younger who began a civil war to take the throne from his brother Artaxerxes II.

Athens, meanwhile, attempted to rebuild their ransacked city-state under the oppressive rule of Spartan-installed tyrants. Their naval empire collapsed overnight, and those ships not destroyed by Sparta were financially untenable. The ever-important grain imports sharply declined, bringing famine when compounded with the burned farmlands outside the Long Walls of the city. Democratic partisans like Thrasybulus led rebellions aimed at reinstating their former government, but factionalism likewise plagued Athens and no political consensus could be found among the citizens.

The Corinthian War occurred during the brief apex of Sparta, shortly after their defeat of the Athenian Empire and when their hegemony was unrivalled by any single Mediterranean power. It was during this period when they best matched their strengths and their weaknesses: their mighty army and cunning diplomatic apparatus was for the only time in their history paired with their economic and infrastructure shortcomings. These mismatched components could survive previous conflicts given the smaller scope of the Spartan Empire, which could be authentically sustained by the limited resources of the agrarian Peloponnesian homeland, a more visibly present military threat, and diplomatic jockeying against the existing Athenian superpower. However, following their defeat of the Athenians, many policymakers in Sparta aimed to massively expand the boundaries of their supremacy in a short time frame, including the ludicrously lofty goal of invading Persia. Sparta's cardinal sin was summarized poignantly by Xenophon in his *Hellenica*: 'in the day of [Sparta's] good fortune, they have planted the tyrant's heel.'[4]

It was the assertion of Spartan hegemony over Greece that effectively overextended the Spartan state. Their empire lacked the diplomatic finesse of the Persians and the ruthless pragmatism of the Athenians. Without the ability to blame Athens for the problems of lesser city-states, the Spartans lacked a true rival until they created one in the anti-Spartan confederacy of the Corinthian War and the later ascent of the Theban hegemony. Aristotle's stinging deconstruction of the Spartan state in his *Politics* aptly synthesized the matter: 'So long as [the Spartans] were at war, therefore, their power was preserved, but when they had attained empire they fell for the arts of peace [of which] they knew nothing, and had never engaged in any employment higher than war.'[5]

Yet Sparta's imperial malaise was not limited to foreign affairs. On the home front, the vision of the Spartan Empire was never truly cast. Interventionism and regime-shifting changed the fabric of Sparta. Since Lycurgus they had ruled the Peloponnese in such a fashion, but needed the Athenians to maintain it effectively.

However, their inheritance of the Athenian Empire created new problems, and none as severe as factionalism in the Spartan *polis*. After the riches and fame of the Peloponnesian War, leaders like Lysander sought to abandon the past and create a modern, seafaring empire in his own image that expanded well into Asia Minor. Traditionalists like Agis II and Agesilaus II staunchly disagreed with endless expansion but desired a Spartan hegemony over Greece and the Aegean world. An even more conservative and more influential contingent sought a return to Lycurgan isolationism and a strategic retreat to the Peloponnesian peninsula to lord over their historic territories. A final group of abolitionist radicals aimed for domestic reform addressing social classes, culminating in the Cinadon conspiracy of 399 and the empowerment of Brasidas' earlier vision of expanding citizen rights beyond the Spartiates, the body of male citizens with full legal liberties. This faction was motivated by a myriad of selfish reasons, though they were also the only group willing to face the foreboding statistical decline of Spartan citizens after a century of warfare.

The Corinthian War was therefore in retrospect a pathology report on the Spartan Empire, revealing the fundamental limitations in the constitution of the Spartan *polis*. It may seem odd to so harshly criticize the Spartans for their actions in the Corinthian War – a war in which they were the victors – but the long-term implications of their actions directly charted their own decline, and indeed the end of the Classical era in Greece.

This book sets out to examine how the Corinthian War serves as a historical microcosm of eastern Mediterranean military and political conflict in the fifth and fourth centuries and explain the origins of Sparta's decline, the end of Persian interventionism in Greece and the short-lived but consequential reassertion of Athenian imperialism across the Aegean. The book therefore does not endeavour to detail the actual fall of Sparta, on which much has been written, but instead to analyze the catalysts that sent the Spartan hegemony into decline despite their ostensible triumph in the Peloponnesian War and the Corinthian War. Further, this project will illuminate how Sparta's diplomatic policies metastasized their imperial and partisan flaws across the Aegean into the quagmires of Athenian and Persian dysfunction, ultimately reshaping the eastern Mediterranean and ushering in the end of the Spartan, Athenian and Persian supremacy in the region. The Corinthian War therefore encapsulated the multi-layered and mercurial political, diplomatic and military developments across Greece that coalesced into a cascading failure of empire.

The Problem of Sources

The extant sources for the Corinthian War are limited, to say the least. While much ink has been spilled over the Peloponnesian War and Athens' Empire, the centrality of Sparta in the Corinthian War means that Athens – our most prolific option for primary sources from Ancient Greece – shared precious little of this time given their own defeat. Unlike the Peloponnesian War, there are no tomes of histories, plays, poems and orations that give special insight into the Greek mind during the war, and Sparta's notorious shunning of literature and writing results in precious few Spartan texts apart from poems or songs.

Given this relative scarcity of sources, modern scholars must rely on the Spartan-loving Xenophon. Though an accomplished military commander and a philosopher trained under Socrates, the position of relying on Xenophon's historical methods is a poor one indeed. As George Cawkwell proclaims, 'there is no safety with Xenophon.'[6] He is a clumsy and inaccurate historian, often mistaking the size and scope of battles, misunderstanding geography, misattributing accomplishments, conflating Persia and Sparta, and favouring Sparta – and particularly its king Agesilaus II – to an often absurd degree. He also has a dazzlingly uneven treatment of the historical record: some events receive suspiciously detailed treatment while others are missing entirely from the narrative.

It is his notoriously pro-Spartan perspective that underpins Xenophon's entire corpus. Spartan culture, or a naively romantic interpretation of it, influences Xenophon's more noble interests of warrior virtue, honour and religious symbolism, but at the same time, Xenophon viewed history writing as a kind of philosophical and political tool, embellishing events or characters to present an ideal of virtue or the state. His *Cyropaedia* is the perfect example. Ostensibly, it is a hagiography tracing the education and formation of Cyrus the Great. In practice, it confuses Persians with Spartans, proclaims Persians were centaurs, and commits a litany of historical sins. Yet at the same time, the ancients considered *Cyropaedia* to be a masterpiece that exposits on the virtues of an ideal ruler and is a worthy refutation of Plato's ideal society and ruler in *The Republic*.

At the other end of the spectrum, the Roman-era Greek historian Plutarch wrote the definitive biographies of the Ancient Greeks and Romans in his *Parallel Lives*, and his research drew from dozens of ancient historians whose works no longer survive. Steeped in such historical writing, Plutarch developed a rather cynical view of certain thinkers, namely his raw hatred of Herodotus. Plutarch so despised the scholarship of Herodotus that he wrote a diatribe entitled *On the Malice of Herodotus*. This same judgmental Plutarch, however, found little to criticize in Xenophon. In a move with which most modern historians would staunchly disagree, Plutarch wrote:

> Xenophon, to be sure, became his own history by writing of his generalship and his successes and recording that it was Themistogenes the Syracusan who had compiled an account of them, his purpose being to win greater credence for his narrative by referring to himself in the third person, thus favouring another with the glory of the authorship.[7]

For the Corinthian War, our primary source is Xenophon's *Hellenica*, a direct continuation of Thucydides' *The History of the Peloponnesian War*. In fact, Xenophon so desired to continue Thucydides' landmark narrative that the opening lines of *Hellenica* pick up where Thucydides was unable to finish: 'After these events…' Apart from ambition and subject matter, the two historians lack similarities. Relative to his time, Thucydides was a consummate researcher and vastly improved on the use of historical methods from his predecessor Herodotus.

What he lacked in historical skills, Xenophon made up for with passion and first-hand experience. His love for Sparta and its leaders peaks in his *Agesilaus*, a biography of the adored king and his military adventures. In addition, Xenophon penned the famous *Anabasis* which chronicled the rebellion of Cyrus the Younger against the Persian king and the subsequent March of the Ten Thousand, an event which Xenophon personally endured. Indeed, Xenophon's consummate advantage – and biggest drawback – is that he himself is a primary source for the Corinthian War and its surrounding events. He fought in the Spartan army and was a colleague of many of the Athenian and Spartan leaders in the war. While his writings should be approached with scepticism, they are by far the most valuable source for the early fourth-century Greek world.

Of course, Xenophon is not our only source for the early fourth century in Greece. The aforementioned champion of biographies, Plutarch, writing in the first and second centuries AD, gives us incredible insight not only into the life of each of his subjects, but also into the evolution of historical writing. His *Parallel Lives* compares the biography of a titan of the Greek world with a titan of the Roman world. Specific to our purposes, Plutarch penned a biography of many key players in the Corinthian War, Lysander, Agesilaus and Artaxerxes among them. Plutarch's richest contribution is not just his text, but the access to many ancient historians and sources now lost to time. His meticulous sourcing and materials are the envy of the modern classicist.

A century and a half before Plutarch, a Sicilian Greek named Diodorus attempted the ambitious project of cataloguing all of history from founding myths to the Gallic Wars in his *Library of History*. Diodorus Siculus gives excellent insight, and like Plutarch many of his sources are no longer extant. He does, however, fall victim to the passage of time and is less prudent than Plutarch in presenting an objective narrative.

Several other ancients give us sources for the Corinthian War. The Roman military commander and historian Cornelius Nepos wrote brief military histories of the great Greco-Roman strategists. For our purposes, his summaries of Lysander, Pausanias, Conon, Iphicrates, Thrasybulus and Agesilaus are quite helpful. By far the most exceptional source is a nameless historian whose work survived in an Egyptian tomb. Dubbed the Oxyrhynchus Historian, this writer concentrated on Boeotia and Theban politics and history from 415 to the advent of the Corinthian War. No other work on this material, and especially from this perspective, still exists. Much of our inherited Greek history is Athenian in authorship and worldview. That a Theban text survived is not only astounding but critical in discerning a non-Athenian perspective, and the depth of analysis and insight into Boeotian political structure is invaluable.

Finally, the Greek world of the late fifth and early fourth century is perhaps best analyzed not by historical writing, but by surviving cultural works of art, philosophy and theatre. The Athenian Aristophanes' plays *Assemblywomen* and *Plutus* continue the rich tradition of social and political commentary, despite being in the twilight of the Old Comedy period. The great philosophical works of Athens are also pertinent to the early fourth century, and works like *The Apology* of Socrates (both Plato's and Xenophon's versions) and *The Republic* by Plato help sketch the cultural landscape of the Corinthian War. Together, these cultural artefacts help inform the political and social context of the Corinthian War and illustrate its enduring legacy, even if it remains in the shadow of the Peloponnesian War and the Theban-Spartan War.

Yet to understand why the Corinthian War deserves further insight, we must first understand the distillation of Greek identity and culture that was the Spartan state.

The Spartan State and the Lycurgan Reforms

It was a butcher's knife that forged Sparta.

In the early ninth century BC, a riot broke out in Sparta. The city-state had been plagued by decades of lawless rule, and it would be centuries before they became the dominant power in the Peloponnese. Despite a rigidly disciplined and honour-focused heritage, it had taken only a single king, ironically the namesake of one of Sparta's royal families, the Eurypontids, to 'relax the excessive absolutism'[8] of the Spartan state in the pursuit of 'seeking favour and popularity with the multitude.'[9] For generations, Sparta's current monarchy had proven feckless in the face of food shortages, social class conflict, military inferiority and bureaucratic corruption. Riots were the natural outcome.

Attempting to fix matters himself, the Spartan king entered the fray and attempted to restore peace. For his efforts, he was stabbed with a butcher's knife by one of the rioters. He died amid the chaos that had engulfed his city-state. The assassin went unpunished.

That king was the father of Lycurgus, the legendary and semi-mythical founder of the Spartan state as we now know it. Lycurgus inherited the throne of Sparta after the similarly short and chaotic reign of his brother. Upon his coronation, he immediately sought to bring order to the chaos of Sparta. Lycurgus' chief ambition was not to create a Panhellenic empire, but instead to simply bring order to his homeland which, according to Herodotus, had gained the reputation of being 'the worst governed of well nigh all the Greeks.'[10]

Lycurgus instituted a set of iron-fisted reforms that transformed Sparta into the militaristic and communalistic state that defined it for the next millennia: the Lycurgan Reforms. They were a fundamental reorganization of the entire state and its people; a sweeping law code that codified the political, economic, commercial, social and military activities of the state under a single authoritative rule.

Overnight, Sparta nationalized personal wealth and property. All male citizens were required to serve in the *agoge*: a brutal and communalistic military education that trained boys as young as 7 to fight with relentless effectiveness in the Spartan army. Sparta and its territories effectively cut off contact with the outside world. Commercial and economic activity was abruptly disallowed, and few outsiders were allowed inside the Spartan home region of Laconia. Just as well, as few merchants would want to visit anyway, considering that the Lycurgan Reforms also abolished gold and silver currency, implementing instead flat iron ingots that were deliberately worthless outside of Sparta. Art, theatre and other cultural activities were discouraged. Communal dining halls were established, where all male citizens ate daily and were held accountable to their peers for social behaviours and conformity. Spartan male citizens similarly lived in the barracks until the age of 30. Sparta's hoplites trained with greater ferocity and skill than their Greek peers, becoming unequalled in combat and forging a dominant land power. Sparta needed no protective walls, since 'the young men were the walls of Sparta, and the points of their spears its boundaries.'[11]

Their entire existence became the military supremacy of Sparta. Aristotle's judgement of the Spartan state was that 'the whole constitution has regard to one part of virtue only – the virtue of the soldier, which gives victory in war.'[12] Those Spartans who survived the *agoge* were awarded with the title of Spartiate or *homoioi*. These Spartiates were the apex of Greek warriors: full-time soldiers with expert discipline, training and an almost cultish warrior spirit. The Spartiates often towered over the seasonal militia of most other city-states in both skill and tactics.

However, not all residents of Sparta were considered Spartiates. For sustenance, the Spartans were thoroughly agrarian since widespread trade was now impossible given the insularity of Lycurgus' Sparta. Although Spartiates could earn acreage and farmland through military service, it was the helots – the 'captives' and enslaved natives of neighbouring Messenia – who bore the main brunt of food and grain production in the Spartan state. The helots were brutally brought to heel as the Spartan government knew that their city-state depended fully on helot food production. The Spartan senate famously declared war on the helots annually and even created a secret police force aimed at rooting out the seemingly annual helot revolts.

Such revolts could stymie even the most successful Spartan military campaigns and needed to be avoided at all costs. Fear of the helots and their superior numbers motivated Spartan policy to be 'at all times…governed by the necessity of taking precautions against [the helots].'[13] The conflict between Spartiate and helot was not only ceaseless, but perhaps the definitive social identity of Sparta after its militarism. The Spartan state and culture existed because of their subjugation of the helots, and only survived as long as that subjugation was maintained.

This fuelled the pride and insularity of Spartan citizenship, and the *agoge* and similar culture-making projects of the Lycurgan Reforms formed the backbone of the new Spartan culture: all citizens were equal, and all citizens would be able to fight for Sparta or support those who did fight in war. The reforms were rooted in the virtue of *isonomia*: the equality of all citizens under the law. While democracies like Athens similarly wrestled with the concept, Sparta's radical implementation of equality turned 'the city into a camp, the *polis* into an army, and the citizen into a soldier.'[14] The reforms bound Sparta together with paramount emphasis being on the community over the individual.

Accordingly, the physical city of Sparta hardly even existed by then. Far from being an urban centre with a bustling marketplace and meeting areas, Sparta was a collection of four small villages built of simple wood and devoid of the beautiful architecture and artwork associated with Classical Greece. For the rest of the Greek city-states, the *polis* consisted of an urban centre and the surrounding countryside. However, Sparta, alone among the powerful states, instead resembled a military camp: a collection of villages lacking proper infrastructure, but abounding in resolute commitment to the community above the individual; a complete veneration of military virtue.

Indeed, Sparta is far from a popular tourist destination in Greece today given the dearth of architectural remains or historical sites. The absence of historical ruins against the rugged and mountainous landscape belies the rich history of Sparta, much as Thucydides predicted two millennia ago:

> For I suppose if Lacedaemon were to become desolate, and the temples and the foundations of the public buildings were left, that as time went on there would be a strong disposition with posterity to refuse to accept her fame as a true exponent of her power. And yet they occupy two-fifths of Peloponnese and lead the whole, not to speak of their numerous allies without. Still, as the city is neither built in a compact form nor adorned with magnificent temples and public edifices, but composed of villages after the old fashion of Hellas, there would be an impression of inadequacy.[15]

The Lycurgan Reforms produced a particular type of citizen, ones who could take hold not of their own destiny but of the destiny of Sparta itself: men like Leonidas, Lysander, Agesilaus, Brasidas and Agis; citizens who earned distinction and added to the renown of Sparta and, despite their faults, seamlessly blended their own identity and ambitions into the state, not losing their individuality but gaining it through the community of the Spartan *polis*. Lycurgus forged a Sparta that was, above all else, the epitome of the *polis*.

For the rest of Greece, Sparta was the quintessential Greek *polis*. Whether they admitted it or not, the other city-states revered the Spartan lifestyle as maximizing Greek identity and virtue.

The Spartan Hegemony and the Persian Wars

With the societal and cultural reforms settled, Lycurgus faced the challenge of political instability head-on with a reorganization of the government's constitution. Prior to the reforms, the social upheavals dominating Sparta's cultural milieu had fallen victim to a pattern experienced by many city-states across Greece. It was a systemic conflict between the populace that demanded democratic participation and the oligarchs who demanded preservation of their own power. This civil conflict was called *stasis*. It was a ubiquitous experience across the Greek city-states during the latter half of the first millennium BC.

Almost every Greek state's *stasis* escalated into violent civil war and often concluded with rewritten constitutions – Greek city-states in Sicily had more than seventy violent civil conflicts alone – and tensions were constantly brewing in those states with populist elements such as Athens or Corinth. The Athenian *stasis* resulted in none other than the world's first democracy by the year 500, but many other city-states simply saw their oligarchs or kings cyclically quarrel with the unprivileged masses every decade or so.

In order to address the *stasis* in Sparta, now punctuated by the murder of his father, Lycurgus invented an entirely new governmental system. In lieu of conforming to the standards of oligarchy, democracy or monarchy, Lycurgus instituted a curious mixture of the three which ostensibly neutered each individual faction and strengthened the state.

Sparta maintained its monarchy but installed two kings, each from a separate royal lineage and each in charge of either the army or the state religion. The Agiad and the Eurypontid families were believed to be direct descendants of Heracles himself, and each king was tasked with keeping the other from seizing absolute power.

In addition to the monarchy, Lycurgus created a 'senate' consisting of twenty-eight men and the two kings. Christened the *Gerousia*, the twenty-eight non-monarchical members were required to be at least 60 years old and served for the rest of their lives. The *Gerousia* was primarily tasked with legislative proposals to the democratic assembly of citizens, who rarely rejected a proposed law out of respect for the *Gerousia*. They were also empowered with judicial authority for those Spartans charged with serious crimes, and were even given the authority to veto decisions of the voting assembly.

Perhaps the most influential group was the *ephors*, a group of five magistrates elected by the voting assembly of citizens for a one-year term. The *ephors* – literally translating to 'overseers' – wielded enormous political and social influence across the city-state. They were the only Spartans to never bow to the kings, and were in fact the ones charged with checking the power of the kings against corruption. Most critically of all, *ephors* controlled all official diplomatic and foreign policy interactions with those outside Laconia, without exception. The *ephors'* power waxed and waned with the particular rosters of kings and *ephors* of the day, but their vice-like grip on foreign policy never slipped.

Aristotle characterized the Spartan constitutional cocktail as quite popular, since many believed that 'the best constitution is a combination of all existing forms.'[16] Sparta's government was with 'the king forming the monarchy, and the council of elders the oligarchy while the democratic element is represented by the *ephors*.'[17] Isocrates, meanwhile, emphasized the pragmatism of Spartan political decision-making, noting that the Spartans 'are governed by oligarchs at home, but by kings on the battlefield.'[18] Bureaucracy was brutally stamped out to streamline the Spartan military machine. Political unity was found in the common identity of the Spartan state, and all diplomats, admirals, generals and other dignitaries on foreign soil were never to sacrifice the Spartan ideal.

The results spoke for themselves. As the foremost *laconophile* – a devout admirer of Spartan culture and state – Xenophon famously marvelled that 'though they were among the least populous city-states, they nevertheless were the most powerful and renowned of all Greece.'[19]

By the first Persian invasion of Greece in 490, Sparta reigned unopposed as the hegemon atop a group of loosely aligned city-states coined the Peloponnesian League. The league was formed in 550 in response to the growing severity of helot revolts and the persistently antagonistic Argos. Argos had perhaps been the prime Peloponnesian state until Lycurgus' reforms in Sparta supplanted all domestic rivals.

Apart from Argos and Athens, most major *poleis* in mainland Greece formally aligned with the Peloponnesian League at some point between 550 and 400, and even Argos and Athens allied with the league during the Corinthian War. Despite this influence, the Peloponnesian 'League' is a misnomer given by modern historians. The ancient label for the league was the more precise *symmachy* which connoted a military alliance against a common foe.[20] This alliance was exclusively for military endeavours, however, and there was a limited element of political allegiance required for league membership. Member *poleis* did not pay financial tribute and only committed military aid to Sparta when called upon. The Peloponnesian League was a clever solution to the statistical woe that always plagued Sparta's military: they were the elite in military prowess, but almost always inferior in raw size and a systemic inability to produce more Spartiates.

Because membership only demanded an alliance with Sparta and not necessarily with other members, individual city-states could and did disregard Spartan command and fight against each other. While Sparta demanded no formal political affiliation, each city-state was given a vote in a council of allies, although Sparta oversaw the vote, demanded that the allied council be held in Sparta and maintained their own parallel council. Consequently, Sparta was often invested in funding the aristocratic factions among member *poleis* that were sympathetic to Sparta in order to secure 'their subservience to [Spartan] interests by establishing oligarchies among them.'[21] Such meddling made the relatively weaker states like Tegea or Elis easier for Sparta to control, but often resulted in troublesome relations with the more powerful league members like Corinth. Despite being labelled full Peloponnesian League members, some *poleis* were wholly subservient to Sparta, while others were only tacitly affiliated with Sparta when military affairs matched their domestic agenda, especially Corinth and Thebes.[22]

In this way, the Peloponnesian League was functionally identified with Spartan hegemony. Their leadership over the Greeks was strictly a military supremacy. Even at the height of the 'empire', Sparta's supremacy could not accurately be labelled an empire. It lacked the economic, social or political nucleus to support its holdings in a meaningful way; it lasted only because of favourable circumstances, Persian benevolence and military strength.

Although sprinkled with some diplomatic expectations from 550 until the end of the Peloponnesian Wars in 404, Sparta's hegemony lived and died by the Spartan spear and not by diplomacy or trade. Expectations of member *poleis* were made clear to Athens after their defeat: 'acknowledge the headship of Sparta in peace and war, leaving to her the choice of friends and foes, and following her lead by land and sea.'[23]

Spartan hegemony was first tested in the Persian Wars, the conflict that had defined and remade the Greek world. The mighty Achaemenid Persian Empire had conquered the Ionian coast of Greece by 500 to create an empire stretching from Pakistan to Egypt, expanding from their homeland on the Iranian plateau. Although the fringe of their empire, their Greek colonies in Asia Minor were of significant strategic value. The Persians subdivided their empire into thirty-six territories named *satrapies* lead by a governor likewise named a *satrap*. Asia Minor constituted several *satrapies* under the authority of the governor of Lydia, one of seven 'great *satrapies*'. Lydia and its regions of Caria, Ionia, Phrygia, Cilicia and beyond counted for approximately 15 per cent of the annual tax revenues for the entire Achaemenid Empire.[24]

Darius I the Great ordered an invasion of Greece after Athenian meddling in local uprisings across Asia Minor. The Athenians were eager to find allies in their new project of democracy, which was about a decade old during the Ionian Revolt of 499. Their ambition led to military aid towards anti-Persian rebellions in various Ionian city-states, an aspiration which begat the burning of the *satrapy*'s capital city of Sardis. Darius ordered an invasion of Greece that was turned away first by a shipwrecked naval expedition and then, quite miraculously, by the undersized Athenian hoplites in the swamplands outside of Marathon.

A decade later in 480, his son Xerxes I oversaw a much larger invasion force that was similarly doomed. The formal invasion forces were turned away first at the naval battle of Salamis near Athens and then on the fields of Plataea near Thebes. Although the Persian Wars would formally conclude in 449, they functionally ended with the Spartan hoplites crushing an elite Achaemenid force at Plataea.

Both invasions failed to conquer mainland Greece, but many Greeks voluntarily joined the Persians and fought against their countrymen. Some major Greek powers like Thebes, Macedon and Thessaly 'medized' and fought for Persia for at least some of the war, either for personal gain or to seek retribution on their rivals. Argos remained neutral for transparently selfish reasons, hoping to reign over the aftermath. Only the Peloponnesian League under Spartan authority – Cyprus, Thespiae, Plataea and the upstart Athens – stood against the tidal wave of the Persian invaders, which Herodotus numbered up to 2 million soldiers.

The Persian Wars challenged the delicate balance of the Spartan *symmachy*, with the allies voting to give Sparta primacy in all military affairs including naval activities. This was surprising given Sparta's naval paucity. While they were capable seafarers, the Spartans had not prioritized sea power to the same extent as their rivals. Instead, their chief contribution to Panhellenic navies was the naval commander. Well versed in Spartan virtue and military prowess, the Spartan commander was given the highest respect and decisively led the allied Greek navy. Sparta dominated the Greek resistance effort in the early parts of the war.

Historically the Corinthian fleet was the mightiest in Greece, and even they were usurped by the newly-minted Athenian navy that had been constructed after the first invasion of 490. Athenian triremes outnumbered their Greek allies by orders of magnitude, quadrupling the Corinthian fleet at the Battle of Artemisium and tripling it at the Battle of Salamis. The Spartans nevertheless maintained a significant navy typically in the upper crust of ship count: ten at Artemisium and sixteen at Salamis.[25] The notion that Sparta lacked a true navy was rooted primarily in the pro-Athenian bias of historians like Herodotus and Thucydides.[26]

Yet the Persian Wars quickly cemented Athens' arrival as the new superpower in the Mediterranean and as the primary threat to Sparta's hegemony. Under the cunning leadership of Themistocles, an upstart politician who masterfully gamed the Athenian democratic system, Athens quickly subverted Spartan command, even outright deceiving Sparta and their Greek allies at Salamis. After destroying the Persian naval fleet at Salamis, Athens turned away the main Persian invasion force, and the Spartans later defeated the Persians outright a few months later at Plataea.

The Athenian Empire and the Peloponnesian War

In short order, the Aegean Sea was divided among those city-states loyal to Athens, to Sparta or to Persia. Athens leveraged its navy – by then the largest in

Greece – into a thalassocratic empire. Themistocles had begun this enterprise shortly after Greek victory at Salamis, exacting tribute from belligerent islands like Andros. Themistocles envisioned a grand sea power headquartered in Athens, with democratic colonies across the Mediterranean. He had realized it within a decade of Salamis. Themistocles had also foreseen the new conflict ripping across Greece: Athens vs. Sparta. He ordered the reconstruction of Athens and the expansion of Athenian walls to protect against the inevitable Spartan invasion of Attica.

Athens meanwhile spearheaded the foundation of the Delian League, an alliance of Greek *poleis* committed to pooling resources to excise Persian presence from the Greek world. Although similar in nomenclature to the Peloponnesian League, the Delian League was no *symmachy* like Sparta's hegemony. In lieu of a military pact like the Peloponnesian League, the Delian League instead demanded tribute from its allies, ostensibly to share among the league to fund the anti-Persian campaign, but in reality to spend on Athenian interests and construction projects.

While the Delian League's campaign against Persia lasted until a formal peace treaty in 449, the true Athenian campaign quickly became against the Peloponnesian League. Less than two decades after the Persian Wars, imperial tension between the two city-states quickly boiled over into armed conflict in 460. Although settled quickly, the underlying cause – 'the growth of the power of Athens and the alarm that this inspired in Sparta'[27] – magnified and led to prolonged civil war from 431 to 404. The Peloponnesian War devastated Greece.

The Spartan strategy played to their strength in land warfare. The Spartan king Archidamus II laid siege to Athens and burned the resources of their home territory of Attica in a war of attrition. Athens survived – barely – through its naval trade systems and the harbour at Piraeus, safely set behind their city walls. Athenian allies fared little better.

In turn, the Athenians embargoed the Peloponnese and harassed all naval activity by Sparta and her allies. Despite life on the brink of starvation for the Peloponnese, the Spartans managed to win many city-states to their league with cunning diplomacy. They cast Athens as the new Persia: enemies of liberty and corrupted by greed and power. To those in the Peloponnesian League and those under the iron-fisted rule of Athens, Sparta represented the glimmer of freedom for Greece.

For victory, the Spartans transformed themselves into a naval power. At the start of the war in 431, Archidamus II sagely articulated a narrow path for the Spartan state to defeat the Athenian superpower:

But a struggle with a people who live in a distant land, who have also an extraordinary familiarity with the sea, and who are in the highest state of preparation in every other department; with wealth private and public, with ships, and horses, and heavy infantry, and a population such as no one other Hellenic place can equal, and lastly a number of tributary allies – what can justify us in rashly beginning such a struggle? Wherein is our trust that we should rush on it unprepared? Is it in our ships? There we are inferior; while if we are to practice and become a match for them, time must intervene. Is it in our money? There we have a far greater deficiency. We neither have it in our treasury, nor are we ready to contribute it from our private funds.

Confidence might possibly be felt in our superiority in heavy infantry and population, which will enable us to invade and devastate their lands. But the Athenians have plenty of other land in their empire, and can import what they want by sea. Again, if we are to attempt an insurrection of their allies, these will have to be supported with a fleet, most of them being islanders. What then is to be our war? For unless we can either beat them at sea, or deprive them of the revenues which feed their navy, we shall meet with little but disaster.[28]

Such a prognosis led the Spartans to a dramatic about-face in their military and political strategy. After decades of bitter conflict against the seafaring Athenians, the Spartans abandoned their emphasis on land warfare along with their stark opposition to the ever-looming Persian threat of Greek conquest and made an alliance with the Persians to fund construction of a new navy.

In 407, a new Spartan naval admiral or *navarch* ascended from obscurity and from outside the privileged Spartiate class. Born from a family of helots or non-citizens, Lysander befriended the Persian prince and *satrap* Cyrus the Younger and secured funds for the construction of a navy out-sizing even the vaunted Athenian fleet. That Athenian fleet had been winnowed by a disastrous invasion of Sicily from 415 to 413. Under the famed orator and admiral Alcibiades, a student of Socrates who in many ways was the embodiment of Athens' greatest virtues and its most terrible vices, the Athenians failed not only to conquer new territory but managed to decimate the strength of both their navy and their empire. Alcibiades fled to Sparta – and then to Persia and then back to Athens – pursuing his own survival and heroic journey.

In 405, at the Battle of Aegospotami on the Hellespont, the Persian-funded Spartan navy finally defeated the Athenians and their fleet. With grain and food trade to Athens now impossible, the city faced starvation and the rebellion of their colonies. A little more than six months later in the spring of 404, the Athenians formally surrendered and the war ended.

For perhaps the first time ever, Greece had an unchallenged hegemon. The Spartans had saved Greece from the Persian invaders and now toppled the Athenian oppressors. For their supporters, true Greek virtue and culture had prevailed. Sparta ruled the Peloponnesian League and with the same combination of military strength and diplomatic finesse found in their homeland, and immediately sought to exert that same influence over all of Greece.

Before Sparta could be coronated as the sole ruler of Greece, however, the Peloponnesian League disintegrated over the future of Spartan influence, the proper punishment for Athens and the complicated relationship between Sparta and Persia. Within a matter of months, Sparta's internal *stasis* crippled her imperial vision and caused her to adopt new, incongruent policies that mutated their hegemony into an empire.

In 395, less than nine years after the Peloponnesian War and less than a century after the Persian Wars, the Corinthian War would reshape Greece yet again.

Chapter One
Inheritance of Empire

Lysander's Personal Empire

When the Spartan admiral Lysander sailed into Piraeus harbour in Athens in 404, he immediately ordered the destruction of the city walls. To the music of flautists and a raucous crowd of supporters, Lysander personally oversaw the dismantling of Athens and her power. He and the Spartans had vanquished the final vestiges of the Athenian navy and with it the oppressive Athenian empire. The Greek world, at long last, 'proclaimed that day the beginning of liberty in Greece.'[1]

Yet it was not to be. Lysander instead took the reins of the Athenian empire and remade the Spartan hegemony in his own image. By the close of the Peloponnesian War, the Spartans – through factional indecision and Lysander's personal ambitions – assumed the Athenian colonial interests as their own. For the rest of Greece, it was simply a change in leadership and there would be no liberation or breaking of chains.

After the calamitous Athenian invasion of Sicily in 415, most Greeks – including the Spartans – assumed that the remnant of the Athenian navy would put up a nominal fight before formal surrender, but the return of the intrepid Alcibiades to naval command reinvigorated the Athenian war effort, if only for a few short years. From 407 to 405, the Spartans grew concerned about an *en masse* defection by the city-states in Asia Minor, tentatively loyal to Sparta, to join the resurgent Athenians. Those city-states were motivated by the Spartan promise to give them liberty from both Persian and Athenian oppression; an oath that Sparta would not ultimately keep. Lysander became the Spartan *navarch* in 407, the same year that Alcibiades returned to Athens, and although he was dispatched to Asia Minor primarily for military purposes, Lysander quickly expanded his duties to laying the groundwork for Spartan imperialism.

Although he was replaced as *navarch*, as per Spartan law, in 406 and only appointed deputy *navarch* in the following year, he effectively administered all Spartan military and diplomatic activity without serious oversight from the *ephors*. Lysander systematically dismantled democracies across Asia Minor and replaced them with oligarchies loyal first to Lysander and then to Sparta. Athens had framed its imperial expansion in the fifth century around the propagation of democratic governments; Sparta now did the same with her new empire, but around oligarchies instead of democracies.²

To accomplish this, Lysander first appointed *harmosts* in each city-state of strategic value. The *harmosts* were the 'overseers', militarily-empowered magistrates that reported directly to Lysander, circumventing the *ephors* and Spartan ambassadors. Some *harmosts* were uniquely empowered to serve more as a deputized general in the Spartan army, often to reinforce Spartan forces or to garrison a strategic location. Such was the case with Thibron, who in the year 400 was sent with 5,000 men to aid in an Ionian revolt against Persian encroachment.³ While the ostensible job of the *harmost* was to command a Spartan garrison and to eliminate the seeds of rebellion in troublesome city-states, increasingly their focus was to replace democratic governments with oligarchies.

The position of *harmost* was often coupled with the installation of decarchies or 'political clubs' in many city-states across the Aegean. These were oligarchies of ten men who effectively served as a military junta, executing duties such as military administration, commercial logistics, the collection of taxes and diplomacy but, like the *harmosts* who often were members of decarchies themselves, their primary objective seems to have been the oppression of democracy and those who supported it. Such anti-democratic behaviour was often brutal and despotic given their presence among former Athenian colonies or close allies, most notably at Samos where Lysander personally besieged the city to ensure the dismantling of democracy and expulsion of Athenian sympathizers.⁴ The historian Paul Cartledge aptly summarized the animating motive of the new Spartan Empire: 'the Spartans also levied tribute and maintained a navy, but whereas the Athenians' Empire had been conceived and largely maintained as anti-Persian, the Lysandrean version of the Spartan Empire was mainly anti-democratic and pro-autocratic.'⁵

From 406 to the outbreak of the Corinthian War in 395, Lysander was patron to the oligarchs of many decarchies and cultivated a close relationship with their leaders, even at the cost of Sparta's interests. In 406, when he was term-limited out of the office of *navarch*, Lysander undermined his successor Callicratidas and funnelled support and funds away from Callicratidas through his network of harmosts.⁶ *Harmosts* became little more than sentinels for Lysander. Plutarch left little doubt as to the fervent devotion of Lysander's personal oligarchs: '[for they] yearned for the zealous support of Lysander, and missed the interest which he took in the welfare of his partisans, so that when he sailed away they were dejected and shed tears.'⁷ For this and other underhand manoeuvres, the ancient historians credited him with inventing the new Spartan diplomatic and imperial model:

Lysander now summoned from their various cities to Ephesus men whom he saw to be most eminent for confidence and daring, and sowed in their minds the seeds of the revolutionary decarchies afterwards instituted by him, urging and inciting them to form political clubs in their several cities, and apply themselves to public affairs, assuring them that as soon as the Athenian empire was destroyed, they could rid themselves of their democracies and become themselves supreme in power.[8]

Harmosts were first appointed late in the Peloponnesian War in city-states including Samos, Megara, Heraclea, Chios and Lesbos. The official reason for these *harmosts* was to heal the city-state from Athenian imperial corruption, and if the citizens of these *poleis* found the decarchies or *harmosts* permissible, it was only in contrast to the threat of Athenian aggression. After the Battle of Aegospotami in 405, however, Athens wielded no navy and therefore no imperial menace. This should have made the position of *harmost* outdated, yet Lysander instead accelerated the pace of appointing *harmosts*; an exhaustive endeavour as it is probable that *harmosts* were term-limited to a single year.

With their directive to dismantle democracies and root out any scent of rebellion, Sparta's decarchies earned a dreadful reputation. Even Xenophon, never one to miss a chance to praise Sparta, was acutely aware that Sparta's new foreign policy departed from Sparta's traditional foundation of the Lycurgan Reforms:

> ...in former times the Lacedaemonians preferred to live at home on moderate means, content to associate exclusively with themselves rather than to play the part of governor-general (*harmost*) in foreign states and to be corrupted by flattery; knowing further, as I do, that formerly they dreaded to be detected in the possession of gold, whereas nowadays there are not a few who make it their glory and their boast to be possessed of it.[9]

Sparta's empire and her foreign policy were now inextricably conflated with Lysander's private imperial projects. Lysander's commandeering of Sparta's statecraft became the first step in the Spartan appropriation of Athenian imperial policy. For generations, the fulcrum of Sparta's hegemony was the steadfast commitment to the Lycurgan model of diplomacy and self-sustenance. Indeed, the very position of *harmost* was modelled on the Athenian *episcopi* who were appointed as overseers of subject city-states in the Athenian empire.

This was not the first time an individual Spartan had seen their personal ambitions eclipse their commitment to the Spartan hegemony. A century earlier, another distinguished Spartan military commander named Pausanias the Regent – notably not the same as the Agiad king Pausanias who ruled

Sparta during much of the Corinthian War – sought to turn a part of Asia Minor into his own fiefdom.

In the aftermath of the Persian Wars in 479, Pausanias the Regent refused to be hobbled by fidelity to the Lycurgan tradition or the standard Spartan diplomacy. Pausanias sailed to Byzantium shortly after distinguished service in the battles of Plataea and Mycale, the final battles of the Persian Wars and resounding victories for the Spartan hoplites. In Byzantium, far from the prying eyes of Sparta and in the chaos of the Persian retreat, Pausanias set up a personal empire and began to transform the city into a new Sparta. For his efforts, he was recalled to Sparta by the *ephors* and stood trial for 'medizing', or giving allegiance to the Persian Empire, and faced the accusation that he had conspired to conquer Greece in exchange for Persian favour.[10]

Pausanias the Regent's escapades in Asia Minor potentially cost the Spartans leadership in the Delian League and the post-war military effort to expel Persians from Greek territory. Pausanias the Regent exposed two animating motives for Spartan exclusion from the Delian League, and thus the rise of Athens' empire. First, the Spartan *ephors* realized they fundamentally could not sustain an overseas expeditionary force. With their political system's primary focus necessarily on the oppression of helots and helot revolts, Spartan foreign policy was, for the time being, limited in scope to the mainland of Greece. Second, the rest of Greece saw that a rogue Spartan leader like Pausanias the Regent – and later Lysander – was capable of remaking the entire political landscape with ambition, talent and clever manipulation of the Spartan military system.

Cyrus the Younger and Spartan-Persian Diplomacy

One distinction of Lysander's new Spartan hegemony was his embracing of finances and commerce shunned by Lycurgus. The Spartan need for triremes and rowers during the final phase of the Peloponnesian War reshaped Sparta's diplomatic approach to finances. Indeed, the very existence of Lysander's financial motivation was a stark departure from Lycurgus' iron ingots that were worthless outside Sparta. Although the Lycurgan disassociation from the Aegean economy was never truly the reality, Sparta clearly pivoted towards an increased participation in the Aegean economy late in the Peloponnesian War.

The chief benefit was tribute. Diodorus remarks that 'although before this time [the Spartans] had not used coined money, they now collected yearly from the tribute more than a thousand talents.'[11] Such tribute was deployed for the maintenance of the city-state, the raising of new triremes and the salaries of their crews. Indeed, it was the trireme that had initially motivated Sparta's grand entry into Aegean commerce that was predicated in large part on the funds that Lysander secured not from Sparta or its *ephors*, but from Persia. The linchpin of his personal empire was Lysander's close relationship with the Prince of Persia and *satrap* of Lydia and Ionia, Cyrus the Younger. Despite the contentious history between Persia and Sparta, the two were as thick as thieves. Making friends with those in proximity to power was a common practice of Lysander, who is described by Plutarch as 'naturally subservient to men of power and influence, beyond what was usual in a Spartan, and content to endure an arrogant authority for the sake of gaining his ends.'[12]

The Spartan admiral and the Persian prince forged a close relationship after Lysander's success at the Battle of Notium in 406. Notium had been a landmark victory for Lysander; it was shortly after his ascent to *navarch* and his strategic acumen – and especially his ability to market his successes afterwards – effectively launched his public career beyond Sparta. Most critically, Notium directly led to Alcibiades' final removal from Athenian leadership and indeed Athens itself as he left in exile.

For ridding Sparta of the threat of Alcibiades' cunning antagonism, Lysander also revitalized Persian support for the Spartan cause in the Peloponnesian War, but now Notium had come in the wake of several years of poor luck for the Spartan and Persian war effort. Since 411, a series of crushing defeats had plagued the Spartan navy. After Athens' failed invasion of Sicily, the Spartans should have made short order of what remained of the Athenian fleet, but Alcibiades' unexpected return to Athens following an oligarchic coup in 411 changed Athenian tactics as they strung together a series of critical victories in battles at Cyzicus and Abydos and costly sieges at Byzantium and Chalcedon. The result almost crippled the Spartan war effort.

On the brink of failure, Sparta turned to their old rivals, the Persians. The Persians had nominally been supporting Sparta through shipbuilding and financing for at least the past year, particularly the *satrap* of Hellespontine Phrygia, Pharnabazus, who had a longstanding rivalry with the *satrap* of Lydia and Ionia, Tissaphernes. However, in 413 the Persian emperor Darius II demanded repayment of tribute from the Greek city-states in Asia Minor, and left it to his *satraps* to figure out how to make it happen. Pharnabazus quickly 'calculated that by weakening the Athenians he should get the tribute better paid, and should also draw the Lacedaemonians into alliance with the [Persian] king.'[13] Pharnabazus' approach to the Peloponnesian War consequently became aggressive Persian interventionism.

Tissaphernes adopted a more discerning strategy. Following first the advice of the exiled Athenian statesman Themistocles, who in the 470s had suggested pitting Athens and Sparta against each other to further Persian influence in the Aegean, the Persians had generally stayed out of the Peloponnesian War.

However, new counsel from another exiled Athenian statesman, none other than Alcibiades himself who had left Athens for Sparta in 415 and then Sparta for Persia in 412, cautioned Tissaphernes 'not to be in too great a hurry to end the war'[14] but to instead divide Greek resources among the Spartans and the Athenians so as to not 'put the power by land and sea into the same hands; but to leave each of the contending parties in possession of one element, thus enabling the king when he found one troublesome to call in the other.'[15]

Tissaphernes immediately set out to ally with Sparta in a treaty focused on shipbuilding to equip Sparta to challenge Athens on the sea and thus elongate the Greek civil war. Although he had success, the Spartans soon soured on dealing with Tissaphernes, even charging one commander with treason for soliciting the *satrap* in a new scheme. Tissaphernes' lack of funds and his links with the hated Alcibiades were too much. The Spartans found themselves far more amenable to Pharnabazus' deeper pockets and more active political support.

The Persian treaty with Sparta in 412 had a heavy price, however. The primary demand of Persia was to regain control of the Greek city-states in Asia Minor. For Sparta, this demand grated against the very purpose of the Peloponnesian War: to stem the growth of Athenian imperial power and the desire to liberate Greece. While the city-states of Asia Minor had been governing themselves since the end of the Persian Wars, the threat of their reoccupation by Persia – or now by Athens – was a sword of Damocles.

Over the last century, Spartan foreign policy had become more fixated on stemming Athenian growth than fulfilling their promises to liberate Asia Minor from Persia, and so their abdication of Asia Minor to the Persians in this treaty was seen as an abandonment of the Spartan *symmachy* itself. The Athenian propaganda almost wrote itself: how could the Peloponnesian League maintain any credibility in the fight against the imperial oppressors if they simply handed over large territories to different oppressors?

Tissaphernes' treaty had a grievous impact on his own ambitions, however. His half-decade of tacitly funding Spartan activity – but often lacking in direct Persian involvement – was able to be cast as incompetence by his rivals, especially his rival *satrap* to the north, Pharnabazus. The latter had taken a far more direct role in the new Spartan-Persian diplomacy, directly funding the construction of Spartan triremes after Cyzicus[16] and even riding his own horse out into the water to stop the Athenians from towing the ships away in the middle of the battle. Compounding matters, Tissaphernes had busied himself with diplomatic matters in an effort to recruit more funds and soldiers in Ephesus and other Ionian city-states. It was a simple matter for Pharnabazus and his courtiers to portray this as dereliction of duty.[17]

The obliteration of the Persian/Spartan navy at Cyzicus initially left Darius II dismayed at further messiness in Greece and refocused his efforts on internal affairs such as a minor uprising in the Persian heartland of Media, but in 408, after still sufficiently receiving his demanded tribute, Darius was newly determined to stop the Athenian resurgence. Proclaiming Pharnabazus' prodigal commitment to Sparta's war effort as the new expectation for his governors, Darius II demoted Tissaphernes to the uncelebrated province of Caria and fully embraced the partnership with Sparta.

Most critical in this rearrangement of power in Persian Asia Minor was the deployment of the young son of Darius II to the *satrapies* of Lydia and Ionia to replace Tissaphernes. That son was none other than Cyrus the Younger. At just 16 years of age, Cyrus was tasked as *karanon* – the Persian title for commander – of all the provinces in Asia Minor that bordered the Aegean. His primary purpose was to unite the dysfunctional Persian *satraps* and support the Spartan naval effort against Athens.[18]

Cyrus the Younger proved to be the effective mixture of vision and pragmatism that Persia desperately needed to centralize power in Asia Minor. A gifted military tactician, Cyrus's greatest strength was a leadership style that harked back to the days of his namesake Cyrus the Great, who had built the Achaemenid Empire with expert foreign policy and relatively kind treatment of conquered peoples. Cyrus the Younger continued the Persian tradition of meritocracy in military and political affairs, and Cyrus actively sought to promote commanders and governors who were most qualified. Cyrus was magnanimous with those under his leadership and garnered quite the reputation with his subjects, from slaves through to governors:

> He made no secret of his endeavour to outdo his friends and his foes alike in reciprocity of conduct. The prayer has been attributed to him, 'God grant I may live long enough to recompense my friends and requite my foes with a strong arm.' However this may be, no one, at least in our days, ever drew together so ardent a following of friends, eager to lay at his feet their money, their cities, their own lives and persons.... Wherever he might discover any one ready to distinguish himself in the service of uprightness, his delight was to make this man richer than those who seek for gain by unfair means. On the same principle, his own administration was in all respects uprightly conducted, and, in particular, he secured the services of an army worthy of the name. Generals, and subalterns alike, came to him from across the seas, not merely to make money, but because they saw that loyalty to Cyrus was a more profitable investment than so

many pounds a month. Let any man whatsoever render him willing service, such enthusiasm was sure to win its reward.

And so Cyrus could always command the service of the best assistants, it was said, whatever the work might be. Or if he saw any skilful and just steward who furnished well the country over which he ruled, and created revenues, so far from robbing him at any time, to him who had, he delighted to give more.[19]

Cyrus's bountiful blessings to highly effective subjects led him to Lysander. Lysander and Cyrus found kinship with each other immediately on their first meeting in 407. Lysander, freshly appointed *navarch* at the time, criticized Tissaphernes' ineffective leadership and lack of financial support for the Peloponnesian navy and its rowers. Cyrus quickly raised the wages of the Spartan sailors by 25 per cent, advanced them a month's salary and even remunerated all unpaid wages.[20] The Spartan rank and file were understandably enamoured with Cyrus the Younger, although traditionalists like King Pausanias were perhaps hesitant about Lysander's ambition and continued remaking of the financial and diplomatic infrastructure of the Spartan state.

Cyrus's infusion of funds directly led to Lysander's tactical victory at the Battle of Notium a few months later, and Lysander quickly became the most powerful figure in Greece after Alcibiades' final exile from Athens. Shortly after Notium, Lysander's *harmosts* and supporters conspired to restore Lysander to *navarch* to replace his successor Callicratidas. Cyrus the Younger escalated the new Persian interventionism and, after undermining Callicratidas by delaying payment for Spartan sailors, directly petitioned for Lysander to be given full authority over the Peloponnesian fleet. This request was in conjunction with several of Sparta's allies, masking the extent to which Persia was now dictating Spartan policy and flouting the Spartan constitution. Lysander was nevertheless appointed 'vice admiral' in name, but *navarch* in practice.[21] He now had full naval authority over the Spartan Empire and full allegiance to Cyrus the Younger.

In 405, Cyrus was recalled to the Persian capital of Susa to attend his father Darius II who was on his deathbed. Intending to inherit the throne or challenging his brother Artaxerxes II should he not succeed his father, Cyrus the Younger took Tissaphernes and a regiment of Greek soldiers with him to Susa. Cyrus had no intention of abandoning Persian machinations in Greece, however. He made the astonishing move to select Lysander as acting *satrap* and treasurer of the Persian territories in Asia Minor, giving to him 'all the tributes from the several cities which belonged to him personally.'[22] Plutarch recounts this unprecedented honour for a sitting Spartan admiral:

Cyrus summoned Lysander to Sardis, and gave him this, and promised him that, ardently protesting, to gratify him, that he would actually squander his own fortune, if his father gave him nothing for the Spartans; and if all else failed, he said he would cut up the throne on which he sat when giving audience, a throne covered with gold and silver. And finally, as he was going up into Media to wait upon his father, he assigned to Lysander the tribute of the cities, and entrusted his own government to him; and embracing him in farewell, and begging him not to fight the Athenians at sea until he was come back, and promising to come back with many ships from Phoenicia and Cilicia, he set out to go up to the King.[23]

Cyrus's sole stipulation of avoiding direct military involvement with Athens was disregarded as Lysander provoked the Athenians into the Battle of Aegospotami in a matter of weeks. The Athenian fleet was annihilated, Sparta was triumphant, and the great Peloponnesian War was in its death throes.

Unlike Pausanias the Regent's doomed 'invasion' of Asia Minor, Sparta's new navy and diplomatic influence with Cyrus the Younger allowed them the luxury of sustaining an expeditionary force for the first time. Lysander had begun the annexation of city-states along the coast of Asia Minor and in former Athenian colonies, demonstrating to the Greek world a desire for Sparta to fully embrace the Athenian imperial model. Lysander had begun the Spartan annexation of Athenian territories and inheritance of their empire, but King Pausanias of Sparta shared no such sentiment. The Agiad king represented a vision for Sparta to return to their rigid Lycurgan traditionalism in contrast to Lysander's new, spendthrift model of empire. Cracks were emerging in post-war Sparta as, for the first time, domestic political figures attempted to rein in Lysander's activities.

Sparta's Brittle Empire: Class Struggle and Factionalism in the Spartan State

After Lysander's victory at Aegospotami in 405, Sparta set its sights on Athens. Sparta's allies, however, became increasingly disgruntled at the appropriation of Athenian imperial power by Lysander and also at the second abandonment of the Greeks in Asia Minor, who continued to languish under Persian rule. Yet despite this growing concern, the greatest threat faced by Sparta from 404 to 395 was the health of its internal political and social system.

Although in its infancy, the Spartan hegemony over Greece was in *agon*. In Greek athletics, the *agon* was the gruelling struggle or contest faced by a competitor to win the glory of a championship. The English word 'agony' retains the same message today. The virtuous fight for honour led the *agon* to also be associated with political debate, especially in democratic assemblies during a contentious deliberation before a vote. The theatre soon incorporated the *agon* into the comedy and tragedy plays of the fifth and fourth centuries, when the 'protagonist' and 'antagonist' – named after the very concept of *agon* – debated and entered into conflict. Despite their resounding victories, Sparta's class struggle – the *stasis* – crescendoed into this *agon* and threatened the existence of the Lycurgan constitution and the brittle empire they were forging.

Before discussing the Spartan assault on Athens itself, it is important to analyze this socioeconomic and demographic turbulence in Sparta. With Spartan foreign policy privatized under Lysander, Spartan domestic policy now dictated the future of the hegemony. The primary issue facing Sparta was demography and population trends. Since the Spartan *polis* was fundamentally premised on the subjugation of the helots and the elevation of the citizen-soldier Spartiates, population management was paramount for the survival of the state. The costliness of the decades-long Peloponnesian War had a dramatic effect on the delicate balance of helots and Spartan citizens.

Like most Greek city-states, the population of Sparta peaked in the sixth century and faced a steady contraction during the fifth century, but the unique anatomy of the Spartan government and social class structure did not allow them to weather the challenges of the Persian Wars and the Peloponnesian War with the same fitness as other city-states. Because Sparta relied on a particular type of citizen – and one that took decades to replace through birth and training in the *agoge* – they had to filter all political decisions through their dominance over the vastly more populous helots. By the end of the fourth century, Aristotle blamed the steady decline of the Spartan population on the progressively institutionalized desire for money and the inequality in wealth and land ownership in Sparta. However, Aristotle specifically pinpointed Sparta's demise by the mid-300s on the staggering decline of Spartiates: 'for the city sank under a single defeat; the want of men was their ruin.'[24] The trend of declining Spartan citizens even earned its own name: *oliganthropia*.

The sharp decline in Spartiates and Spartan citizens afforded an opportunity for the helots to fulfil their yearning for liberty. Helot revolts were a constant threat that even the Spartan secret police, whose sole duty was to identify and suppress rebellions, had trouble inhibiting. Aristotle characterized the helots as 'constantly awaiting the ruination of Spartan citizens',[25] while Xenophon described how 'not one of [the helots could] conceal the delight it would give him if he might eat up every Spartan raw.'[26] Such fervour left no flexibility in state affairs: all policymaking must actively suppress helots and strategize around any potential helot revolution.

Both the decline of Spartan citizen-soldiers and the tenuous helot-Spartiate dynamic were inflamed in 464 when a catastrophic earthquake struck Laconia and the Spartan villages, reportedly killing 20,000 Spartan citizens.[27] The helots seized the divine opportunity. Specifics on this revolt are elusive, but it is clear that it took several years, perhaps even up to a decade, for the Spartiates to quell the revolution. Partisanship in Sparta complicated their ability to effectively address the matter. The traditionalist camps blamed the failure to stop the revolt on the lingering influence of the corruption of Pausanias the Regent, while other factions called for the opportunity to call for outside aid and further depart from their historic Lycurgan isolationism.

When the Spartans were forced to request aid from their allies in the Peloponnesian League, Sparta's domestic troubles bled over into foreign affairs. Thucydides reports that Athens attempted to send aid, but was forcefully rebuffed by the Spartans who feared the growing interventionism of Athens. This was reportedly the 'first open quarrel' between Athens and Sparta after the Persian Wars, and the Athenians returned home 'deeply offended and conscious of having done nothing to merit such treatment'[28] and quickly formed a new alliance with Sparta's enemies of Argos and Thessaly. There is little doubt that Spartan insecurities about their domestic *stasis* contributed to the Peloponnesian War itself.

The population of Spartan citizens and their proportion to helots and other Spartan non-citizens never recovered from the earthquake of 464. A statistical survey of these demographics in the fifth and fourth centuries reveals the attenuation of Spartiates due to the earthquake, the high price of the Peloponnesian War and the inability to produce sufficient graduates of the *agoge*.

Taking statistics given from ancient writers such as Herodotus, Thucydides and Xenophon, we can chart a rough sketch of the decline of male Spartan citizens. During the Persian invasion in 479, Sparta had approximately 5,000 Spartiates and 5,000 *perioeci*, the free non-citizens under Spartan rule but without full legal rights.[29] For comparison, Herodotus notes that there were seven helots appointed to serve each Spartiate, illustrating the massive disproportion of helots and Spartiates.[30] In 425 at the Battle of Pylos during the Peloponnesian War, the numbers had dwindled to 2,755 Spartiates and up to 4,500 non-citizen soldiers.[31] By the Battle of Nemea in 395 during the Corinthian War, the number of Spartiates had dropped to about 1,800 with about 3,000 *perioeci*.[32] By the final stand of the Spartan hegemony at the Battle of Leuctra in 471, there were fewer than 1,000 Spartiates and only 2,150 *perioeci*.[33] In summary, despite the Spartan hegemony over Greece and her consistent victories in the Peloponnesian War and the Corinthian War, fully-trained Spartan citizen-soldiers steadily declined until there was less than a quarter of their original number and only a fraction of their non-citizen soldiers.

To combat the citizen-helot asymmetry, the Spartan government introduced a new social class: the *neodamodes* or 'new citizens'. This new class comprised former helots who had earned their freedom through special service to the state. They were likely awarded land and a status underneath the *perioeci*. Their origin is murky, but it is apparent they were seen as a solution to the decline of Spartiates in Sparta's military and that they became a major force by the time of the great commander Brasidas early in the Peloponnesian War. Sometime in the late 430s and 420s, Brasidas distinguished himself as remarkably hospitable and eloquent for a Spartan general; traits that earned him the distrust and ire of the *ephors* despite his vaunted military achievements.

For the Spartan *ephors*, kings and elders, however, Brasidas' most problematic trait was his treatment of the helots. By the time of his death in 424, Brasidas actively promoted helots into his army. They were given the nickname of *Brasidoi*, 'the men of Brasidas'.[34] After earning distinction in combat under Brasidas, sometime late 430s or early 420s it was 'decreed that the Helots who had fought with Brasidas should be free and allowed to live where they liked'[35] and settled them alongside the land of the *neodamodes*. Brasidas' was the first substantial attempt to address the growing problem of manpower in the Spartan military and citizenship.

If Brasidas opened the door to helot promotion as a means of addressing demographic decline, Lysander flung it open. However, his policies were more than a simple ripple effect of the destabilized socioeconomic situation in Sparta. Lysander embodied the Spartan *stasis* of the day: a discordance of imperial expansion fuelled by domestic class struggle. Lysander's imperial projects were perhaps directly motivated both as personal ambition to reform the Spartan state into an Athenian empire, with himself at the head, and as a means of addressing the Spartan civil conflict. Lysander's complex system of *harmosts* and decarchies fundamentally required the empowerment of sub-elites and non-Spartiates to maintain the vast colonial network.[36] Lysander's vision of empire employed an Athenian-style promotion of the common population and would comprehensively expand the contours of Spartan power well beyond that of Brasidas' manumission of helots. It would certainly solve the problem of Spartan *oliganthropia*, but would come at the cost of the Spartan identity and constitution.

To appreciate the revolutionary steps taken in pursuit of a new Spartan Empire, it is important to emphasize the non-elite and non-Spartiate heritage of Lysander. He was 'reared in poverty'[37] and was possibly the child of a helot mother. Yet he also claimed ancestry from a non-royal branch of the Heracleidae line, the origin of the two Spartan monarchical families. The dichotomy between his unprivileged birth and his unparalleled accomplishments incensed Lysander, and he sought to remake the Lycurgan Reforms themselves.[38] Already stifled by his term limits as *navarch*, Lysander proposed the radical idea of reforming the monarchy of Sparta itself, 'putting an end to the kingship of the Heracleidae and making every Spartan eligible to election as king; for he hoped that the kingship would very soon come to him because of his achievements.'[39] Although he attempted to bribe the oracle at Delphi in pursuit of this reform, it was unsuccessful, and the oligarchs of Sparta even formally charged him with sedition. Although the plot to reform the monarchy failed, Lysander's influence was nevertheless insurmountable and the trial quickly found him not guilty without the general population even being aware of the matter.[40]

Lysander's ascension to leader of Sparta, and indeed Greece, did not directly solve the problem of class struggle. Aristotle took up the reforms of Lysander in his *Politics* when he argued that oligarchies can see revolutions

> when great men who are at least of equal merit are dishonoured by those higher in office, as Lysander was by the kings of Sparta; or, when a brave man is excluded from the honours of the state, like Cinadon, who conspired against the Spartans in the reign of Agesilaus.[41]

In 399, early in the reign of the new king Agesilaus II, a war hero named Cinadon coordinated a social class uprising rebellion that would have overthrown the Spartiates and established a more democratic state.

Xenophon's account of the conspiracy is lacking – perhaps intentionally as to avoid angering his Spartan patrons – but Cinadon's coup assuredly destabilized any temporary balance between helots, Spartan sub-elites and their Spartan overlords. The non-Spartiate Cinadon leveraged his social position with a covert, Athenian-style populism that had allowed the helots and sub-elites to see how vastly they outnumbered the Spartan citizens. Massive upheaval and change was imminent in Sparta, and even though Cinadon was betrayed by an informant, his message of liberation for the helots of Sparta did not vanish. Before his torture and execution, Cinadon plainly stated his mission: 'I wished to be inferior to no man in Lacedaemon.'[42] The message echoed across the Spartan homeland, even while Lysander won honours for the hegemony overseas. The conspiracy of Cinadon was a referendum on Sparta's inability to manage their domestic *stasis* and their further inability to support a Lysandrean-style empire beyond their borders.

Resistance to Lysander's reprogramming of Sparta's foreign affairs was more avoidable given its distance from Sparta's centre, but direct opposition to

Lysander's new domestic and constitutional changes was now palpable. Despite the undisputed power of the Spartan hegemony, the Spartans could not discern their own vision for leadership or treatments of their subjects. The combination of the decline of Spartan citizens, the rise of helots under Brasidas and Cinadon and the rise of Lysander led to factionalism in the Spartan government.

Several partisan groups emerged, each with a dedicated solution to solve the demographic challenge facing Sparta and each with a sharply different understanding of the purpose of the Spartan hegemony. The historian C.D. Hamilton identifies three key political factions in Sparta at the end of the fifth century.[43]

First were the traditionalists. Strictly adhering to the Lycurgan model of isolationism, a miserly economic system and a preservation of the Spartan class system, this faction heralded the Peloponnesian League and Spartan *symmachy* as the tools to long-term prosperity in Laconia, even if Athens survived. They looked within the boundaries of Sparta and saw little value in imperial projects, generally only finding interest in foreign affairs or military campaigns if it helped the Lycurgan system survive. The Agiad king Pausanias was their primary champion, and they held a strong influence over the *ephors* for much of the waning years of the Peloponnesian War and the interlude before the Corinthian War, although lacking in substantial diplomacy with outside allies.

The next faction was the empire-builders, who wanted Spartan imperial power to extend even beyond the Aegean world into Persian territory, commandeering the Athenian empire and restructuring the Spartan government and class system to support their imperial vision. This faction was, unsurprisingly, spearheaded by Lysander. As discussed, the Spartan Empire would inherently recreate the Spartan social structure with the liberation of helots and enfranchisement of sub-elites across their new power. This was both the most influential and most radical faction by Lysander's ascendancy in 403 after the Peloponnesian War, and was also the most active in diplomacy with Persia and the rest of the Peloponnesian League.

The third faction might be called the 'hegemons of Greece': those who wished to coalesce Spartan power exclusively in the Peloponnesian peninsula and maintain influence north into Delphi, Thebes and Athens. This group synthesized Spartan expansionism and traditionalism, and saw Sparta's historic role as the dominant force in the Greek mainland as both their past and their future. Alterations to the Spartan class system or political structure were possible but limited as this faction was still tethered to the Lycurgan Reforms, despite finding flexibility in interpreting them. The Eurypontid King Agis II and especially his successor Agesilaus II led this faction.[44] Though initially the least influential of the three, this faction became the most dominant both domestically and diplomatically as Agesilaus' influence increased over the course of the Corinthian War and the waning years of the Spartan hegemony.

I propose a fourth faction of the Spartan partisanship of the late fifth and early fourth centuries: the pragmatists. This group was in fact compatible with the multiple imperial visions, but their primary motive was stabilization of the Spartan class struggle and a secured future for Sparta. They would do whatever it took to ensure the survival of Sparta as a state, even if not an empire. They were also determined to end the rapid decline of citizens, even if it included the radical move of manumission for helots. Cinadon, Brasidas and Lysander all overlapped with this group to varying degrees as they each empowered the non-citizens of Sparta with policies that would have addressed the economic and manpower challenges in the Spartan state, and Antalcidas would eventually try to synthesize the imperialists and pragmatists when he negotiated the war's end in 387. Whether ideologues or populists, they saw the resolution of Sparta's *stasis* and domestic affairs as key to the survival of the *polis*.

No matter what their vision for the Spartan Empire, the partisan factions of the city-state crippled their future and undermined their own ascendancy after Aegospotami. Hamilton successfully argued that 'Sparta failed because her policies were constantly subject to revision and change through the workings of factional rivalry.'[45] This disharmony descended on the rest of Greece as Lysander fused Sparta's complex domestic problems with the oppression and expansionism of Athens' empire. When Lysander set out for the dismantling of Athens in 404, he brought the full weight of Sparta's internal entropy and immediately angered Sparta's allies, Athens' former colonies and even the then friendly Persians. Within weeks, Athens became both the crowning jewel of Lysander's private colonial projects and the most egregious example of Sparta's new maladapted empire.

Chapter Two
Thirty Reasons to Despise Sparta

The Demise of the Athenian Empire

Late in the night the fastest Athenian ship, the trireme *Paralos*, sailed into the harbour of Athens with the news that the Athenian fleet had been shattered at Aegospotami. Within minutes, the howls and cries of the people rose up 7 miles into the city proper. No one in the city was spared the suffering, and no Athenian slept that night as they realized that their city and their empire were now awaiting certain death. Lysander and the Spartans would arrive soon.

Directly after the defeat of the Athenian navy at Aegospotami, Lysander sought to eliminate all Athenian influence in the Aegean. Plutarch notes that he 'sailed to the various cities, and ordered all the Athenians whom he met to go back to Athens, for he would spare none, he said, but would slaughter any whom he caught outside the city.'[1] Corralling the citizens of Athens home was not a selfless strategy. Lysander intended to expedite famine in Athens. He paralleled this move with the throttling of grain shipments from the Hellespont to Athens; the only source of food for most Athenians as they sheltered behind their city walls.

Such brutal treatment was directly aimed at inflicting such pain on the Athenians that they quickly submitted. The more Athenians Lysander could pack into the city, 'the more quickly the want of necessaries of life would make itself felt'[2] and the more quickly the Athenians would finally succumb to Spartan – and Lysandrean – rule.

However, by the end of the war in 404, there were far fewer Athenians left to starve. Like the Spartans, Athens experienced a massive decline in population, with their citizenship halved since the advent of the war in 431. The plague of 430 killed 100,000 Athenians alone, almost a quarter of the overall population. Direct casualties of the war led to a steep decline from 40,000 to about 22,000 male citizens by 403.[3] In 406, almost three dozen triremes had to be abandoned in mid-campaign since they could not find sufficient men to row them, and Athens was forced to offer citizenship to slaves and foreign residents in order to man ships.[4] Most strikingly, the number of Athenian hoplites had withered from 25,000 in 431 to barely 9,000 by 411.[5]

Population decline in Athens was such a dire issue that in 355 it was addressed by Xenophon in his *Ways and Means* when he proposed a dramatic step: offering citizenship to the city's foreign residents as a means of saving the Athenian economy. He wrote:

> But these natural blessings may be added to: in the first place, by a careful handling of our resident alien population. And, for my part, I can hardly conceive of a more splendid source of revenue than lies open in this direction. Here you have a self-supporting class of residents conferring large benefits upon the state, and instead of receiving payment themselves, contributing on the contrary to the gain of the exchequer by the sojourners' tax.[6]

At some point during the Peloponnesian War, Athens was forced to make the radical move of allowing polygamy as a means of population growth: 'wishing to increase the population, [the assembly of Athens passed] a decree permitting a citizen to marry one Athenian woman and have children by another.'[7] The philosopher Socrates, aged 70 in 399, had multiple wives by this law and it was apparently still allowable by the time of Aristotle two generations later. Losses from malnutrition and disease behind the walls of the overcrowded Athens caused substantially more damage to the rest of the populace, especially among women, children, foreign residents and slaves, although these statistics are virtually impossible to verify.

It was the socioeconomic trends of the Athenian population decline that were especially damning. The historian Barry Strauss demonstrates that Athenian citizenship losses were highly concentrated in the lowest social class, the *thetes*, who were typically employed as labourers in the workforce and as light skirmishers or rowers on triremes when at war. The sinking of the Athenian fleet, and Athenian naval trade with it, either directly killed off many such *thetes* or cut off their employment opportunities with the end of Athenian naval dominance.

By contrast, the contraction among the middle-class hoplites was far less severe. The final decade of the Peloponnesian War primarily saw naval warfare, such as at Cyzicus, Notium, Arginusae and Aegospotami. The land-based hoplites therefore saw far fewer casualties and enjoyed a newly disproportionate representation in the Athenian voting assembly. Nevertheless, many wealthier hoplites recognized the danger of serving in a dilapidated army and paid their way into the cavalry, traditionally reserved for only the aristocrats and viewed as a safer alternative.[8] The result was the devastation of the lower class and the survival but debilitation of middle- and upper-class Athenians.

A unique consequence of this was uneven distribution of land and wealth in the aftermath of the war. Instead of the expected enrichment of the wealthy and oppression of the poor, many of the Athenian middle classes saw their crops and livestock destroyed by the Spartan land strategy of destroying farmland. Those farmers who by chance lived near strategic locations targeted by Sparta such as Decelea or Eleusis saw their livelihood ruined. Meanwhile, other farmers across Attica capitalized on their fortuitous locations and saw a windfall in wealth, trade and political opportunity.[9] In short, it was a matter of simple luck and location that determined the socioeconomic fate of many Athenians by the end of the war.

Yet despite their obvious grief at the loss of Athens' empire, some middle-class hoplites and still more aristocrats reached a point sometime around 403 where they were happy to see the end of the Peloponnesian War given its high economic and political cost, and the potential boom in their new personal fortunes. This striking development was not matched by the lower classes and *thetes*. The lower classes categorically welcomed warfare since it provided stable employment and consistent wages. The population drop among *thetes* had empowered the middle class, and eventually ultimately facilitated a new aristocratic power grab by some former middle-class hoplites.

This new aristocracy was disconnected from the landed families of old Athens. The commercial and economic empire of Athens had enriched the merchants and manufacturers, creating a new layer of upper-middle-class Athenians. The uneven land distribution of the hoplite middle class towards the end of the war meant those families who did benefit did so in spades, accumulated substantial wealth and land that made them indispensable to the Athenian political and economic machine. Due to the manpower demands of the Athenian empire and the Peloponnesian War, these new aristocrats now dominated Athenian politics. By 403 '[traditional] aristocrats in Athenian politics were the exception, not the rule'[10] in contrast to the previous century of generations of politicians primarily localized in ruling clans like the Alcmaeonids.

Many of the old-money aristocrats took a pessimistic perspective on the future of Athens, and placed the blame squarely on the lower classes and, ultimately, on democracy itself. Since the start of the Peloponnesian War, anonymous aristocrats spread their dissent in evangelistic writings that were covertly distributed. One aristocrat took the pseudonym of the 'Old Oligarch' and penned scathing criticisms of democracy and the lower classes:

> In every corner of the earth, the best principles are in opposition to democracy. Among the greatest and most powerful men, there is little incontinence and injustice. Instead, they have a great desire to promote goodness. But among the common people, it is ignorance, chaos and evil that prevails. The hardships of life drive them to commit terrible

deeds – it is often because of their poverty that many men are so uncouth and immoral.[11]

Although both old and new Athenian aristocrats were relatively united in their welcoming of the end of the war, they were staunchly divided in how to welcome Sparta into Athens in 403. With *thete* depopulation and the unbalanced hoplite developments, these aristocrats held firmer to the levers of power in Athens by the time of Lysander's grand arrival. Some aristocrats were, for personal expediency or genuine worldview, *laconophiles*: supporters of Spartan culture and society. Many more, however, supported either their democratic heritage or an oligarchy unbeholden to any foreign power.

What united them, however, was a mixture of incompetence and corruption. In Aristophanes' play *Assemblywomen*, written in 391, such malfeasance from Athenian bureaucrats led the protagonist to despair for the future of her beloved Athens:

> My country is as dear to me as it is to you, and I groan, I am grieved at all that is happening in it. Scarcely one in ten of those who rule it is honest, and all the others are bad. If you appoint fresh chiefs, they will do still worse.[12]

The *stasis* in Athens was therefore no less contested than in Sparta. The gruelling cost of war had so crippled agriculture, commerce and labour that the socioeconomic landscape of Athens was nigh unrecognizable from the heights of Pericles' day. In fact, the civil strife became so turbulent that Athenian democracy itself was overthrown for the first time in its century of existence. In 411, a select group of aristocrats seized power.

Motivated both by their declining position in the new socioeconomic complexion of Athens and the political and economic turmoil caused by the failed invasion of Sicily in 413, these wealthy oligarchs blamed democracy for the mismanagement of the Athenian empire. As Aristotle would later diagnose, democracy had been perverted for the selfish and immediate interest of the voters and not for the good of the *polis* itself. The oligarchs labelled themselves 'The Four Hundred' but could not build sufficient consensus even among themselves, still less among the lower classes. An attempt to cultivate a relationship with Sparta failed. Their oligarchy crumbled just a year later in 410 after the Battle of Cyzicus.

In summary, Athenian decline began long before their defeat at Aegospotami, and even before the doomed invasion of Sicily. Compounding socioeconomic and social class challenges led directly to a loss of Athenian demography and, ultimately, democracy. That loss of identity led to a loss of discipline, and then a loss of war. The Roman historian Cornelius Nepos argued that Lysander and the Spartans defeated Athens not because of his own ingenuity or by Spartan discipline, 'but by the want of discipline among the [Athenians], who, from not being obedient to the commands of their leaders, but straggling about in the fields, and abandoning their vessels, fell into the power of their adversaries.'[13]

Athenian democracy had finally unravelled, and her empire along with it.

The Conquest of Athens

Only nine Athenian ships survived the final battle of the Peloponnesian War at Aegospotami. While the *Paralos* set off for Athens to warn them of their doom, the Athenian admiral Conon and the remaining eight ships set out for a very different destination: Cyprus.

Conon saw it unfit to return to Athens, knowing that the surviving Athenians would soon surrender the city to his Spartan rival Lysander. Conon was perhaps the prominent Athenian admiral of the final years of the Peloponnesian War. He commanded the strongest fleet, the Samian fleet, in the final three years of the war and mostly excelled at avoiding heavy losses instead of earning outright victories. Conon had restored confidence in the Athenian fleet in 406 after their loss at Notium, inspiring the new rowers with successful raids along the Spartan-controlled coast of Asia Minor, despite his triremes being undermanned and underequipped.[14] Conon further distinguished himself in the fleet's unlikely survival after being vastly outnumbered by Spartan triremes at the Battle of Mytilene. His sterling reputation had allowed him to avoid a contentious trial of Athenian admirals after heavy losses at Arginusae, which saw eight admirals put to death.

Conon and the Athenian fleet were defeated at Aegospotami, however, and his flight to the Cypriot city of Salamis was motivated by pure survivalism. Salamis was chosen for one simple reason: their king, Evagoras I.

Evagoras of Cyprus claimed mythological ancestry from Telamonian Ajax from the Trojan War, whose family later migrated to Cyprus and founded the city of Salamis, named after the island of Salamis, their traditional home near Athens. Evagoras had apparently recently recovered the Salamian throne for his bloodline in 410 through a coup overthrowing Persian-loyal tyrants who likely came from Phoenicia. Despite eliminating a tyrant who claimed close friendship with the Great King of Persia, Evagoras somehow managed to thread the needle of avoiding provoking Persia and maintaining semi-sovereign rule in Salamis. He certainly envisaged complete autonomy from Persia, and laid the foundation for a future outright rebellion. For now, Evagoras maintained friendly diplomacy with the Persian Empire and potentially even mediated Persian diplomatic agreements between Tissaphernes and Greek city-states.

Most critically, Evagoras was adored by Athenian politicians. The Athenian orator Isocrates said that 'should there ever be appropriately beautiful words to summarize the accomplishments of Evagoras, his virtuous life would be forever remembered among all peoples.'[15] For Athenians experiencing the slow crawl of defeat against the Spartans, Evagoras' revolution in Salamis represented liberty, and since Athenians historically claimed Salamis as their own island, they saw Evagoras as distant kin and his liberty as their own.

Conon would remain at Salamis for the next several years, watchfully awaiting a return to Athens when the time was right. Evagoras' military and political support, and his diplomatic connections within Persia, would prove a valuable ally for the exiles as they hoped to soon restore Athenian democracy. In 405, however, Conon and Evagoras bided their time. It would take a full decade.

The post-Aegospotami Spartan trajectory was quite different.

Immediately after their victory at Aegospotami, Lysander dispatched messengers to send all Athenians away on military campaign and demanded they all return home to Athens or else face execution.[16] To encourage obedience, Lysander 'made it a rule to give them safe conduct to Athens, and to Athens only.'[17] With the exiles returned, Lysander could realize his plan of hastening starvation behind the walls of Athens and bring about the final capitulation of the city. Athenian imperial power crumbled in on itself as every single colony, with the exception of Samos, rebelled and proclaimed either a short-lived independence or the inevitable loyalty to Sparta.

Lysander quickly subjugated Mytilene, the island of Lesbos and the entirety of Thrace before sailing for Athens with 200 ships.[18] In his departure, however, Lysander broke the longstanding Spartan promise to liberate the Greeks of Asia Minor. This was now the second time Sparta had abandoned the Greeks of the region, and no forgiveness or mercy would be forthcoming from these Greeks who had endured Persian, Athenian and now Spartan oppression. Lysander's imperialism through decarchies and *harmosts* compounded by his friendliness with the Persian *satraps* and now his outright neglect of Spartan diplomatic agreements in Asia Minor made him reviled. Before even seizing Athens, the Spartans antagonized the subjects of their new empire.

Lysander, for once, worked in lockstep with the Spartan *ephors* and kings to take the city of Athens itself. He quickly coordinated with the two Spartan kings to surround Athens by land and by sea. King Agis II encamped to the north of the city at the fortress of Decelea while King Pausanias entered the city proper and seized the gymnasium known as the Academy, the first formal Spartan occupation of the Athenian city. Before formally blockading the

Athenian harbour of Piraeus, Lysander liberated strategically symbolic city-states that had been uniquely tyrannized by Athens: first their long-time naval rival Aegina, then the island of Melos whose population they had infamously murdered, and finally the island of Salamis where Themistocles had defeated the Persians and given Athens the foundation of their empire.[19]

Lysander and the Spartan fleet then surrounded the Athenian harbour with 150 ships. With no way to import food or reinforcements into the overcrowded and panicked city, Sparta let chaos descend upon Athens.

At first, the Athenians desperately wished to avoid the negotiations of surrender with Lysander, and instead engaged Agis with an offer of pledging allegiance to Sparta. Agis, ever in deference to the Lycurgan monarchical model, refused and deferred to the Lycurgan model that all diplomatic agreements must be approved by the *ephors*. Lysander had no such qualms about constitutional impropriety and entered into negotiations with Theramenes, an Athenian admiral and former lieutenant to Alcibiades. Theramenes had been elected by the Athenian assembly to discern the intentions of Lysander in his conquest, be it enslavement, murder or subjugation.

However, Lysander refused to speak to Theramenes for three full months, intentionally tarrying in order for the Athenians to become more starved as food supplies dwindled. Theramenes was then sent all the way to Sparta to negotiate in person with the *ephors*, delaying the surrender even further and starving more Athenians with it. The enthusiasm surrounding the long-awaited victory over Sparta apparently caused the Spartan factional politics to be quelled for the time being. Pausanias' traditionalists, Lysander's empire-builders and Agis' Greek-focused imperialists all worked with the *ephors* to seamlessly subdue Athens and no partisan even attempted to undermine the negotiations, as was evident by Agis' refusal to parley with the Athenians who had sought him out.

With surrender now certain, the primary question for the Peloponnesian League was what to do with Athens, its allies and its client states. Sparta's allies – especially Corinth and Thebes – strongly advocated for the utter devastation of Athens and the enslavement of its citizens. One Theban even called for a destruction so thorough that Athens and 'the country about it was left for sheep to graze.'[20] This sentiment was not limited to the Peloponnesian League: Xenophon notes that Greece at large was supportive of the call to destroy Athens once and for all.[21] However, Xenophon also suggests that Sparta simply ignored the input of the rest of the Peloponnesian League, while Plutarch includes a poignant story where a poet sings an Athenian chorus that so moved the assembly that they mercifully 'felt it to be a cruel deed to abolish and destroy a city which was so famous, and produced such poets.'[22]

The Spartans were unmoved. Their stance was that they 'would never reduce to slavery a city which was itself an integral portion of Hellas, and had performed a great and noble service to Hellas in the most perilous of emergencies.'[23] Lysander, acting on direct instructions from the Spartan *ephors*, demanded several specific terms of surrender: the dismantling of the city walls and all military fortifications in Athens, the eradication of the Athenian navy, the reinstatement of all exiles (many of whom had been ostracized for having Spartan sympathies), and the formal acknowledgement of 'the headship of Sparta in peace and war, leaving to her the choice of friends and foes, and following her lead by land and sea.'[24]

Lysander decided that only twelve Athenian ships were allowed to remain, excluding those ships still commanded by Conon in exile, and Athens would never again be allowed to exceed twelve ships. The rest of the Athenian ships were grafted into the Peloponnesian fleets.

Dissatisfied with the final terms, Sparta's allies held their tongues for now, but they retained a palpable bitterness over the survival and potential revival of Athens, and it would not fade with time. Theramenes persuaded the Athenian

Lysander's celebration of the destruction of the walls of Athens. (*Wikimedia Commons, 2022. Public domain*)

voting assembly to accept the terms. There was little pushback as, by now, dozens of Athenians were dying each day from starvation.[25]

In 404, Lysander sailed into the Athenian harbour as 'a man who had the greatest power, and who was, in a manner, master of Hellas.'[26] In his first edict, he ordered beautiful young flautists to play a celebratory tune as the walls and fortifications of Athens were dismantled. The Spartans and the rest of the Greeks who had been oppressed by Athens declared this the first day of liberty in Greece.[27] Yet for those in Athens, having survived plague, war, siege and starvation, their suffering was only just beginning.

The Thirty Tyrants

Lysander wasted no time in the systematic deconstruction of Athenian democracy. Athens was too special for a simple *harmost*, although he did install one to lead a garrison at the acropolis, and its combination of democratic empowerment and class struggle too precarious to be governed by a decarchy. Lysander instead opted for a new style of oligarchy that placed thirty men in command of the state. Diodorus Siculus aptly describes these men as 'directors ostensibly but tyrants in fact'.[28] These men became known as the Thirty Tyrants.

The selection of these thirty men was of the utmost importance. In order to convey a sense of legitimacy, Lysander ordered that Athens vote for the men in a show of democracy, and that the state be governed by the 'ancient constitution'.[29] Xenophon, then a citizen in Athens in his 20s and an eyewitness to the events, records that the primary purpose of the Thirty was to compose a new constitution that would be amenable to Sparta but remain true to their ancestral traditions.[30] Writing just a few decades later, Aristotle described how the nature of that 'ancient constitution' was not so settled, and comprised a brief struggle between political factions favouring democracy and those preferring oligarchy. Diodorus Siculus, writing almost four centuries later, paints a very different picture and says that 'the people, being struck with terror, were compelled to dissolve the democracy by a show of hands.'[31] Either path led to the same destination: the death of Athenian democracy.

Sparta had a long history of patronage among ambitious Athenian aristocrats. Great Athenian leaders like Themistocles, Aristides the Just, Cimon, Alcibiades and Xenophon all cultivated Spartan benefactors or became outright *laconophiles*. For many years, Sparta had a *proxenos* in Athens, a citizen who hosted foreign ambassadors and brokered negotiations and diplomacy between the two city-states. Despite the long war between them, an unbroken stream of Athenian aristocrats maintained admiration of Sparta and would have preferred a

Spartan-friendly oligarchy. The Athenian coup of 411 was the briefly-realized manifestation of at least some of that pro-Spartan sentiment.

The voting assembly was quickly compelled to formally vote in the thirty oligarchs, shortly after the walls of Athens were destroyed. Each oligarch was loyal to Sparta and each was sympathetic to the coup of 411. Some men, such as Theramenes, were oligarchs in both governments despite opposing Spartan rule. Theramenes was voted into his role after his noble approach to the surrender negotiations, and the Athenians perhaps hoped that his presence would soften Sparta's treatment of Athens. Theramenes was instead quickly chastised and threatened by Lysander for the crime of advocating for Athens and appealing to the peace terms. Theramenes would not be able to hinder Lysander's methodical takeover of Athens.

The Thirty's first action was to determine what the 'ancient constitution' actually was. They set out to formalize the new Athenian government via erasure of its past. The Thirty ordered a heavy-handed rewriting of the law system of Solon, the founder of Athenian democracy. These reforms were inscribed on the walls in the centre of the governmental buildings in Athens and were the symbolic cornerstone of democracy itself. Accordingly, while the Thirty re-established traditional institutions of Athenian democracy such as the Council of 500 and the elected military generals, their main purpose was to break Athens and her democratic foundation.[32] Under the auspices of streamlining the government and eliminating the bureaucracy, the Thirty made bold reforms that restricted the court system, dismissed the voting assembly, neutered the council of former magistrates known as the *areopagus*, installed a decarchy to oversee the Athenian harbour of Piraeus, persuaded Sparta to install a Spartan garrison and *harmost* in the city and, finally, appointed a lesser council of 3,000 to champion their new government as field personnel in the daily affairs of Athens.[33]

Their governmental reforms accomplished, the Thirty Tyrants turned their attention to what would become their legacy: culling the Athenian population. The first targets were the informants who had supported Sparta through their espionage – a popular move given their reputation as traitors to Athens – but the list soon extended to any who did not fully submit to their authority, and then to any individual of social or political status.[34] The Tyrants even hired 300 'lash-bearers' to whip the public and stamp out any lingering resistance.

Xenophon mourned the devastation: 'Day after day the list of persons put to death for no just reason grew longer. Day after day the signs of resentment were more significant in the groups of citizens banding together and forecasting the character of this future constitution.'[35]

Anti-democratic bloodshed was an expensive affair, however, and the Thirty soon found themselves starving for coin. After passing a law that allowed them to execute any resident not included in their council of 3,000, they began to select victims 'from the rich such men as suited their ends, they proceeded to arrest them as revolutionaries, put them to death, and confiscated their possessions.'[36]

Sensing a dangerous upheaval of the *stasis*, Theramenes protested these new practices. Butchery and despotism were acceptable, but targeting aristocrats was not. Theramenes had begun the oligarchy as a moderate, but the violent nature of the regime pushed him to the extreme. Xenophon recounts a lengthy and honourable trial for the former Athenian admiral, but in the end he was outmanoeuvred by his fellow tyrant Critias, a close associate of the philosopher Socrates. Critias persuaded the Thirty's council of 3,000 to sentence Theramenes, the most powerful Athenian at the end of the war, to death. He was forced to drink hemlock, but not before a caustic toast to his rival before he drank the poison: 'This to the lovely Critias.'[37]

The death of Theramenes was only an accelerant for the Thirty's bloodshed. In just eight months, up to 1,500 Athenians were killed by the Thirty Tyrants and their lackeys, up to a tenth of the remaining population of the *polis*. Even the rural regions of Attica, the historic refuge far from the metropolitan centre of Athens, were unsafe as the lash-bearers and prosecutors raided homesteads and farms. Citizens began to flee Athens in droves. Megara and Thebes received countless refugees while Athenian depopulation showed no signs of ceasing.

The reign of the Thirty Tyrants was a reign of terror, but despite their efforts the will of the Athenian populace was unbroken. Most critically, Athens was not without its own hero to rival Lysander. The admiral and politician Thrasybulus, a hero of the ill-fated late Peloponnesian War effort, emerged as Lysander's Athenian foil. Where Lysander embodied the modernized Spartan Empire, Thrasybulus embodied the old empire of Athens and its absolute refusal to capitulate.

Thrasybulus led a resistance to the Thirty Tyrants and became 'not only the first, but the only man at the commencement, to declare war against them.'[38] Strikingly, Thrasybulus was not driven by a heartfelt love of democracy. He had been an oligarch during the Athenian coup of 411, but had found the extremism of even those oligarchs distasteful and so found the Thirty downright villainous. His actions in the Peloponnesian War, in his rebellion against the Thirty and then in the coming Corinthian War won him many admirers in the Classical World. Cornelius Nepos adulated his virtue:

> If merit is to be valued by itself, without regard to fortune, I doubt whether I ought not to place him first of all the Greek commanders. This I can say without hesitation, that I set no man above him in integrity, firmness, greatness of mind, and love for his country; for while many have wished,

and few have been able, to deliver their country from one tyrant, it was his lot to restore his country, oppressed by thirty tyrants, from slavery to freedom. But though no man excelled him in these virtues, many, I know not how, surpassed him in fame.[39]

In 403, Thrasybulus had taken the Thebans' offer of residency to Athenian refugees, and with only a team of thirty soldiers took a strategic Athenian fortress at Phyle. His campaign to regain Athenian independence was then headquartered at the fortress, and was therefore named the Phyle campaign.

Critias and the Thirty overplayed their hand by seizing Eleusis on the frontier of Attica, and arresting all their citizens and installing a new garrison to counter the Phyle rebels. Thrasybulus' success and the continued oppression of the Thirty swelled the numbers of his forces, by then numbering 1,000. With the majority of the tyrants' soldiers overextended in Eleusis, Thrasybulus and his militia swooped into the Athenian harbour of Piraeus in the night.

Upon hearing of the rising tide of rebellion in Athens, Lysander quickly returned from his work subduing Samos and persuaded the Spartan *ephors* 'to aid the oligarchies and chastise the democracies.'[40] Spartan reinforcements came to assist the Thirty's forces and attacked the Phyle rebels' camp at Piraeus, which was located at the fortified hill of Munichia. This hill was first fortified by Themistocles, architect of the Greek and Athenian victory in the Persian Wars, and was ironically where the Persian king Darius the Great sat and watched Themistocles defeat his navy at the Battle of Salamis in 479. Munichia was again home to an Athenian and democratic victory when Thrasybulus orchestrated two victories in successive battles and overwhelmed the Thirty's soldiers, despite being outnumbered. The Phyle rebels took Piraeus and Munichia, but still lacked the manpower to take the urban centre of Athens just yet.

Seeking to preserve a future for Athens, Thrasybulus 'forbade those that fled to be injured, thinking it just that "countrymen should spare countrymen"; nor was any one wounded except such as would attack him first.'[41] Critias was the exception. He was killed in the second battle, and with him died the power of the Thirty Tyrants.

The remnant of the Thirty, however, did not surrender and instead retreated to Eleusis while appealing to Sparta for more aid. Lysander saw the danger and blockaded the Athenian harbour yet again, installed himself as *harmost* in Athens and his brother as *navarch* and sent the Thirty 100 talents.[42] These were clever moves as Thrasybulus and the rebels were then surrounded in Piraeus, unable to take Athens itself with their limited numbers, and cut off the hopes of reinforcements or supplies.

Lysander's strategies were crippled by Spartan factionalism. His domineering interventionism grated on the traditionalists among the *ephors*, and so they instead sent Pausanias. As champion of the Lycurgan non-intervention strategy, Pausanias led a limited engagement with the Phyle rebels that aimed solely at containing Spartan hegemony and reputation but cared little for the internal politics of Athens. Pausanias' main concern was for Sparta's future, as he was 'touched by a certain envy of Lysander'[43] and wanted Sparta to return to the Peloponnese and maintain her hegemony without overextending their resources.

Pausanias accordingly fought a conservative strategy and in a battle near Piraeus fought Thrasybulus' hoplites to a stalemate, though with a high cost of two Spartan *polemarchs* ('warlords') and one Olympic victor.[44] Both Thrasybulus and Pausanias saw no reason to continue the fighting, and so Pausanias sent emissaries to negotiate a ceasefire. Spartan law required that two *ephors* oversee the campaigns of the kings in order to avoid corruption, and it so happened that the two *ephors* with Pausanias 'shared the political views represented by Pausanias, rather than those of Lysander and his party.'[45] Xenophon made such an observation in order to emphasize the deepening divisions with the Spartan system; it is clear that Lysander's influence, while extraordinarily strong across Greece, was beginning to wane within Sparta.

Thrasybulus and the Phyle rebels heartily accepted the offer of peace, and while the remnant of the Thirty protested, they held no more influence. Thrasybulus and his soldiers finally marched into Athens proper and formally ended the reign of the Thirty Tyrants. Thrasybulus called the voting assembly to reinstitute Athenian democracy, which quickly passed. Most astonishingly, he also called for clemency for those Athenians who had supported or worked for the Thirty, and even for some of the tyrants themselves. All those who feared vengeance by the democrats were offered protection in Eleusis. Although not a popular move with the most loyal supporters of democracy, Thrasybulus' decision appears to have reconciled Athens. Xenophon wrote that 'to this day the two parties live amicably together as good citizens, and the democracy is steadfast to its oaths.'[46] For his deeds, Thrasybulus was enthroned a hero in Athens and given an olive crown and hundreds of acres of land for his descendants.

Though doubtlessly in decline, Athenian democracy survived the Peloponnesian War and the Thirty Tyrants. Its new challenge was to survive the dysfunction of the Spartan Empire, and in this they would have the company of the Thebans, Corinthians, Argives and the rest of the Peloponnesian League. Although recently bitter rivals, Athenians were not alone in their fury against Sparta's new imperial model.

Chapter Three

The Anti-Spartan Confederacy

Disgruntled Allies in the Peloponnesian League

The terror of the Thirty Tyrants simply did not satisfy the bloodlust of Sparta's allies in the Peloponnesian League. Athens had to pay more for their crimes against Greece.

While some aristocrats from Athens and Thebes had made new alliances during the overthrowing of the Thirty, the official position of Thebes, Corinth and their many allies in the Peloponnesian League was that Athens had not suffered enough in the aftermath of the Peloponnesian War. Even while Thebes and Corinth offered residency to those Athenians exiled for resisting the Thirty, their leaders had no desire to see a resurgent Athens, but Sparta's continued needling of her allies in the Peloponnesian League caused the inconceivable: sympathy for Athens. Of the Peloponnesian League's response to the Thirty, Diodorus Siculus writes:

> The [Spartans], seeing the city of the Athenians abased in power and having no desire that the Athenians should ever gain strength, were delighted and made their attitude clear; for they voted that the Athenian exiles should be delivered up to the Thirty from all over Greece and that anyone who attempted to prevent this should be liable to a fine of five talents. Though this decree was shocking, all the rest of the cities, dismayed at the power of the Spartans, obeyed it, with the exception of the Argives who, hating as they did the cruelty of the Lacedaemonians and pitying the hard lot of the unfortunate, were the first to receive the exiles in a spirit of humanity. Also the Thebans voted that anyone who witnessed an exile being led off and did not render him all aid within his power should be subject to a fine.[1]

If the Spartan *symmachy* was still predicated on military headship, their position was increasingly precarious. While the rest of the Peloponnesian League joined King Pausanias' fight against Thrasybulus and the Phyle rebels, Thebes and Corinth did not. They outright refused to join, claiming that they 'saw nothing contrary to the treaty, was inconsistent with their oaths'[2] in the actions of Athens. Such disobedience to Sparta was uncommon before their victory over

Athens. Thebes and Corinth had not received just compensation for their role in winning the Peloponnesian War. The Spartans, through Lysander's diplomatic policies and the oppression witnessed in the Thirty Tyrants' reign, were losing their closest allies.

Sparta's factionalism was not abated by their latest defeat of Athens. Upon return from the campaign to assist the Thirty Tyrants, King Pausanias faced charges of treason for his peace agreement with Thrasybulus' democracy.[3] These charges were trumped up by the Eurypontid king Agis and his cohort that desired Sparta to maintain hegemony over Greece and Athens. Of the thirty senators in the *Gerousia*, fourteen voted Pausanias guilty, including Agis.[4] As Pausanias himself was a senator given his role as Agiad king, the acquittal was a razor-thin 15–14 margin. No political damage may have occurred through Pausanias' trial, but the ordeal continued to harm Sparta's prestige – perhaps the most valuable commodity in the Greek world – among the city-states.

Sparta's inability to contain their domestic partisanship further undermined their position as hegemon of the Peloponnesian League and united their allies in their dissatisfaction with Sparta's policymaking. New alliances were being forged between Athens and the malcontent members of the Peloponnesian League, sowing the seeds of pushback against Spartan supremacy. Thrasybulus had fostered connections with Theban aristocrats during his rebellion at Phyle, and those relationships both paved over many old wounds between the two states and continued into the new manifestation of Athenian democracy. The fact that all the remaining Thirty and their supporters were effectively quarantined in Eleusis only softened Athens' image to the rest of Greece, who perhaps saw Athenian politics as somehow purged of its corruption and dross.

Sparta had long used the Peloponnesian League to propagandize against tyranny and small-party oligarchies, appealing to *isonomia* and pointing to their own constitution as the standard-bearer of Greek liberty. When juxtaposed to Athenian imperialism, this marketing fared quite well, but with Lysander's nepotism and public Spartan support for the despotism of the Thirty, the notion of Sparta as representing any sort of Greek liberty was far-fetched. Thebes and Corinth were the first to disobey Sparta, but the first to publicly condemn and rebel outright was Elis. Sparta sought to make them an example from which the rest of the Peloponnesian League was to learn.

The Elis Provocation

The city-state of Elis had not been the most faithful ally during the Peloponnesian War. It had been only an occasional member of the Peloponnesian League and considered itself independent considering Elis's chief contribution to Greek culture was the Olympic Games, which were celebrated within their territory. In 418, Elis left the Spartan hegemony to join Argos and Athens in the Peloponnesian War, but was quickly subdued at the Battle of Mantinea. Sparta renounced Elean-Spartan diplomacy at the time, but later welcomed Elis back into the Peloponnesian League.

The Olympics became the catalyst for the Elean rebellion when Sparta formally accused Elis of disallowing their participation in the games of 401.[5] Elis provoked Sparta irreparably when they forbade Agis, the other Spartan king alongside Pausanias, from making the traditional religious sacrifices at the games. Sparta's response was to send ambassadors who unabashedly proclaimed that Elis should liberate all its territories and colonies and allow them to govern themselves.[6] These were territories conquered by Elis and integral to their economic and political health and Elis refused; yet another refusal to acknowledge or obey Sparta's primacy in the Peloponnesian League. Sparta responded with an invasion led by Agis himself aimed 'to bring the men of Elis to their senses.'[7]

The war with Elis was at first impeded by yet another earthquake in the Peloponnese. Agis retreated out of religious caution, interpreting this as a portent from the gods. When the Spartans regrouped and sought help from other allies in their hegemony. While the Athenians acquiesced and joined the expedition, perhaps since Thrasybulus did not wish to risk the delicate state of Athenian democracy, the Thebans and Corinthians both declined. This was now the second time that Sparta's closest and strongest allies had openly defied Spartan command after the invasion of Athens to stop the Phyle rebels. It was clear that Sparta's hegemony was increasingly challenged in the Greek political arena, marking the start of the consolidation of anti-Spartan resistance, both within the Peloponnesian League and in Greece at large.

Undeterred, Agis succeeded in the 'liberation' of many Elean territories and seized Olympia where he was able to make his long-awaited sacrifices. Agis soon conquered Elis itself and exerted little restraint in Spartan vengeance on the Elean countryside:

> Multitudes of cattle, multitudes of slaves, were the fruits of conquest yielded, insomuch that the fame thereof spread, and many more Arcadians and Achaeans flocked to join the standard of the invader and to share in the plunder. In fact, the expedition became one enormous foray. Here was the chance to fill all the granaries of Peloponnese with corn.[8]

The city of Elis itself was spared, both as a show of Spartan strength and a wordless threat about any future rebellions against Sparta. In this, the Spartans lost the Elean War. Elis had given a voice to the discontented members of the

Spartan hegemony when they, as Diodorus describes, 'not only paid no heed to [Sparta] but even accused them besides of enslaving the Greeks.'[9] The enduring impact of Elis's rebellion was the Peloponnesian League's growing dissatisfaction with Spartan leadership and the increasingly viable option of rejecting Spartan command.

Unfortunately for Sparta, the Elean War was not the only pushback against their precarious new empire. Elis's rebellion was timed equally with the Persian hostility against Lysander's personal imperial projects.

The Diminishment of Lysander

Sparta's fading fortunes in the Elean War were ill-timed as Lysander's close Persian ally Cyrus the Younger was facing his own setbacks. After leaving Lysander in charge of the Persian city-states in Asia Minor, Cyrus had returned to Persia and attempted to lay claim to the throne upon his father's death, but the *satrap* Tissaphernes, still incensed by his earlier demotion by Cyrus during Persia's interventions in the Peloponnesian War, had betrayed Cyrus's ambitions to the new king Artaxerxes II. Cyrus was imprisoned for treason, but shortly released and sent back to languish in the *satrapies* of Asia Minor.

Still zealous for the Persian throne, Cyrus the Younger instead waged civil war against the *satrap* Tissaphernes and then against his brother Artaxerxes II for the throne of Persia. In the spring of 401, Cyrus the Younger asked for Spartan military aid in his expedition to march on the Persian homelands and seize the crown. Cyrus hired almost 13,000 Greek and Spartan mercenaries to buttress his own forces and march into Mesopotamia. The deal was likely brokered by Lysander, who assumed his friend Cyrus was sure to win the throne and enhance his own standing across the Greek world.

Come summer, Cyrus's expedition failed outside the historic city of Babylon. At the Battle of Cunaxa, Cyrus the Younger fell in battle in a valiant charge on his brother's bodyguards, and his death broke his army's formation as they fled.[10] The 10,000 Greeks who had been positioned on the right flank were the sole survivors of the rebel army.

Wishing to send a clear message about his revived governorship over the Greeks in Asia Minor, Tissaphernes entreated the Greek generals with promises of reconciliation but quickly executed them all. The remaining Greeks, strong enough to withstand an attack but utterly stranded in the heart of the Persian Empire, escaped and fled north all the way to the Black Sea. Their journey was peppered with attacks from Persian forces, but the 10,000 endured and, battered and beleaguered, reached the sea and eventually returned home. Their journey became known as the March of the Ten Thousand and famously was recounted by the historian Xenophon in his work *Anabasis*. Xenophon was, for once, a reliable source. An Athenian philosopher who studied under Socrates and fought for Sparta, Xenophon had been an officer in Cyrus's mercenary army and survived the march himself.

For Lysander, however, the greatest loss of the Persian civil war was the revenue stream that came from the now-deceased ally Cyrus the Younger. So in 401, Lysander's troubles began where trouble so often does: with the financial reports. After establishing the Thirty in 404, Lysander had set out for Samos where he put down the final vestiges of Athenian democracy in Greece. Victorious at last, Lysander sailed for Sparta. He travelled at the head of the Athenian navy and with a rich coin purse filled with Persian gold.

Yet the defeat of Athens, of course, was also a Persian project. As the tribute and taxes that Cyrus the Younger had left to Lysander began to flow in, Lysander soon found himself with a veritable fortune. Cyrus's funds totalled 470 gold talents, a massive war chest that was likely the most wealth Sparta had ever seen, and was certainly its largest foreign financial investment.[11]

In so doing, Lysander continued his practice of 'modernizing' the Spartan hegemony and its economy. The Lycurgan Reforms had forbidden such a practice and warned against corruption and dysfunction where the money was involved. Lycurgus proved correct when Lysander dispatched a Spartan war hero, the general Gylippus who had massacred the Athenians in Sicily a decade earlier, to bring the treasure to the Spartan homeland. Despite earning his honours for valour in battle, Gylippus could not overcome his love of money. He cut open the money sacks and stole a sum from each bag.

He was found out when the ledgers did not balance, but fled Sparta instead of facing prosecution. He died in obscure exile. In the aftermath, one rattled Spartan elder 'fervently besought the *ephors* to purify the city of all the silver and the gold, as imported curses.'[12] Gylippus' corruption was emblematic of Lysander's brazen infection of Sparta's financial and diplomatic systems. The Spartan state as designed by Lycurgus was simply not structured to support such large quantities of foreign investment, and the Spartan state as designed by Lysander was not yet fully remade to support it either.

Persian bookkeepers meanwhile discovered Lysander's abuse of funds. The governor Pharnabazus was first to call Lysander out on his misappropriations of Cyrus the Younger's fortune. Pharnabazus sent emissaries to Sparta to reveal his crimes, and the *ephors* were apparently so enraged that they executed Lysander's close friend Thorax, an accomplished military commander who had been serving as *harmost* of Samos.[13] Lysander was recalled from campaign to face charges.

This was a staggering change in Spartan-Persian diplomacy. Pharnabazus had previously been a steadfast supporter of Sparta, enthusiastically joining the

Spartans in battle late in the Peloponnesian War during his own rivalry with his fellow governor Tissaphernes. Pharnabazus likely even conspired with Lysander himself to assassinate Alcibiades in Persian territory the year before, but now, when Lysander desperately sought an audience with Pharnabazus to settle their dispute before facing the formal charges in Sparta, Pharnabazus sent Lysander away with a letter for the Spartan *ephors*. Lysander left persuaded that the sealed letter announced their reconciliation and the retraction of Pharnabazus' accusations. Instead, the letter outlined Lysander's avarice in greater detail.[14]

Elsewhere across Greece, many of Lysander's decarchies were declining in their ability to control the *stasis* and class struggle of their particular city-state. It seems that the model of the Thirty Tyrants had now extended to Lysander's other holdings: '...the prizes [Lysander] awarded to his friends and allies were irresponsible lordships over cities, and absolute sovereignties, while the sole punishment that could satisfy his wrath was the death of his enemy; not even exile was allowed.'[15]

One political rival in Sparta remarked that Greece was so irreparably damaged that it 'could not have borne two Lysanders',[16] and Lysander earned a dreaded comparison to Alcibiades in his unique ability to meld virtue and chaos across the Aegean world. Lysander's policies had succeeded in amassing power, but also in uniting Sparta's allies in a curious phenomenon: sympathy towards Athens. While the Thirty Tyrants and the Elean War sowed discontent back on the Greek mainland, Persia was now incensed with Lysander's embezzlement and the Greek city-states of Asia Minor felt similarly betrayed at Lysander's handing over of their polity to the Persians, despite long-held Spartan promises of liberty. Sparta finally realized that their Lysandrean problem had to be addressed.

The two Spartan kings, Pausanias and Agis, put aside their own disagreements for the rare opportunity to constrain Lysander's power and charged him with treason sometime around 401. It is nevertheless clear that Lysander's position diminished substantially, perhaps even including revoking his admiralship and the recalling of some decarchies and *harmosts*. Lysander would never regain his personal hegemony over Sparta's hegemony. He would, however, remain an authoritative voice in Spartan policymaking and diplomacy. His final contribution to Sparta was one of his most reverberating: persuading the Spartans to appoint Agesilaus II as their next king.

Agesilaus II and the Spartan-Persian War

Upon his ascent to the Spartan throne in 400, Agesilaus quickly filled the power vacuum left by Lysander's diminished status. After his demotion, Lysander had initially revived his attempts to institutionalize his leadership and allow the

Spartan kings to be democratically chosen, culminating with his previous attempt to bribe the Delphic Oracle. This and his simultaneous effort to empower the sub-elites of Sparta and win the monarchy for himself were unsuccessful, however, and so he instead turned his eye towards the patronage of a new king. When Agesilaus' elder half-brother King Agis died of illness upon his return from the Elean War in 401, Lysander saw the opportunity to play kingmaker. While Agis did in fact have a son and heir, this child was reputed to be illegitimate.

Sparta had long feared an ancient omen about their kings: 'Beware of the lame reign.'[17] This was a thorny point for Agesilaus who was born with a disability; most likely one leg shorter than the other. He was a rare Spartan to survive infancy with any such condition. This was almost entirely due to Sparta's worsening population crisis; Sparta needed all the full citizens they could muster and the *ephors* likely stopped abandoning 'weak' infants on Mount Taygetus. Agesilaus bore his burden with aplomb: 'the ease and gaiety with which he bore such a misfortune, being first to jest and joke about himself, went far towards rectifying it.'[18] Agesilaus was perfectly situated to be admired by all factions of the clashing Spartan social classes. The Spartiates respected him given his graduation from the *agoge*, a feat most kings could not risk given the high mortality rate. The liberated helots came to value his enfranchisement of their new status, and the traditionalist oligarchs valued his royal heritage and military acumen.

Yet when Agis' heir claimed that this prophecy regarding a doomed king was about Agesilaus, Lysander instead spun the rather opaque prophecy to say that Sparta's ruin would come 'if bastards and ill-born men should be kings.'[19] No man in Sparta could contest Lysander's skills at rhetoric and information warfare, and Agesilaus soon became king.

According to Plutarch, Lysander especially desired to install Agesilaus since the two had previously been lovers, and he felt that Agesilaus would be a pliable pawn. While Plutarch credits Lysander, Xenophon leaves Lysander almost entirely out of the narrative of Agesilaus' coronation.[20] In Xenophon's account, Agesilaus suggested that Agis' heir was really the son of Alcibiades and therefore an anathema to Sparta.

Xenophon was keen to give Agesilaus credit for the simplest of reasons: he was his friend and, eventually, his biographer. In fact, Xenophon was so inspired by the honour and deeds of Agesilaus that he considered him among the great Homeric heroes such as Achilles and Odysseus. Xenophon lavishes praise on the Spartan king in the opening words of the biography:

> To write the praises of Agesilaus in language equalling his virtue and renown is, I know, no easy task; yet must it be essayed; since it were but an

ill requital of pre-eminence, that, on the ground of his perfection, a good man should forfeit the tribute even of imperfect praise.[21]

Agesilaus would soon earn his place among the most revered Spartan leaders. His first challenge as king came at the end of his first year with the aforementioned Conspiracy of Cinadon in 399. Agesilaus had performed the religious sacrifice that Xenophon and the Spartans credited with exposing the scheme, and while the sources are scant, the affair clearly cemented his position as the new populist leader of Sparta. Cinadon's almost-rebellion spotlighted the Spartan class struggle given that Cinadon had broad support among 'helots, enfranchised, inferiors, provincials, one and all.'[22] Even members of Sparta's military were said to have compiled weapons and supplies for the coup.

Agesilaus is not said to have led the investigation into Cinadon, but instead apparently showed deference to the *ephors* and the *Gerousia*; this in itself was a wise move that earned a layer of bureaucratic support with the Spartan government that Lysander never fully enjoyed. Such unity from the Spartan state was a remarkable development that likely disarmed any of Cinadon's co-conspirators. Instead of the tense division that Lysander's personal projects had cultivated in Sparta, the co-conspirators now faced a unified front among the kings and magistrates. It did nothing to heal the long term *stasis*, but Agesilaus' steady leadership and populist appeal inspired a brief solidarity that kept Sparta's domestic struggles from boiling over. By 399, Agesilaus was supplanting Lysander as the pre-eminent Spartan leader.

Plutarch paints their relationship as a kind of spirited competitiveness akin to Odysseus and Achilles, a Homeric dialectic that Sparta had been designed to cultivate:

> The Spartan lawgiver [Lycurgus] seems to have introduced the spirit of ambition and contention into his civil polity as an incentive to virtue, desiring that good citizens should always be somewhat at variance and in conflict with one another, and deeming that complaisance which weakly yields without debate, which knows no effort and no struggle, to be wrongly called concord.[23]

Agesilaus and Lysander were not yet true rivals, though. Their antagonism had scant opportunity to truly develop before rumours seeped into Sparta of a vast navy being raised in Phoenicia, a Persian client-state. The Greeks were convinced that this looming third invasion of Greece, almost a century after the first invasion ordered by Darius the Great, was retribution for Greek participation in the revolt of Cyrus the Younger and a result of Tissaphernes' desire for vengeance.

As reward for his distinction in the rebellion of Cyrus, Tissaphernes inherited all of Cyrus's lands in Asia Minor. Upon return to the Ionian coast in 399, Tissaphernes' first action was to demand 'the absolute submission of the Ionic cities, without exception, to his authority.'[24] The Greeks of Asia Minor loathed Persian rule, but had settled into an understanding with Cyrus the Younger on account of his Greek sympathies and duly paid tribute for a tacit sovereignty. John O. Hyland suggests that Tissaphernes' demand for submission was more likely a demand for tribute to Persia for Ionia's support of Sparta, and that the Ionian leaders were more motivated by a fear of retribution against their political class than actual Persian oppression.[25] No matter the Ionian intentions, Tissaphernes' return to Asia Minor upended the equilibrium. The Ionian Greeks refused Tissaphernes entrance into their cities, and swiftly sent diplomats to Sparta to plead for intervention. War was coming.

The first wave was an expeditionary force led by the *harmost* Thibron, chosen because he was one of the few *harmosts* in Asia Minor not under Lysander's thumb. Thibron led an army of 1,000 *neodamodes*, the new citizens composed of freed helots, and 4,000 soldiers from the Peloponnesian allies.[26] Thibron even paid out of his own pocket for 300 Athenian cavalry to join them, although the Athenians slyly sent former soldiers of the Thirty Tyrants and were happy to see them go. While Thibron raised a local militia of Ionian Greeks to further support his army, he saw limited success.

Tissaphernes' forces forced Thibron to retreat from Ionia and instead head towards Tissaphernes' own *satrapy* of Caria on the south coast. After running low on supplies, Thibron's army became desperate and looted Ionian cities. The *ephors* were dissatisfied with his ineptness and recalled Thibron, replacing him with a more capable commander named Dercylidas. Dercylidas laboured for two years in Asia Minor against Tissaphernes and his old rival Pharnabazus, who briefly reconciled with his fellow governor in the face of the Spartan threat. In lieu of direct engagement, Dercylidas eventually cosied up to both *satraps* in a summit after a series of cat-and-mouse encounters, but Dercylidas' terms for a peace treaty were entirely incompatible with the Persians. The Persian *satraps* demanded a complete evacuation from Asia Minor and the retaking of the Ionian city-states, yet the Spartans insisted on Greek control of the entire Ionian coast.[27] At an impasse, each army sent messengers back to their lords for further orders. Sparta had the option to withdraw their forces or double down their efforts and engage Persia in a more comprehensive invasion.

So in 397, Sparta made plans to invade Persia. Despite or perhaps because of recent tensions, Sparta consulted the other members of their Peloponnesian League. Xenophon does not report that the *symmachy* members needed much persuasion, but it is noteworthy that Sparta was aware of the growing dissatisfaction with their hegemony. Upon his return to Greece, Thibron faced charges of treason when the Peloponnesian allies accused him 'of allowing his troops to plunder their friends'.[28]

The prospect of war further split Spartan factionalism. Agesilaus and his partisans, who wished to rule Greece alone, viewed the war as necessary for their own survival and pragmatic for Sparta's imperial interests, but also as a dangerous overextension. Yet Agesilaus had an earnest desire to prove his leadership in warfare, and persuaded the *ephors* that a limited campaign would secure Sparta's holdings in Asia Minor and only reinforce her hegemony. The *ephors* preferred his aggressive defensive mindset to Lysander's imperial vision, and he was approved to 'carry on the war at the expense of Persia rather than that of Hellas; but it was the perfection of policy, they felt, so to change the arena of battle, with Asia as the prize of victory instead of Hellas.'[29]

Agesilaus legitimized the new Spartan social classes by requesting 2,000 *neodamodes* to join just 30 Spartans in the invasion.[30] Their forces would be strengthened by 6,000 soldiers from the allies in Sparta's empire. This striking imbalance showed both the severity of Spartan depopulation and the *ephors*' hesitancy to risk their Spartiates in a foreign land war. Agesilaus bolstered both the freed helots, who were quickly becoming a burgeoning middle class, and the pragmatist-abolitionist faction within Sparta's *stasis*.

Through this pre-emptive invasion, Agesilaus sought to succeed where the Spartans had failed the Ionians so many times before, and 'endeavour to effect a peace; or, if the barbarian preferred war, he would leave him little leisure to invade Hellas.'[31] Yet Plutarch instead reports that it was Lysander and not the spirit of liberty that was the driving force persuading Agesilaus to invade. Lysander and his imperialist faction relished the opportunity to win back his former decarchies and reconnect with many of his former oligarchs in Asia Minor. It was to be a springboard to their new Spartan Empire.

Agesilaus gathered the invasion force at Aulis in the Theban region of Boeotia. Aulis was a symbolic launching-point for the Greeks as none other than the Mycenaean king Agamemnon had gathered the Greek army there as they sailed to invade Troy, thus beginning the events of *The Iliad*. The departure of Agamemnon's army had come at a great cost: the goddess Artemis demanded that Agamemnon sacrifice his own daughter. According to tradition, Agamemnon had told his daughter she was to marry the great Achilles: the young girl dressed in her bridal gown before being killed by her own father. Her sacrifice cleared the skies for the Greek ships to sail to Troy.

Agesilaus' own invasion required a similar sacrifice for their departure. In his quest to become a reincarnated Homeric hero like Agamemnon, Agesilaus deeply offended the Thebans when he tried to make animal sacrifices without following Boeotian custom or asking their permission. Agesilaus even intended to use his own priest and not a Theban soothsayer. The Theban oligarchs, military commanders named the *Boeotarchs* who functioned as chief magistrates with full political and diplomatic authority, sent a cavalry to intervene. The Thebans forced Agesilaus to 'desist from further sacrificing; and lighting upon victims already offered, they hurled them from off the altars, scattering the fragments.'[32] The simmering tension between Sparta and Thebes had now boiled over into outright conflict. Agesilaus and his army quickly vacated Boeotia, but the Thebans were incensed at the perceived disrespect. Agesilaus, in turn, blamed the Thebans not just for a failed offering but for a failed invasion of Asia Minor.[33] The poor omens of the unfinished sacrifice were to Agesilaus the prophecy of an unfinished invasion. He was convinced that the Spartans would not resolve the Persian war due to Theban meddling in Spartan piety.

Thebes never recovered from the doomed sacrifice. Although they had approved of the Spartan invasion, they refused to send assistance at least in part due to the lingering animus over Spartan imperialism, maltreatment of the Peloponnesian allies, the war on Elis and now the sacrifices of Agesilaus. Sparta was keenly aware of the delicacy of their fraying relationship with Thebes, and had sent the father-in-law of Agesilaus as the ambassador to request Theban participation in the invasion.[34] They clearly hoped to assuage Theban disaffection with this personal touch, but it was of no avail. This marked Thebes' second refusal of Sparta's demand for military aid after they likewise refused to support the Elean War. As of 397, Thebes was functionally no longer a member of the Peloponnesian League, and as the strongest ally after Sparta, Thebes was the first domino to fall. Corinth and Athens similarly refused to send aid to Agesilaus.

Agesilaus' antagonism of the Thebans was the final affront in the plagued Peloponnesian League. While Agesilaus had envisioned a united Greek army much like Agamemnon's, the invasion force was almost entirely Spartan and Peloponnesian, but while Sparta's now former allies refused aid, they were not yet provoked into outright war. It took Persian desperation and interventionism to bring about military conflict.

After arriving in Asia Minor, Agesilaus was at first overshadowed by his own general Lysander. Plutarch remarks that the public displays of affection for Lysander were so overwhelming that 'Agesilaus had the command in name and outward appearance, to comply with the law, while in fact Lysander was master of all, had all power, and did everything.'[35] Plutarch further reports that Agesilaus was reluctant to cast Lysander off, despite the fanfare of his return to Asia Minor, and still considered Lysander a close ally and friend.[36] The relationship between the two Spartan leaders soon soured.

Agesilaus and his army arrived in Ephesus and were immediately entreated by Tissaphernes' messengers for peace while the *satrap* sought further instructions from the king Artaxerxes II. Agesilaus' sole terms were the 'liberty' of the Ionian city-states. Tissaphernes was, of course, instead raising reinforcements, which Agesilaus suspected.

While Agesilaus tolerated Lysander's public adoration, the thirty Spartans who accompanied the invading force did not. Agesilaus sought to appease his Spartan aristocrats over his political mentor, and accordingly promoted each of the thirty Spartans to governor positions in Ionia. He meanwhile had a different job in mind for Lysander: his meat carver, but the demotion to meat carver was far too demeaning for the mighty Lysander and it brought about the final split between the two great Spartan leaders:

> Lysander determined to have a conference with him, at which a brief and laconic dialogue passed between them. 'Verily, thou knowest well, Agesilaus, how to abase friends.'
>
> To which Agesilaus: 'Yes, if they would be greater than I; but those who increase my power should also share in it.'
>
> [Lysander replied] 'Well, perhaps thy words, Agesilaus, are fairer than my deeds; but I beg thee, even because of the strangers who have their eyes upon us, to give me a post under thy command where thou believest that I shall be least annoying to thyself, and more serviceable than now.'[37]

Agesilaus sent Lysander off to an ambassadorship in the Hellespont, and then turned his attention to the invasion itself. With his army now supported by the Ionians, Aeolians and Hellespontines, Agesilaus ravaged the Persian territories in Asia Minor from Ephesus to Caria.[38] Over the next year, Tissaphernes proved no match for Agesilaus' tactical mind, and was consistently outmanoeuvred both by Agesilaus' military movements and by his information warfare.

The Spartan king took plenty of territories in Asia Minor back from the Persians, and was able to build up the infrastructure and logistical systems needed for Sparta to sustain an expeditionary force overseas.[39] By winning over the loyalty of the Ionian Greeks and subsequently mobilizing their industrial powers from smiths to tanners to hoplites, Agesilaus briefly created a template for Sparta's sluggish Lycurgan economic model to authentically coordinate a military campaign on foreign soil. Xenophon tells us how 'the bronze-worker, the carpenter, the smith, the leather-cutter, the painter and embosser, were all busily engaged in fabricating the implements of war; so that the city of Ephesus itself was fairly converted into a military workshop.'[40] It was the closest Sparta came to fully emulating the Athenian empire that preceded their own. The logistical foundation was matched with a heavy-handed bullying of allies as Agesilaus conscripted Ionian Greeks into his own army, akin to the Athenian model. Unlike the Athenians, Agesilaus was charismatic and skilled enough, and the threat of Persian subjugation salient enough, to minimize any serious resistance.

It was the apex of Sparta's empire, but it would only last a matter of weeks. Back in Greece, the Spartans could still not manage to rein in their allies' discontent. Persia decided that the best way to stop Agesilaus was to further drive the wedge between Sparta and the rest of Greece.

The Outbreak of the Corinthian War

Persia's inability to contain Agesilaus' invasion caused a chaos of two kinds. First, the governorship and command of Tissaphernes, who had so redeemed himself against Cyrus the Younger, was now deeply in peril. Tissaphernes had few allies within Persian politics, and fewer still now that he was falling out of favour with the King of Kings. Tissaphernes was executed for his failures on orders from Artaxerxes II himself.[41] His successor, Tithraustes, thought that Agesilaus would withdraw, but Agesilaus marched now for the provincial capital of Sardis and boasted of plans to capture the Persian king.[42]

The second chaos came from the desperate Persian turn to bribery and spycraft among the Peloponnesian League members. The new *satrap* Tithraustes sent a cunning diplomat named Timocrates of Rhodes to bribe Thebes, Corinth, Argos and Athens into an official rebellion against the Spartan Empire. Timocrates' mission was an elegant solution to the Agesilaus problem: domestic war in Greece would force Sparta to recall Agesilaus' army. Timocrates brought 50 talents of gold with him to spread among influential aristocrats in each city; only the Athenians rejected the money.[43]

Thebes was quick to accept the offer, though they determined that the shrewdest approach was an indirect instigation. They funnelled the Persian money to their allies in Locris who were involved in a long-running territorial dispute with their neighbour Phocis. With their new funds, the Locrians claimed the territory and increased taxation on its Phocian residents. Phocis immediately declared war on Thebes.[44] Phocis was a dutiful Spartan ally and beseeched Sparta to come to their aid, exactly as the Thebans had anticipated.

Sparta was all too happy to march on Thebes. Their bitterness over Thebes' varied slights against the Spartan *symmachy* had not abated. Xenophon summarizes the list of offences: refusal to pay tithing during the Peloponnesian War at Decelea, collaboration with Corinthians on defying orders to march on the Phyle rebels and on Elis, abstention from the invasion of Asia Minor and the bellicose defiling of Agesilaus' sacrifice at Aulis.[45] Corinth and Thebes had likewise accepted the Persian bribe and were soon to join Thebes, with Athens still deliberating and not far from supporting the rebels. The *ephors* saw no choice and eagerly approved an assault on Thebes, therefore ordaining yet another civil war in Greece.

Sparta could simply not look past the expansion of its new empire to the cost of its maintenance. The Spartans somehow managed to be both myopic in their domestic partisanship and farsighted in their desire to conquer the vast Persian territories in Asia Minor, despite their logistical shortcomings. The Oxford historian George Forrest deftly described the fragility of Sparta's relationship with her allies by 395: 'when single-minded brutality might have worked, indecisive aggressiveness merely won enemies for Sparta and at the same time gave those enemies heart.'[46]

The departure of Thebes, Corinth and their many territories hollowed out the Peloponnesian League and reconfigured the diplomatic landscape of Greece. Thebes, Corinth and Argos were now all united in what would become an anti-Spartan confederacy, with Athens soon to join. This uneasy alliance of formerly bitter rivals was bound by one thing alone: their hatred of the new Spartan hegemony. In the Theban town of Haliartus, the Spartans would meet their old friends and new enemies in battle.

The stage was now set for the Corinthian War.

Chapter Four
Dawn of War: The Battle of Haliartus

Prelude to Battle

Spartan optimism was at an all-time high as their armies set out from Laconia in the late summer of 395:

> [Sparta] reasoned that now, if ever, was the favourable moment to conduct an expedition against the Thebans, and once for all to put a stop to their insolent behaviour towards them. Affairs in Asia were prospering under the strong arm of Agesilaus, and in Hellas they had no other war on hand to trammel their movements.[1]

To bring the impudent Thebans back under their thumb, Sparta plotted a twin assault of two armies led by Pausanias and Lysander. Lysander's standing in Sparta in 395 was complicated. By the end of 396, he had journeyed home to Sparta after his ambassadorship, seething over the failure to regain his decarchies in Asia Minor. Despite Sparta's successful invasion, it was a personal failure. Lysander and Agesilaus had reversed their roles among the Ionian Greeks. He again tried to rewrite the Spartan constitution to allow non-royalty to become king, resolving 'to put into execution at once, and without delay, the plans for a revolutionary change which he is thought to have devised and concocted some time before.'[2] His scheming was unsuccessful, although primarily due to his steadfast discipline to never truly break Spartan law. Plutarch would later remark in his *Parallel Lives* that this distinguished Lysander from his Roman analogue Sulla:

> A peculiar virtue in Lysander [was] that he obtained all his high offices with the consent of his fellow-citizens, and when affairs were in a sound condition; he did not force anything from them against their will, nor did he acquire any power which was contrary to the laws.[3]

Lysander maintained enough residual influence to be appointed command of the second invasion force into Thebes. He was sent ahead to Phocis to raise an army of non-Peloponnesian allies, including the Phocians, Oetaeans, Heracleotes,

Melians and Aenianians.[4] Lysander conscientiously followed his orders from the *ephors*, but decided to add to them by also marching on the city-state of Orchomenus. The enterprising Lysander sought to prise Orchomenus' loyalty away from the Thebans.

Sparta's grand strategy against Thebes was akin to Persia's with Sparta: to leverage dissatisfied allies into rebellion against their leader. Lysander therefore took it upon himself to select the Boeotian city-state of Orchomenus which held a long grudge against Thebes and was more amenable to joining Sparta. The Spartans aimed to convince the Orchomenians to revolt and subsequently disintegrate the Boeotian Confederacy, a smaller but influential *symmachy* that Thebes led as hegemon. The eleven *Boeotarchs* led the Confederacy and were elected for one-year terms to represent their home territory in a federal model.[5] To get Orchomenus to abandon Thebes was no small feat, since their territory controlled two of the eleven *Boeotarchs*, in comparison to Thebes itself which controlled four.[6] Thebes surely had an outsized influence; however, winning over Orchomenus not only destabilized the Confederacy but was a threatening invitation from Sparta to its other smaller members.

This was a template employed by Athens in the 420s, when they likewise invaded Boeotia in an attempt to subdue Thebes while simultaneously fomenting rebellion with her allies.[7] The Athenian invasion had been clever in design but poor in execution. They had been distracted by northern tactical movements in Thessaly and Macedon, and the Boeotian campaign had a punctuated implementation over five years that culminated in Athenian defeat at the Battle of Delium.

The Spartan battle plan aimed to efficiently accomplish both Athenian phases of invasion at once.[8] Lysander was to attack the western front of Boeotia with his non-Peloponnesian allies, now including the Orchomenians, while Pausanias was to attack the eastern front with the Spartan and remaining Peloponnesian League armies. Thebes would be caught in the pincers. Full battle would not be required since, if things went according to plan, the Boeotian Confederacy would lose its key allies and Thebes would be forced to negotiate for peace.[9]

The two armies were to meet at the city-state of Haliartus, a minor member of the Confederacy which shared their two *Boeotarchs* with two other *poleis*.[10] Haliartus was a strategic location in a flat, agrarian stretch of land nestled between the large Lake Copais and mountain foothills to the south and west eventually leading to the mythical Mount Helicon. The city itself was on the crossroads from Thebes to the north of Greece and equipped with a small acropolis and respectable walls. Before the Corinthian War, it was perhaps best known as a member of Agamemnon's army listed by Homer in his 'Catalogue of Ships' in *The Iliad*. With the armies aiming to merge at Haliartus, the Thebans would be in a double bind: either they march west to meet Lysander and abandon Thebes to Pausanias, or they march east to meet Pausanias and leave western Boeotia undefended and its city-states prone to defection to avoid Lysander's wrath.[11]

José Pascual suggests that the Spartan battle strategy was another ploy by Lysander to alchemize the resuscitation of his political power. Lysander had persuaded the *ephors* into the two-army strategy, allowing him to assume the position of *harmost*.[12] This further allowed him to both equalize his rank with King Pausanias for the campaign and become autonomous enough to 'shift the centre of gravity of Spartan politics towards Europe [and away from Agesilaus' Asian campaign] so he could play a leading role.'[13] Lysander, his eye ever on the prize of dominating Sparta and Greece, marched on Haliartus. Back in the Peloponnese, Pausanias' Spartan army made the customary sacrifices and found only good auguries. He camped at Tegea while raising the banners of the *perioeci* and other Peloponnesian allies, but his delay risked the delicately-timed convergence at Haliartus. There is no indication that Pausanias intentionally delayed his arrival at Haliartus, but it is hard not to consider the possibility.

Meanwhile, the Thebans were preparing for the invasion they knew was coming. The Boeotian Confederacy's strategy appears to have logically prioritized defence of Thebes proper and keeping the majority of their forces safe in the city until they could determine where and when the Spartan armies would attack. They would then join with the reinforcements and engage Sparta in a defensive war effort.[14] With Corinth and Argos needing to secure their homelands in the Peloponnese before the offensive campaign began, the Thebans hoped that those reinforcements would come from Athens.

Despite their antipathy to Sparta, Thrasybulus and the Athenians were so far taciturn about the outbreak of war in Greece and had not seceded from Sparta's hegemony. Theban ambassadors, no doubt influenced by the Theban *Boeotarchs* and not by the rest of the Confederacy, arrived in Athens in 395 to spur the Athenians into joining their growing anti-Spartan coalition.

Thebes' negotiating position was precarious considering that they had so recently advocated for Sparta to brutally punish Athens after the Peloponnesian War, but Thebes was quick to point out that they had not tried to march on the Thirty Tyrants despite Sparta's commands. The Theban orators focused instead on casting the Spartans as the new tyrannical power. Their speech to the Athenian assembly was a masterpiece in Classical rhetoric. They began with the following:

> As then you are to a large extent the cause of the resentment which the [Spartans] feel towards us, we consider it only fair that you in your turn should render us assistance. Still more do we demand of you, sirs, who

were of the city party at that date, to enter heart and soul into war with the [Spartans]. For what were their services to you? They first deliberately converted you into an oligarchy and placed you in hostility to the democracy, and then they came with a great force under guise of being your allies, and delivered you over to the majority, so that, for any service they rendered you, you were all dead men; and you owe your lives to our friends here, the people of Athens.[15]

Well aware of their audience, the Thebans employed an appeal to emotion. The Athenians desperately wished to re-establish their empire and reclaim their position as the cultural and political hegemons of Greece. The Thebans pressed this sore point with zest:

But to pass on – we all know, men of Athens, that you would like to recover the empire which you formerly possessed; and how can you compass your object better than by coming to the aid yourselves of the victims of [Spartan] injustice? Is it their wide empire of which you are afraid? Let not that make cowards of you – much rather let it embolden you as you lay to heart and ponder your own case. When your empire was widest then the crop of your enemies was thickest. Only so long as they found no opportunity to revolt did they keep their hatred of you dark; but no sooner had they found a champion in [Sparta] than they at once showed what they really felt towards you. So too today. Let us show plainly that we mean to stand shoulder to shoulder embattled against the [Spartans]; and haters enough of them – whole armies – never fear, will be forthcoming.[16]

Finally, the Thebans delivered their thesis and identified the deepest offence of Sparta: 'in the day of their good fortune, they have planted the tyrant's heel.'[17] The Athenian assembly voted unanimously to join the new anti-Spartan confederacy. With no more neutral parties, all of Greece was now united against the Spartan *symmachy*.

The State of Thebes

Before moving to the Battle of Haliartus itself, it is important to explore the context of Thebes in 395 and overcome the gravitational pull of historians towards Athens and Sparta. It would be improper to reduce this historic Greek power to a middling malcontent or a grey eminence, frustrated over the failure to destroy Athens in 404 or over Spartan abuse of power. Indeed, Thebes had been a great power since the genesis of the Greek identity. In the 'Catalogue of Ships' in Homer's *The Iliad*, the first group of Greeks listed as joining Agamemnon's war was the Boeotians. They sent fifty ships to the Trojan War and held the distinction of having the most individual *poleis* named by Homer.

Culturally, Thebes still held their traditional influence. From Hesiod's *Theogony* to the Seven against Thebes to the myth of Cadmus and Europa, Thebes played a more central role in Greek mythology than perhaps any other Greek political power of the Classical era. Yet more works championing Thebes did not survive until the present day. A series of four epic poems centred on Thebes entitled the Theban Cycle rivalled the Trojan War's Epic Cycle, which includes *The Iliad* and *The Odyssey*. A strong argument can be made that Thebes and Troy are the two great Greek cities of myth. Then passing from the age of heroes into the Classical era, Thebes remained ever on the lips of orators or in the pens of playwrights. In Athens, Thebes became a punching-bag for criticism of their own *stasis*. Wrapping their themes in Theban mythology, playwrights like Sophocles offered criticism of the Athenian and Greek society by scapegoating Thebes. Plays like *Antigone*, *Oedipus Rex* and *Oedipus at Colonus* were set in Thebes as a vehicle to skewer Athenian culture and politics. Criticism of Thebes was socially acceptable; criticism of Athens less so.

By 395, the Boeotian Confederacy had seventeen city-states of varying sizes across Central Greece. Thebes was, of course, the mightiest, but by no means held unchecked power. Their support of Persia during the Persian invasions a century earlier had substantially diminished their status, making them something of a pariah in Greek affairs shortly after the Persian Wars. Even though there were 700 hoplites from Boeotian Thespiae at the Battle of Thermopylae, the Theban reticence to act in the invasion was seen as cowardice. As such, the Boeotians were something of a vassal state of both Athens and Sparta in the late fifth century, but regained their status as a great power by the end of the century with Athens' decline. During this century of restoration, the Boeotian Confederacy grew from eleven city-states to their current seventeen, and could contribute as many as 7,000 hoplites when at full force. After Sparta, the Boeotian Confederacy wielded the mightiest land army of the early fourth century in Greece.

The federal system of the Boeotian Confederacy had no parallel in the Greek world. Its innovative system was lauded by Thucydides and Herodotus. Its most unique contribution was a fusion of *polis* and regional identity. Somehow, the Boeotians managed to maintain the political autonomy and cultural identity of their individual *polis*, no matter how small, yet still participate in broader Greek politics by unifying with their neighbours. Unlike Sparta or Athens, no single *polis* managed to subvert the *symmachy* through raw strength, largely due to the constitutional constraints embedded in the Boeotian Confederacy's charter. Proportional allotment of representatives and *Boeotarchs* ensured the legitimacy and safety of each city-state, no matter how minor.

Had the geopolitical winds of the fifth century blown in a slightly different direction, then it would have been Theban federalism and not Athenian democracy that the Western world may have inherited. Several notable historians have argued this in the past few decades, including Simon Hornblower and Hans Beck. Beck argues:

> Just as Athens exported democracy...Thebes exported federalism. By doing so, it contributed largely to the process of overcoming the narrow boundaries of the Greek *polis*. The influence of Thebes on Greek political culture thus seems to be obvious: it is – as Simon Hornblower once put it – 'the export of the federal principle.'[18]

Thebes was, however, no paradise, and they were not immune to *stasis* and political factionalism either. The Oxyrhynchus Historian is our most reliable ancient source for Thebes in the late fifth and early fourth centuries, and the picture that historian paints is steeped in the customary *stasis* of the day. Thebes had been on the verge. This ancient historian argues that it was Spartan meddling – perhaps especially growing Theban resentment towards Agesilaus – that finally peeled Thebes away from their Peloponnesian League loyalties. Since the latter part of the Peloponnesian War when Athens attempted to fully seize Boeotia, both Athens and Sparta funded pro-democratic or pro-oligarchical powers in Boeotia. Their federal system was pressure-tested by such interference.

The democrats were led by Ismenias, while the Spartans funded the efforts of Leontiades. The two factions oscillated in power until the Spartan fortification of Decelea in 413, which swayed the tide towards the oligarchs given Decelea's proximity to Boeotia and the Spartan need to firm up support as they tightened the screws on Athens. Yet even while pro-Spartan powers gained power, Ismenias and the democrats knew that the Boeotians were too divided to unite against a powerful rival in Sparta, especially when many in Thebes considered Sparta an ally. The democrats therefore found a more calculating method of subverting Spartan supremacy in Thebes. By the opening years of the fourth century, Ismenias and the Boeotian Confederacy had been approached by Timocrates of Rhodes with the Persian offer to fund a war effort against Sparta. Acting with alacrity to take advantage of the opportunity, Ismenias persuaded the Phocians to invade the western Locrians. In short, the Oxyrhynchus Historian casts the Corinthian War's outbreak as a cunning manoeuvre of pro-Athenian partisans in Boeotia, disrupting the Persia-Athens-Sparta axis that so often narrates Greek history. By the onset of the Corinthian War and the Battle of Haliartus, the Boeotians aimed to shatter that traditional power structure further.

The Battle of Haliartus

The rendezvous city of Haliartus had strong fortifications, so Lysander camped on a hill – the 'Fox Hill' – within view of the city walls, a foreboding sight meant to intimidate the Haliartians. The Fox Hill was a strategically sound position. It had natural defence with the Hoplites River nearby and it overlooked both the city of Haliartus and Pausanias' anticipated route of arrival from Plataea.[19] The foothills of Mount Likophios protected his army's rear.[20] Upon arrival at the Fox Hill, the primary issue for Sparta was communication: Lysander and Pausanias had no practical means of synergizing their armies to meet in Haliartus at the exact time. Exacerbating this was Pausanias' procrastinated arrival in Boeotia; Pausanias spent several unnecessary days in Tegea gathering his arm, resulting in a major delay. Lysander arrived near Haliartus on the appointed day, but Pausanias did not. Spartan communication failures continued when Lysander sent a messenger to Pausanias' army in Plataea. Shortly into the 30-kilometre journey to Plataea, the messenger was intercepted and the Thebans deciphered Lysander's letter. The Thebans were then able to fortify Haliartus with their own troops and even a vanguard of Athenian hoplites.[21]

Before turning to the course of the battle, it is helpful to understand the composition of both the Spartan and Theban armies. While the precise makeup of Lysander's army remains disputed, it is safe to assume that he took at least one Spartan tactical unit named a *mora*. The *mora* was the backbone of the Spartan army and consisted of about 600 heavy infantry hoplites. Unless there were dire circumstances, the *ephors* only dispatched *moras* for expeditionary forces and invasions. Lysander would have certainly had a *mora* supplemented perhaps by light infantry from Sparta or their Peloponnesian allies. It is likely that Lysander's had less than a full *mora* as some Spartans stayed behind to garrison Orchomenus. Lysander's incomplete *mora* was further supported by at least 5,000 hoplites and infantry from the allied city-states in Boeotia and Phocis.[22]

Based on analysis of the Boeotian Confederacy's political makeup and previous expeditions during the Peloponnesian War, Pascual suggests that the average Theban battalion similarly hovered in the 5,000–6,000 range.[23] As for auxiliary forces, we know from Diodorus that Pausanias' army had 6,000 soldiers, though his army was yet to arrive.[24] This number roughly matched the reinforcements sent by Athens to the Thebans.[25] Therefore, as Pascual theorized, had the Battle of Haliartus proceeded as Sparta intended it would have pitted approximately 12,000 Spartans and allies against approximately 12,000 Thebans and Athenians.[26] Sparta traditionally thrived with such odds, which made Lysander's next steps seem out of character.

Lysander, perhaps frustrated by Pausanias' delay or perhaps out of desire to regain his status in Sparta, became impatient and threw out the careful Spartan battle strategy. He departed the Fox Hill and marched on the walls of Haliartus. After this, the course of battle is murky and the ancient historians diverge on details. In fact, Xenophon outright admits his uncertainty: 'This only is clear: a battle was fought beside the walls, and a trophy still exists to mark the victory of the townsfolk before the gates of Haliartus.'[27] No Theban accounts of the Battle of Haliartus survive, and Xenophon's retelling is hearsay due to his Spartan sources not being present at the battle. We can, however, glean the basic course of battle.

The Thebans were lying in wait for Lysander's approach to the city walls. Lysander approached the gates with his army, probably presuming that Haliartus would capitulate as Orchomenus had,[28] but Lysander misdiagnosed the size of the Haliartian army due to ignorance of the Theban and potentially Athenian reinforcements hidden behind the walls.

Critically, at least some of the Theban auxiliary forces were already outside the city gates. After intercepting Lysander's letter to Pausanias, the Thebans had inside access to the Spartan timing and battle plans and therefore Theban reinforcements had set out from Thebes early the night before and arrived at Haliartus under cover of darkness.[29] The Theban commanders then cunningly split their forces with a small contingent outside the walls and a stronger force within. These Thebans 'had remained outside, taking the city on their left, [and] advanced upon the rear of their enemy, at the spring called Cissusa.'[30] Lysander confused this Theban battalion for the full reinforcement forces that the anti-Spartan coalition was offering. Feeling no serious threat from such a small force, he was confident in approaching the city gates against the paltry Haliartian army and the allegedly small Theban reinforcements.

The Thebans sprang the trap when Lysander's army reached the walls of Haliartus. The remaining Theban hoplites burst out of the city gates and caught Lysander's army by surprise. There is no surviving account of how the battle proceeded, but its outcome is undisputed: Lysander was killed outside the walls of Haliartus. A Theban hoplite named Neochorus, who had a dragon emblem on his shield, killed Lysander.[31] The great Spartan reformer and empire-builder was dead.

Lysander's forces would have been at least partially surrounded by the combination of the city walls, the Thebans from outside the walls and the Thebans who came from inside the city. Pascual argues that the outside Thebans attacked Lysander's rear and left flank from the west, while the Haliartians and Thebans ambushed from the northern front in a delayed attack.[32] With only a narrow escape route to the south-west available, the remaining Spartan and

Peloponnesian fighters fled past the Fox Hill and into the rocky hills of Mount Likophios beyond. The Thebans aggressively pursued the Spartans into the hills, but encountered fierce resistance in the steep terrain, narrow space and the array of arrows, volleys and rocks desperately thrown by the Spartans.[33] The Spartans managed to kill 200 overzealous Thebans.[34] By contrast, at least 1,000 of Lysander's army were killed.[35] The remainder of the Thebans settled for their victory and, most importantly, their prize of Lysander's body.

The Battle of Haliartus was a resounding catastrophe for Sparta. The gravity of their grim start to the Corinthian War was apparent when Pausanias' army finally arrived at Haliartus and surveyed the defeat: 'Deep, we are told, was the silence and abasement which reigned in their host.'[36] Lysander's personal failure was the foremost concern of the historian Plutarch. While Lysander made a career of pushing beyond Spartan traditions, Plutarch suggests he lost sight of the discipline of a Spartan warrior:

> What occurred in Boeotia and at Haliartus was due, perhaps, to a certain evil fortune; but it looks as though he was injudicious in not waiting for the large forces of the king, which had all but arrived from Plataea, instead of allowing his resentment and ambition to lead him into an inopportune assault upon the walls, with the result that an inconsiderable and random body of men sallied out and overwhelmed him.... But Lysander threw away his life ingloriously, like a common targeteer or skirmisher, and bore witness to the wisdom of the ancient Spartans in avoiding assaults on walled cities, where not only an ordinary man, but even a child or a woman may chance to smite and slay the mightiest warrior, as Achilles, they say, was slain by Paris at the gates.[37]

Someone had to pay for Sparta's debacle. The *ephors* selected Pausanias as the scapegoat. Even after his long-awaited arrival at Haliartus, Pausanias refused to engage the enemy. Xenophon reports that it took three full days for Pausanias to make any tactical move. He was not immobilized by his fear, but rather by his analysis of the battle: if his Spartans joined the Battle of Haliartus, they were certain to suffer heavy losses due to low morale and being substantially outnumbered by the Theban cavalry. Most tempting was the need to rescue the Spartan bodies from the base of the city walls, but that was prime range for Haliartian arrows and therefore out of the question.[38] While tactically sound, Pausanias' many delays were interpreted as an abdication of duty by the belligerent *ephors*.

The Spartan king instead offered a peace treaty with the Thebans. Pausanias was allowed to retrieve the bodies from the city walls, but with strict warnings

52 The Corinthian War, 395–387 BC

Battle of Haliartus 395 BC

City-State of Haliartus

Athenians — City Gates — Thebans

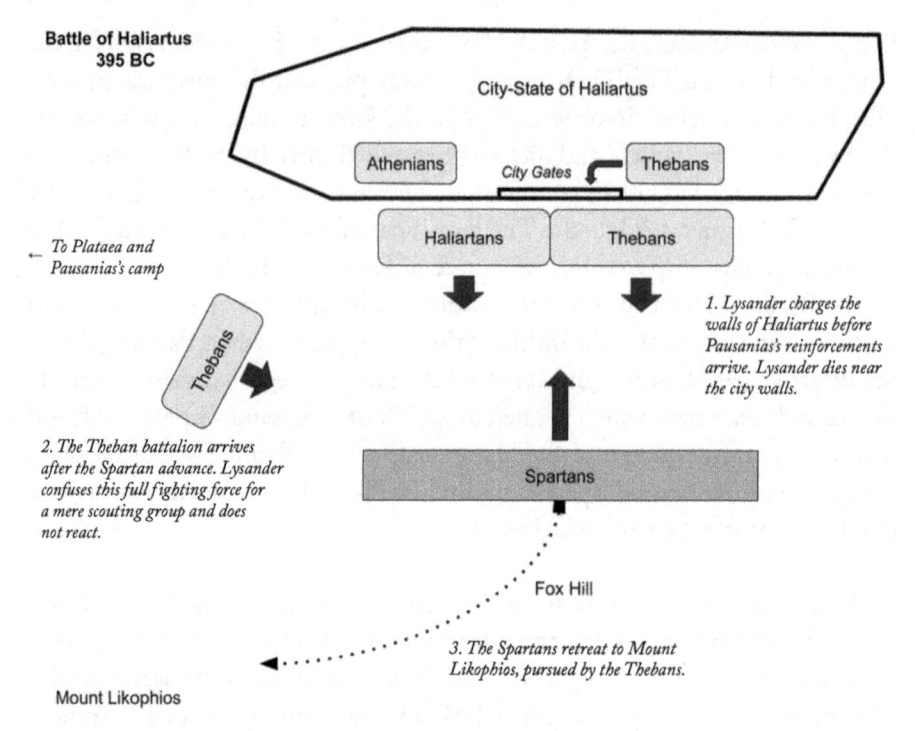

Haliartans — Thebans

← To Plataea and Pausanias's camp

Thebans

Spartans

Fox Hill

Mount Likophios

1. Lysander charges the walls of Haliartus before Pausanias's reinforcements arrive. Lysander dies near the city walls.

2. The Theban battalion arrives after the Spartan advance. Lysander confuses this full fighting force for a mere scouting group and does not react.

3. The Spartans retreat to Mount Likophios, pursued by the Thebans.

A depiction of the Battle of Haliartus' events.

that the Spartans thereafter retreat from Boeotian territory. After gathering their dead, the Spartans soberly turned homeward while Theban enthusiasm – and enmity – overflowed: 'Despondent indeed was the demeanour of the [Spartans], in contrast with the insolent bearing of the Thebans, who visited the slightest attempt to trespass on their private estates with blows and chased the offenders back on to the high roads unflinchingly.'[39]

Upon return to Sparta, Pausanias had to pay the price for the loss. The *ephors* charged him, again, with treason for sabotaging Lysander's army through his delayed arrival at Haliartus and his further delay in joining the battle once there. The *ephors* contended that this was now a pattern, given his cautious disengagement at Piraeus against the Phyle rebels a few years earlier. While he was able to defeat previous attempts to convict him, Pausanias made no attempt to even defend himself this time. He skipped the trial entirely. He was sentenced to death *in absentia*, and fled in exile to Tegea where he died of illness shortly afterwards.[40]

The Rise of Conon and Parallel Developments in Asia Minor

In his letter to the Thebans before Haliartus, the Athenian leader Thrasybulus justified anti-Spartan diplomacy by citing Theban refusal to march on Athens when Sparta demanded retribution against Thrasybulus' own Phyle rebels. He also directly pledged Athenian support for the looming revolt against Sparta's empire: 'we are prepared to fight your battles with you against the enemy, if he attacks you.'[41]

While not entirely dishonest, Thrasybulus was withholding the entire truth. While the Thebans accurately diagnosed many of the Athenian sentiments against Sparta, there were more concerns for Athens than the romantic reassertion of her empire and vengeance against Sparta. Athens was particularly concerned about the rising tide of Spartan imperialism in Asia Minor under Agesilaus. Agesilaus' conquests had destabilized Athenian-Persian relations. Despite their complicated history, Thrasybulus and the Athenians viewed Persia as a potential ally, and the diplomacy of Timocrates of Rhodes provided positive momentum towards cultivating Persian intervention in the revival of Athens' empire.

Their most pressing concern, however, was that the Persians had found a swashbuckling new admiral for their Aegean navy: Conon of Athens. The Athenian admiral Conon had been living in exile in Cyprus for five years by this time. He had been approached by Pharnabazus the *satrap* in 396 when the Spartan expedition into Asia Minor first saw success. With approval from his patron king Evagoras of Cyprus, Conon sailed with forty ships to the Cilician coast to cut off the retreat of the invading Spartans. Conon now commanded at least part of the vast fleet that had inspired the Spartan invasion of Persian territory. Athens was now forced to watch their own hero join their adversary Persia. This was a frustratingly common pattern for many Athenians who found their new patronage in the deep pockets of the Persian Empire after running afoul of Athenian democracy, such as Themistocles or Alcibiades.

Much as in the Peloponnesian War, Sparta realized her need for naval power. While Agesilaus succeeded in the logistical support structure for his army in Asia Minor, shipbuilding on a scale to match Persia was beyond Sparta's economic and industrial reach. Since they could not secure the Persian funds they had enjoyed a decade earlier, they went to Egypt. The Egyptian pharaoh contributed a hundred triremes plus a healthy amount of grain to feed their rowers and essential materials to repair the undermanned Spartan ships that were likely in disrepair.[42] Egyptian intervention was not benevolence, but instead a clever tactic by the pharaoh. The Persian king Artaxerxes II was plotting an invasion of Egypt when the Spartan challenge waylaid his plans. In fact, the rumoured 300 Persian triremes that had instigated Agesilaus' invasion was likely a fleet aimed to conquer Egypt and not Greece. By supporting the Spartan navy, Egypt successfully distracted Persian designs to reacquire Egypt, and Sparta was desperate to keep her naval strength.

The Spartan admiral Pharax headquartered the new Spartan fleet in Rhodes. The Rhodians, however, were more loyal to the Athenians and happily joined the ex-Athenian Conon after expelling the Spartans.[43] The seizing of Rhodes would be a significant strategic advantage for the Persian fleet as they aimed to vanquish the Spartan fleet, and Conon garrisoned Persian triremes off the north coast of Rhodes from 396 to 394 which severely limited the movement of the Spartan fleet.

Conon's tactical acuity also impeded Agesilaus' conquests in Asia Minor. Largely avoiding direct conflict, Conon was able to position the Persian navy to disrupt supply chains and block escape routes for the Spartans, hampering Agesilaus' opportunities to advance beyond the coastline and into Cilicia and the south of Asia Minor. Cornelius Nepos would later remark that 'if Conon had not been there, Agesilaus would have taken all Asia, as far as Mount Taurus, from the king.'[44] Conon was officially attached to Pharnabazus' defensive campaign as a lieutenant, but quickly assumed true command. He curried favour not just with Tissaphernes' successor Tithraustes, but with the King of Kings himself. Artaxerxes II personally appointed Conon to lead the Persian navy and lavishly endowed him with riches and honours.

Conon's heart, however, never left Athens. Indeed, he only accepted the Persian command 'in the hope not only that he would recover the leadership in Greece for his native country.'[45] Conon even refused to meet with the Persian king, not out of a lack of respect for the Persians but out of a heartfelt patriotism to Athenian custom to not show adoration to foreign kings.[46] His time in Cyprus, his mercenary work for Evagoras and now his mercenary work for Persia had always been designed as stopgaps until the political situation in Athens would be amenable to his triumphant return, and despite his Persian employment, his policymaking was decidedly Athenian. He installed an Athenian-style democracy in Rhodes and modified the size and style of the Persian ships to fit the Athenian standard. He hired, with Persian gold, the best Athenian sailors and rowers to man the ships. Conan's Persian fleet was, ironically, the most Athenian navy since Aegospotami. He was laying the groundwork for the re-emergence of Athenian imperial interests in the Aegean, even as he headed a Persian fleet.

Conon likely figured that matters in Persia were a helpful financial and political opportunity, but that the overextension of Sparta's empire would create enough diplomatic turmoil across the Aegean world for Athens to need its best commanders to return. Such tumult was certain to come: Evagoras himself was plotting to rebel against Persian rule soon, and Conon's fickle loyalty was a helpful catalyst in weakening the Persian grip on the southern coast in the aftermath of Agesilaus' invasion. Conon patiently waited out the Thirty Tyrants, the Phyle campaign, Agesilaus' invasion and now the official start of the Corinthian War for his opportunity to return to Athens as a hero.

By early 394, Conon's navy was ideally situated to both challenge Agesilaus' ascendancy in Asia Minor and distract Spartan policy from the land war on the Greek mainland. In a move that would have astonished the Greeks of a century earlier during the Persian Wars, an Athenian commander would soon lead Persian ships into battle against the Spartans.

Sparta's Post-Lysandrean Paralysis

With the loss at Haliartus, Sparta was now overextended with a land war both in Asia Minor and in Greece, and her forces divided between them. The proven leaders of their empire were either dead, exiled or on foreign soil. Lysander's empire-builders had no cogent vision or leadership after his death at Haliartus. Agis 'hegemons of Greece' faction had endured his death with the rise of Agesilaus, but he was now in Asia Minor and fighting on their second front. The traditionalists led by Pausanias now saw their leader exiled and powerless. The final pragmatist faction, which transcended these groups, had lost both Lysander's utility of freed helots and his attempts to rewrite the constitution of Sparta.

Hamilton described how even though Haliartus was a major loss, in the long term it alleviated Spartan factionalism and gave their empire cogency: 'The irony of Haliartus and its sequel [trial of Pausanias] is that the last of the… faction leaders whose rival foreign policies after 404 had prevented Sparta from consistently following a single line of action was now removed from influence.'[47]

The remaking of Spartan political leadership would not be complete until Agesilaus' return from his campaign in Asia Minor. Agesilaus alone now commanded the respect of the Spartiates and the *ephors*, and while the factions continued to exist they would coalesce their political vision around Agesilaus. Sparta, at long last, had a coherent imperial vision behind a single leader. However, before he could eclipse the factional politics of Sparta, he would need to return from his overseas campaign and face the growing threat against Sparta's empire.

Chapter Five

The Bloody Year 394

The Recalling of Agesilaus

'A thousand Persian archers have driven me out of Asia,'[1] Agesilaus quipped when his invasion force was recalled back to Sparta to fight the rebels. Agesilaus was not referring to actual archers. It was instead the thousand gold coins sent by Artaxerxes II that bribed the Thebans, Corinthians, Argives and Athenians into the Corinthian War. Those coins, emblazoned with Persian archers on them per the Persian custom, were the only reason why the Spartan invasion of Asia Minor ended prematurely.

In just over two years, he had conquered large swathes of territory and even captured the *satrapal* capital of Sardis. The Greeks of Asia Minor adored him, with him supplanting even Lysander as the most admired leader. In contrast to the ostentatious Persian *satraps*, Agesilaus ruled with simplicity and humility: 'went about in a paltry cloak, and at one brief and laconic speech from him conforming themselves to his ways and changing their dress and mien.'[2] The Greeks of Asia were ready to revolt against Persian rule entirely, and Agesilaus even entertained the delusional idea of marching all the way into the Persian homeland.

However, Agesilaus' invasion had begun to flat-line by 395. After Tissaphernes' execution, Agesilaus had entered into a six-month peace treaty after rejecting an offer from the King of Kings to return the Greek city-states of Asia Minor to paying Persian tribute. In 396, Agesilaus had both naval and land supremacy; by the middle of 395, Conon's leadership over the Persian fleet had changed Spartan naval fortune and limited their land campaign.

Agesilaus made a rare tactical failure in his appointment of his brother-in-law Peisander as the Spartan fleet's new admiral. In an unusual move, Agesilaus had been granted the role of *navarch* in addition to army commander. This was both out of desperation and in response to the crisis at Rhodes when Conon conquered the strategic location and expelled the Spartan triremes. Peisander was, at best, inexperienced in the construction, command and maintenance of a naval fleet.[3] He was no match for Conon. While Agesilaus marched for Phrygia, Peisander floundered against Conon's Persian fleet.

Compounding matters, Agesilaus was distracted by the more pressing land campaign and his *satrapal* adversaries. In the overland campaign, the *satrap*

Pharnabazus proved a more cunning rival than Tissaphernes. Pharnabazus had been a steadfast supporter of Sparta during the Peloponnesian War and funded Sparta's naval construction, but now he was fighting against his former allies. By the autumn of 395, Agesilaus' army entered Pharnabazus' home region of Phrygia. Agesilaus' army burned the land beyond recognition, but Pharnabazus was undeterred in his efforts to end the Spartan invasion. When a mutual friend brokered a clandestine negotiation between Pharnabazus and Agesilaus, Pharnabazus opened the dialogue with an eloquent entreaty:

> While you were at war with the Athenians I was your friend and ally; it was I who furnished the wealth that made your navy strong on sea; on land I fought on horseback by your side, and pursued your enemies into the sea. As to duplicity like that of Tissaphernes, I challenge you to accuse me of having played you false by word or deed. Such have I ever been; and in return how am I treated by yourselves to-day? – in such sort that I cannot even sup in my own country unless, like the wild animals, I pick up the scraps you chance to leave. The beautiful palaces which my father left me as an heirloom, the parks full of trees and beasts of the chase in which my heart rejoiced, lie before my eyes hacked to pieces, burnt to ashes. Maybe I do not comprehend the first principles of justice and holiness; do you then explain to me how all this resembles the conduct of men who know how to repay a simple debt of gratitude.[4]

Agesilaus was moved by the words and agreed to show renewed amity to Pharnabazus and to spare his homeland of Phrygia. They even entered into a Homeric-style 'guest-friendship', but their ceasefire would not extend to the rest of Persia's city-states in Asia Minor. Agesilaus withdrew from Phrygia and camped at Cilician Thebe near the coast. Despite the setbacks, Agesilaus made preparations for a deeper invasion into Asia and peeling away the Persian king's cities one by one until the Spartans reached Mesopotamia. His goals were lofty:

> …to transfer the war from the Greek sea, to fight for the person of the King and the wealth of Ecbatana and Susa, and above all things to rob that monarch of the power to sit at leisure on his throne, playing the umpire for the Greeks in their wars, and corrupting their popular leaders.[5]

Agesilaus' vision was not to be. In the spring of 394, a messenger named Epicydidas was sent from Sparta to relay a message to Agesilaus: the king had to return home to assist in the Corinthian War. The *ephors* were in a panic after the loss at Haliartus and the death of Lysander: '[Sparta was] quite alive to the fact that moneys [from Persia] had been sent into Hellas, and that the bigger states were leagued together to declare war against them. It was hard to avoid the conclusion that Sparta herself was in actual danger, and that a campaign was inevitable.'[6]

Agesilaus was enraged at the order, but acquiesced. Plutarch compares his virtue in laying aside hubris and obeying orders with the vices of Hannibal and Alexander the Great, who were resolutely unwilling to end their ambitious campaigns for the greater health of their empires. To Plutarch, Agesilaus never 'performed a nobler or a greater deed than in returning home as he now did, nor was there ever a fairer example of righteous obedience to authority.'[7] The residents of Asia Minor were more heartbroken than Agesilaus, and pre-emptively invited him to return as their king when the war was over. Xenophon paints a rather biased picture of the renown earned by Agesilaus among the Ionian Greeks who 'deplored his departure [at the end of the invasion], as though they had lost, not simply a ruler, but a father or bosom friend, and in the end they showed that their friendship was of no fictitious character.'[8]

Agesilaus refused to make his return easy, however. After his laconic banter about being recalled by 1,000 Persian archers, Agesilaus charted a path home that mirrored Xerxes the Great's infamous invasion of Greece in 480.[9] The route crossed the Hellespont, through Thrace and the north of Greece, then through Thessaly and into Phocis in central Greece. It was a gaudy and unnecessary display, but it was an important piece of theatrics for the Spartan hegemony in the wake of their loss at Haliartus. As Agesilaus entered each region, he 'sent envoys to each people asking whether he should traverse their country as a friend or as a foe.'[10] Much like his time in Asia Minor, he cultivated both personal and institutional friendships on which he would soon come to rely. Much like Lysander, these would forge the future of the Spartan Empire, although Agesilaus' methods avoided the personal ambitions and entanglements of Lysander, likely due to Agesilaus' undisputed role as king and *navarch*. Agesilaus was not beyond holding a grudge, however, and he blamed the Thebans for their continued rebellion against Spartan leadership. This rivalry between Agesilaus and Thebes, which had climaxed at the ruined sacrifice at Aulis, would continue for decades.

Agesilaus would arrive in Central Greece at Boeotia later in 394. Many of his Peloponnesian soldiers remained behind, garrisoned in Asia Minor. The bulk of Agesilaus' army was now of Ionian Greeks, who likely hoped for Agesilaus' quick return to Asia. Peisander and the remnant of the Spartan navy stayed in Asia Minor. Peisander's navy would soon fight against the Persians and the allied Greeks at the Battle of Cnidus off the coast of Asia Minor later in 394, but for now the anti-Spartan confederacy gathered in Corinth to prepare for

The meeting between Agesilaus (left) and Pharnabazus (right). (*Wikimedia Commons, 2022. Public domain*)

Agesilaus' triumphant return and prepare a counter-attack. The bloodiest year of the Corinthian War had begun.

The Congress at Corinth

In Corinth in the spring of 394, the allied Greeks deliberated on how best to exploit the deepening cracks in Sparta's empire. Though Xenophon does not name each party, the entirety of Greece's anti-Spartan league was present: Athens, Thebes, Corinth and Argos. While Persia was not present, Persian money and influence still loomed large over the confederacy. With Conon now leading the Persian navy and eyeing a return to Athens, the prospect of linking with the Persians reassured the anti-Spartan league about the daunting prospect of continuing war on Sparta.

This congress marked Argos' first main contributions to the Corinthian War, and Argos' anti-Spartan history deserves special analysis. Argos was an anomaly in the Peloponnese: they were a democracy yet abhorred Athens, and militaristic yet despised Sparta. Argos and Sparta historically jockeyed for Peloponnesian dominance. Argos had been brutally defeated by Sparta in battle in the 490s which ended Argive claims to Peloponnesian dominance. Their loss transformed the state from an oligarchy into a democracy, but their sphere of influence had been further relegated when they remained neutral in the face of the Persian invasion. The Peloponnesian War had been a chance of regaining their status among the Greeks. Argos formed a considerable anti-Spartan alliance in 421 and coordinated with the Athenians in an effort to end the war and decimate the Spartan military. Their efforts failed in 418 at the Battle of Mantinea when the Spartans and the Peloponnesian League overwhelmed the Argives and Athenians. Sparta attempted to install pro-Spartan oligarchs, but the democrats soon regained power, with a deeper hostility towards their southern Peloponnesian neighbours.

For now, the Argive goal was the same as the other allied Greeks: breaking Sparta's empire and, at least until Agesilaus' return, Sparta's leadership was in a historically weak position after the death of Lysander and the exiling of Pausanias. The new Agiad king was Agesipolis, the teenage son of Pausanias, but he was considered too green to effectively lead the Spartiates and so the *ephors* appointed a regent named Aristodemus. Under Aristodemus, a seasoned military officer and member of the royal family, the Spartans raised their banners and began preparations to march north out of the Peloponnese with another vast army of 6,000 Spartiates plus up to 12,000 Peloponnesian League soldiers. Undaunted, the allied meeting at Corinth aimed to resolve their mission before that army arrived in Corinthian territory.

The primary question of the congress was simple: how could they lead a coordinated resistance against Spartan hegemony? Despite their imperial weaknesses and logistical challenges, Sparta's military might and diplomatic reach made them the dominant favourite even when outnumbered. A Corinthian named Timolaus took charge of the congress. He had been a recipient of Persian gold from Timocrates of Rhodes at the start of the war, and harboured both a unique sympathy for Argos and an antipathy towards Sparta.[11]

Timolaus used a pair of metaphors to propose a solution. He first said that the Spartan hegemony was akin to the mouth of a river: small and easy to cross, but gradually expanding and difficult to traverse the further out you travelled as more rivers and creeks converged with it. For Sparta, their home territory was that river mouth, but it was formidable only when supported by the Peloponnesian League allies. Timolaus said, 'Take them at the starting-point and they are but a single community, but as they advance and attack city after city they grow more numerous and more resistless.'[12]

The eloquent Corinthian's next metaphor was a wasps' nest: 'When people wish to take wasps' nests – if they try to capture the creatures on the wing, they are liable to be attacked by half the hive; whereas, if they apply fire to them ere they leave their homes, they will master them without scathe themselves.'[13] Timolaus' strong recommendation was to strike Sparta in its homeland. An assault on Laconia would be unprecedented. It would be the furthest from their discontented allies, the closest to their rebellious helots and would drive a wedge into the *stasis* that plagued the state, and the time to attack was now, while Sparta was leaderless and her armies were split across the continents.

The congress voted in favour of the offensive assault on Sparta, but there were plenty of logistical questions to settle first. Namely, who was in charge of this new *symmachy*? Also how could that party avoid the trappings of Sparta's hegemony? How would they arrange their armies in a way that was strategically sound and evenly spread the opportunities for renown and glory? These questions soaked up the remaining time at the conference.

Unfortunately, the allies waited too long. While they were deliberating the details and logistics of their new alliance, the Spartan army entered Corinthian territory and began to pillage the land, trying to draw out the allied forces. Such questions were avoided, for now, due to the urgency of tactics. With the Spartans on the move both from the Peloponnese under Aristodemus and from the north under Agesilaus, the anti-Spartan league needed decisive and effective action.

The Spartan army travelled north to Corinthian territory past Tegea and joined a major road network near Kleonai that connected Argos and Corinth. They approached Corinth from the south-east and camped near a dry riverbed. Both Xenophon and Diodorus Siculus name this river as the Nemea. This battlefield was not especially close to the city of Nemea, home of the mythological Nemean Lion defeated by Heracles and also to the famous Nemean Games, one of the four major Panhellenic athletic contests.

Nemea, the city-state, was situated about 30 kilometres from the city centre of Corinth, but J.F. Lazenby suggests that it makes more sense for the Nemean battlefield to be situated between the Nemea River and the Longopotamos River near Sicyon, a bit closer to Corinth and a more strategically sound angle of attack.[14] At only 10 kilometres from Corinth, Lazenby's positioning makes logical sense, especially since the Sicyonians were part of the Peloponnesian League and fought in the upcoming battle alongside the Spartans. César Fornis pinpoints the battlefield as slightly south of Assos, a modern suburb of Corinth en route from Sicyon and in the foothills of the mountains, closer to the Longopotamos than the Nemea.[15] This would make the battle site not far from Corinth itself and, critically, on the path to the Corinthian harbour of Lechaeum which was a valuable target that Sparta would soon prioritize.

The precise location notwithstanding, the allied Greeks were forced to spring to action and defend Corinth and their confederacy. The ensuing battle would be the largest land battle of the Corinthian War and change the course of the war. For Sparta, another loss might be insurmountable.

The Battle of Nemea

The two main sources for the Battle of Nemea, Xenophon and Diodorus Siculus, give divergent reports on the number of fighters for each side. Xenophon's pro-Spartan history is quite detailed: 6,000 Spartan hoplites (it is unclear how many were Spartiates, *perioeci* or helots), 3,000 Elean, Triphylian, Acroreian and Lasionian hoplites, 1,500 Sicyonians and 3,000 hoplites from Epidaurus, Troezen, Hermione and Halieis. A further 600 Spartan cavalry, 300 Cretan archers and 400 skirmishers and slingers from Margiana, Letrini and Amphidolia rounded out the Spartan army.[16] In total, Xenophon's account has 13,500 hoplites supported by 1,300 other fighters. Writing a few centuries later, Diodorus Siculus, who uses decidedly pro-Athenian forces, gives a streamlined number of 23,000 hoplites and 500 cavalry.[17] Hamilton astutely notes that Xenophon's composition did not include their closest allies in the Peloponnesian League.[18] Hoplites from Achaea, Tegea and Mantinea were certain to have joined such an important campaign. Hamilton reconciles the dichotomy in the army sizes from the two ancient historians by suggesting 9,000 total hoplites from these Peloponnesian allies, bringing the total Spartan army to about 22,500 and closer to Diodorus' account.[19]

For the anti-Spartan allies, Xenophon reports the following hoplite statistics: 7,000 Argives, 6,000 Athenians, 5,000 Thebans and Boeotians, 3,000 Corinthians and 3,000 Euboeans for a total of 24,000 hoplites.[20] A further 1,550 cavalry reinforced those numbers along with an unspecified number of light infantry and skirmishers that Xenophon describes as 'more numerous' than the cavalry.[21] Diodorus Siculus does not give any numbers for the allied Greeks. If Hamilton is correct in the support of the unlisted Peloponnesian League allies, then the armies were roughly equal at 22,500 Spartans versus 24,000 allied Greeks.

Upon arrival in Corinthian territory, the Spartan army had hugged the coastline of the Gulf of Corinth, passing through Sicyon and towards Lechaeum and Corinth. They had been harassed by the light infantry of the allied Greeks, perhaps diverting their planned course, and camped on the bank of a large ravine. The allied Greeks camped less than 2 kilometres away on the other side of the ravine.[22]

When the two armies met in battle the next day, it was a 'classic in hoplite warfare, occurring under prime conditions on fairly level ground and between two armies of almost equal size.'[23] Despite such enthusiasm from historians, the Boeotians were anxious. Dysfunction among the congress at Corinth had apparently bled over into battle preparations, and the allies bickered over the positioning of each *polis*'s hoplites. The Boeotians had been assigned the left flank, which made them opposite the Spartans and sure to experience the fiercest

The few remains of the city of Sparta, with Mount Taygetus and the Eurotas River valley in the distance. In this valley, the Spartans forged their mighty army through the *agoge* training camp. (*Used with permission. ID 159525490 © Leonid Andronov | Dreamstime.com*)

The ruins of the Temple of Artemis Orthia in Sparta. At this temple, one of the key rites of passage of the *agoge* occurred as Spartan trainees were beaten as they made their way to the steps of the temple. (*George E. Koronaios. Wikimedia Commons, 2020. Creative Commons CC0 1.0, Universal Public Domain Dedication*)

The Kerameikos Cemetery in Athens. Named after the potters that frequented this area, this was the main cemetery in urban Athens for hundreds of years. The Grave Stele of Dexileos, the Tomb of the Spartans, parts of the Themistoclean walls and parts of Conon's rebuilt walls converge here. (*Used with permission. ID 98189321 © Lucian Milasan | Dreamstime.com*)

At the top right of this photograph from the Kerameikos Cemetery of Athens lies the Tomb of the Spartans or the Tomb of the Lacedaemonians. This tomb was the burial place of several Spartan warriors who died during Thrasybulus' rebellion against the Thirty Tyrants in 403. They are the only Spartans buried in this Athenian cemetery. (*Used with permission. ID 199655462 © Andreas Giannakis | Dreamstime.com*)

Adrien Guignet's painting of the Battle of Cunaxa and the retreat of the Ten Thousand. (*Wikimedia Commons, 2013. Creative Commons CC0 1.0, Universal Public Domain Dedication*)

A painting of the meeting between Cyrus the Younger (left) and Lysander by the Italian painter Francesco Antonio Grue. The alliance between Cyrus and Lysander would empower Lysander and eventually lead to Cyrus' rebellion for the Persian throne and then the Corinthian War. (*Wikimedia Commons, 2019. Creative Commons CC0 1.0, Universal Public Domain Dedication*)

A forest grove in Haliartus in Boeotia, close to the site of the first battle of the Corinthian War, the Battle of Haliartus in 395. (*Thodoris Karakozidis, Wikimedia Commons, 2013. Creative Commons Attribution 3.0*)

The ruins of a temple in Nemea. In the foothills beyond was the site of the Battle of Nemea in 394, the first victory for the Spartans in the Corinthian War. (*Used with permission. ID 81107113 © Znm | Dreamstime.com*)

A recreation of the funerary stele of the Athenian cavalryman Dexileos from Kerameikos Cemetery in Athens. The aristocrat Dexileos perished at the Battle of Nemea in 394. (*George E. Koronaios, Wikimedia Commons, 2021. Creative Commons Attribution 2.0*)

The funeral stele of the Athenian cavalryman Dexileos from Kerameikos in Athens. Dexileos perished at the Battle of Nemea in 394. (*Tilemahos Efthimiadis, Wikimedia Commons, 2010. Creative Commons Attribution 2.0*)

A landscape near Coronea in Boeotia, Central Greece. Not far from this lake was the site of the Battle of Coronea in 394. (*Used with permission. ID 229655009 © Dariya Maksimova | Dreamstime.com*)

An aerial photograph of the city-state of Cnidus, or where the city was relocated to during the Roman era. A bit further to the west, at the edge of the Carian Chersonese peninsula, was the site of the Battle of Cnidus in 394. (*Used with permission. ID 259282838 © Emiralikokal | Dreamstime.com*)

The archaeological remains of the city-state of Cnidus, with its harbour in the distance. (*Used with permission. ID 142792164 © Özgür Şenergin | Dreamstime.com*)

An artist's recreation of a Greek trireme like those used at the Battle of Cnidus in 394. Note the battering ram at the ship's prow, as well as the three rows of oarsmen, from which the name trireme is derived. Photograph from the Museo Naval Madrid. (*Used with permission. ID 173978955 © Whpics | Dreamstime.com*)

A recreation of the armour of a Spartan hoplite, complete with a Corinthian-style helmet which was used by the Spartan hoplites during the Peloponnesian and Corinthian Wars. (*Used with permission. ID 32211380 © Angellodeco | Dreamstime.com*)

A peltast in the style of Thrace and Iphicrates, complete with a crescent shield, light armour and javelins. (*John Shumate, Wikimedia Commons, 2006. Creative Commons CC0 1.0, Universal Public Domain Dedication*)

The ruins of two fortifications from Conon's rebuilding of the walls of Athens in 393. (*George E. Koronaios, Wikimedia Commons, 2019. Creative Commons CC0 1.0, Universal Public Domain Dedication*)

The remains of the road leading to Corinth's Lechaeum harbour, with the Acrocorinth in the distance. This road, paved in its present form during Roman times, was near the site of the Battle of Lechaeum, the final land battle of the Corinthian War in 390. (*Used with permission. ID 243003573 © Prakich Treetasayuth | Dreamstime.com*)

The city of Corinth, with the Gulf of Corinth and the remains of the harbour of Lechaeum in the distance. (*Wikimedia Commons, 2020. Creative Commons CC0 1.0, Universal Public Domain Dedication*)

A colourized recreation of the Spartan admiral Teleutias' burning of the Athenian harbour of Piraeus in 389. (*Copyright: author's own*)

The tomb of the Persian king Artaxerxes II, who ruled the Persian Empire during the Corinthian War and made the King's Peace of 387 to end the war. (*David Stanley, Wikimedia Commons, 2013. Creative Commons Attribution 2.0*)

fighting. They were loath to enter the fray, but shortly before the fighting began a 'rearrangement'[24] gave them the opposite right wing and they switched with the Athenians. It is unclear what precipitated this change, but it is probable that the Thebans advocated for the swap to avoid the fearsome Spartan hoplites. The allies likely used a rotating command structure, as was common in many Greek armies, but Thebes circumvented the current commander and leveraged their influence to switch flanks and instead fight against the more palatable Achaeans.

The Theban-Athenian switch led to pandemonium. The main problem was that the Thebans disregarded the generally accepted sixteen-man-deep phalanx structure. A phalanx of this depth was unusual, as most Classical Greek phalanxes numbered eight men in depth or less. A sixteen-man-deep phalanx was more characteristic of the Hellenistic period. It is likely that the allied Greeks, concerned about Sparta's military discipline and expertise, intended to overload the phalanx depth, yet evenly distribute the numbers. The Thebans apparently added many more than sixteen men into the phalanx lines, which flouted the allies' plans. Lazenby suggests that the Thebans made their phalanx twenty-five men deep.[25] An optimistic interpretation of this manoeuvre is that the Thebans intended the deeper lines to help fight against the Spartans, but failed to adjust properly when their positioning was switched. Xenophon takes a pessimistic evaluation and casts the Thebans as selfish opportunists. While the rest of the allies used the planned sixteen-man structure, the entire right flank was now unbalanced.

In phalanx fighting, the first lines execute a shield wall that pushes against the opposing hoplites' shields. The primary goal of a first-row hoplite is to push against the enemy in unison with their fellow soldiers and to create opportunities for those behind them to strike. The second and third lines use their 8ft-long spears to stab and attack the enemy, and if those in front of them fall in combat or are injured, they move forward in the line. The glaring weakness of the phalanx was its right side. Each hoplite wore up to 90lb of heavy equipment, but only used a shield named an *aspis* on their right side. When the entire front line interlocked their shields to form the shield wall, the individual hoplite covered their own left half and the right half of the hoplite directly next to them. This meant that the hoplites on the right side of a phalanx were the most vulnerable as they had no neighbours to shield their right side. Phalanx combat, therefore, invariably drifted to the right as the hoplites fought to both exploit this weakness of their enemy and to cover their own right's liability.

In the march to the Battle of Nemea, the Thebans' self-serving behaviour caused the allied Greeks' battle formation to become unwieldy. Xenophon describes how the Theban overloading of the right wing caused erratic movements as the allies overcompensated for their vulnerability. The phalanx 'kept veering more and more to their right, with the intention of overlapping their opponent's flank'[26] even before formally engaging with the Spartan army. The Spartans were at first unaware of their enemies' disarray given the rough terrain, but quickly identified it through listening to the *paean* or fighting song of the allied Greeks. These hymns were sung by hoplites entering into battle, both to inspire their own soldiers and to intimidate the enemy. When the Spartans heard the uneven and disparate *paeans*, it was clear that the allied Greeks were not only attacking first, but were already disorganized.

The Spartans sprang into formation and met the allies on more even ground. The *polemarchs* under the regent Aristodemus were allowed latitude to strategically innovate, a feature that immediately paid dividends:

> The order was passed to 'follow the lead', and then the [Spartans] on their side also began edging to their right, and eventually stretched out their wing so far that only six out of the ten regimental divisions of the Athenians confronted the [Spartans], the other four finding themselves face to face with the men of Tegea.

When the two armies finally met, the allied Greeks were disjointed. The Athenians were immediately at a disadvantage and partially surrounded, while the Thebans were so far to their right of the Spartan army that they had to bend to their left significantly just to engage the enemy. Meanwhile, the Spartans began to push from their right side and enclose the Athenians. Xenophon describes the Spartan hoplites 'wheeling round their overlapping columns to outflank his left.'[27] The result was both armies attempting to encircle each other, fumbling awkwardly in a counter-clockwise rotation.

The Athenians disrupted that equilibrium when they broke rank in the face of the Spartan hoplites' superiority. The Spartans capitalized on their strategic positioning and massacred six of the ten Athenian tribes: 'they slew man after man of them; and, absolutely unscathed themselves, their unbroken columns continued their march, and so passed behind the four remaining divisions of the Athenians.'[28] It was not an evenly won fight, however, as the remaining four tribes of Athenians earned distinction themselves. They were towards the centre of the battle and fought the Tegeans instead, emerging generally unharmed from the battle.'[29]

The Spartans eventually rounded the corner against the Athenian flank. The remaining Athenians retreated east to their camp to avoid being surrounded, and with that the allied lines were broken. After the Athenians, the Argives engaged the Spartan forces. The Argives had been in a similar retreat, and the original Spartan plan was to engage them head on. However, a clever Spartan *polemarch* shouted, 'Let their front ranks pass!'³⁰ and the Spartans stopped advancing. This forced the Argives to move perpendicular in front of the Spartans, fully exposing their shieldless right sides. The Spartans stayed stationary and used their spears to butcher many fleeing Argives. After the Argives, many Corinthians and then an unfortunate contingent of Thebans suffered the same unforgiving fate during their own retreat.

At the Battle of Mantinea in 418, the Spartans had found themselves in a very similar situation. King Agis had commanded that battle, and out of fear of being surrounded as the Athenians eventually were at Nemea, ordered his hoplites 'to move out from their place in the ranks and make the line even with the Mantineans, and told the *polemarchs* Hipponoidas and Aristocles to fill up the gap thus formed, by throwing themselves into it with two companies taken from the right wing.'³¹ Agis' theory was that by drawing from the overbalanced right side, he could even out the left flank that was directly engaging the enemy. That was so unprecedented an order that his *polemarchs* refused outright, fearing that the unpractised manoeuvre would result in a disorganized chaos. At the Battle of Nemea three decades later, the Spartans under Aristodemus allowed individual *polemarchs* both autonomy and input on tactical strategy. This was perhaps due to the savviness and experience of Aristodemus, or perhaps due to the lack of a true king and centralized commander at the battle. Nevertheless,

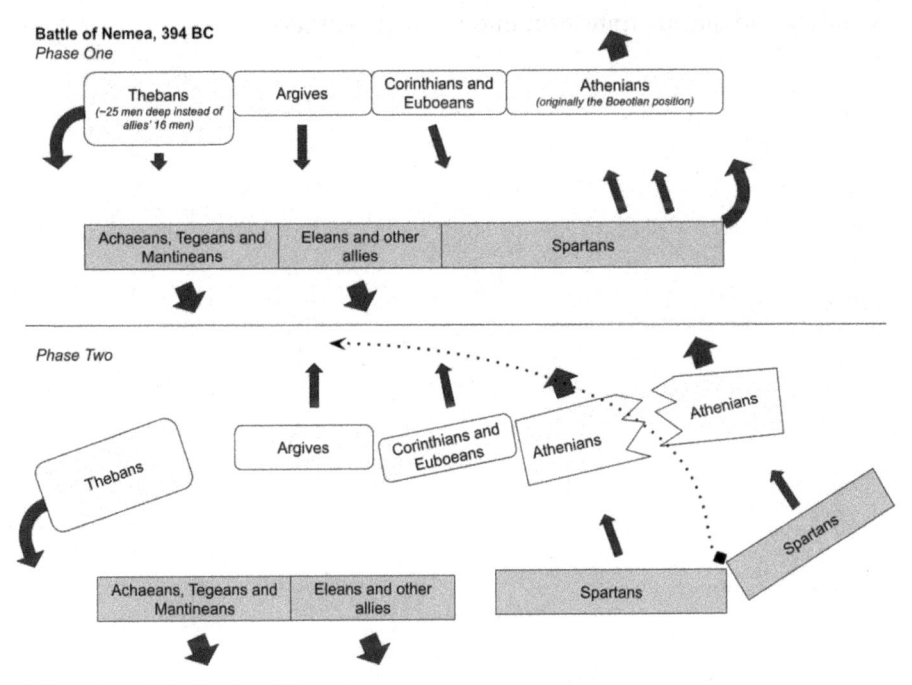

A depiction of the Battle of Nemea's events.

it displayed the sophisticated evolution of Spartan phalanx strategy and the recognized need to increase tactical communications that had cost them so dearly at Haliartus.[32]

By the battle's end, the Spartans had chased the allies all the way back to the gates of Corinth 10 kilometres away. The Corinthians inside, however, refused to open the gates even for their countrymen.[33] The Spartans claimed to have lost only eight men, although Diodorus gives the number as 1,100.[34] Almost all those casualties were from the Peloponnesian allies; a tactically sound decision, but nevertheless a glaring example of Sparta's ruthless treatment of her allies. The lesson was not lost on the rest of the Greeks. Meanwhile, the anti-Spartan league saw a staggering 2,800 men perish, shattering their momentum from Haliartus.[35]

It was a thunderous victory for Sparta, re-establishing their hegemony and weakening the anti-Spartan confederacy. There were only good omens on the horizon for Sparta as Agesilaus inched closer to home with his army. Upon hearing of the victory at Nemea, Agesilaus quickly sent Dercylidas to the Ionian Greeks to deliver the good news of Spartan victory and reassure his Ionian patrons of a quick return, but while Dercylidas brought glad tidings from Greece, there was only misfortune to come from Asia Minor. The Spartan navy under Peisander had engaged the Persian fleet at Cnidus. If the untried Peisander lost that battle, Sparta would effectively lose its navy. Spartan momentum from Nemea would quickly transform into inertia at Cnidus.

Chapter Six

Disaster at Cnidus

Sparta's Naval Infirmity

By 394, Sparta's navy was suffused with her incoherent imperial vision. Of particular concern for Sparta was their inability to maintain the fleet they had constructed at the end of the Peloponnesian War. In the decade after 404, Lysander had benefited from a freshly-constructed navy of 200 triremes.[1] After Aegospotami, this was the strongest navy in the Aegean and Sparta did not require any ships from the Peloponnesian League to buttress her navy, but by late 394 the number of Spartan triremes had withered to just eighty-five at the Battle of Cnidus.[2] It is hard to overemphasize this failure in Sparta's empire. Hyland suggests that their naval neglect 'cut short the possibility of a Spartan empire encompassing both sides of the Aegean'.[3]

However, Sparta's problems were not just limited to trireme numbers. Plaguing their ability to sustain their hegemony were 'the problems of trireme maintenance, manpower and naval finance.'[4] Sparta had perhaps believed that Persian naval power was at a low point when they authorized Agesilaus' invasion in 396, but Conon's cunning leadership had reversed Persian naval fortunes while Sparta's stagnated. Sparta mustered 120 triremes at Rhodes in the stalemate against Conon, but with the outbreak of the Corinthian War, the Spartans had no allies to support their shrinking navy. The Spartan fleet did have sporadic injections of ships, bolstered primarily by a surge of supplies and reinforcements from Egypt in 395 to 396 who were aiming to distract Persia, and a shipbuilding project by Agesilaus, but true Spartan ships were in short supply despite their naval supremacy just ten years earlier. Persia, meanwhile, had substantial reinforcements to which Conon could add, swelling the Persian fleet potentially up to 300 triremes.[5] Sparta's retreat from Rhodes had been ruinous for their navy: they forfeited both ships and supply lines to the rest of the Aegean.[6]

Agesilaus was earning plenty of gold in his land conquests, but that money never fully materialized into adequate ship construction, repair or sailors' wages. Agesilaus did embark on an aggressive shipbuilding project in 396 or 395, adding more than 100 triremes to Sparta's fleet. Yet even though Xenophon had complimented Agesilaus' military industrial skills in Asia Minor, that success did not translate as well to shipbuilding and the new fleet was not completed in time to eclipse Persia's advantage.[7] It is likely that these ships were not all finished on time or fully equipped, as evidenced by an intercepted Egyptian convoy sending supplies to Sparta for 100 triremes.[8] By the summer of 394, Peisander should have had more than 200 triremes, given almost a full year of construction, but he only had 85 battle-ready triremes at Cnidus.[9] Like their population decline, Sparta simply could not overcome the logistical and demographic challenges of maintaining naval supremacy.

Conon had remained quiet for much of 395, primarily antagonizing Agesilaus' land army and liberating several Spartan allies like Rhodes. After seizing Rhodes, Conon waited just off the mainland of Caria at Loryma, due north of the island of Rhodes. Conon's fleet had been headquartered there for two years by this point, waiting for Peisander's Spartan navy to make a move.

Conon and the Persian fleet had a decisive edge over the Spartan navy: their sailors. Due to both the deep Persian pockets and Conon's stellar reputation, the Persian navy attracted the best sailors in the early fourth century, especially those from Athens who were the highest regarded seamen in the Aegean. Conon's leadership also brought substantial connections between Persia and both Athenian voters and anti-Spartan politicians.[10] Despite their undisputed hegemony, Sparta lacked both the funds and the relational capital to consistently recruit sailors of the highest calibre. In theory, the Persian navy should have been flourishing in comparison to the struggling Spartan fleet.

Supplying proper wages to Persian sailors had not come easily, however. In the years before Conon's appointment, Persian *satraps* neglected sailor salaries and had several months of wages in arrears.[11] The Oxyrhynchus Historian blames the Persian king Artaxerxes II himself, who allegedly sent small sums of money to his *satraps* and developed a miserly reputation that apparently extended to the entire Persian navy.[12] Cyrus the Younger had improved matters during his ambitious networking with the Greeks, but since his death the lack of wages risked the disintegration of large parts of the unpaid and discontented Persian fleet.

Conon's first initiative as a Persian admiral was to secure sufficient wages, bluntly telling Tithraustes the *satrap* that the Persian vision for the Aegean would crumble if they could not make the payroll. Tithraustes managed to obtain funds from the king, but not before the sailors from Cyprus led a significant rebellion against Conon and the *satrap*. A revolt involving the Cypriots was especially damaging considering that Conon lived in exile with his Cypriot patron Evagoras. Conon's social aplomb and strategic leadership quelled this rebellion after a series of ruthless executions. Conon immediately pivoted and took it upon himself to travel all the way to the Persian homeland and appeal personally for funds to the King of King's courtiers, and perhaps Artaxerxes II himself.[13] While this was in part a mission to finance the navy, it also served as a way to repudiate the Persian war strategy against Sparta's invasion and highlight Conon's alternate vision of reasserting naval supremacy to cut off Sparta's army. He was successful in both. Artaxerxes II soon appointed a treasurer to oversee proper wages for all sailors.

Yet despite Conon's personal successes, the Persian navy was nevertheless decaying much like Sparta's, if at a slower rate. To argue that Persia's navy in 394 was objectively superior to Sparta's would be inadvisable. These two declining navies met north-east of Rhodes in the seas off the renowned city of Cnidus at the first naval battle of the Corinthian War. The Battle of Cnidus would change the fortunes of Sparta and imperil her hegemony.

Trireme Warfare in the Early Fourth Century

It would first be beneficial to survey the state of trireme warfare in the early fourth century. During the Peloponnesian War, naval warfare became the preeminent diplomatic and political tool, and the trireme was the crowning jewel of a strong navy. Named after its three levels of rowers, the trireme was about 120ft long but held an astonishing 200 crewmen.[14] The 170 rowers worked in teams of three that synergized each of the three levels, led by the rowers on the deck crew who were the only ones who could actually see the water. This teamwork was to ensure that the oars reached the water at maximum velocity and in sync with the other rowers, generating the ship's manoeuvrability and ramming power. A small deck crew, about a dozen marines and a handful of archers complemented the rowers. The marines and archers shared a small platform at the bow of the ship, while the deck crew and commander could walk a narrow catwalk across the confined rowers' posts.

In Athens, whose written records are the most extant, the rowers were not slaves but freedmen. They were of significant political capital in Athenian democracy as the *thetes*. While rich and poor alike served as rowers, the *thetes* were statistically the largest and most influential voting bloc. Appeasing the *thetes* was therefore paramount for Athenian political leaders. Historically, Persian client-states constituted the strongest navies, with the Phoenicians as the undisputed major power, but the Persian Wars reshaped both Mediterranean navies and politics, and the unexpected Greek victory there was on account of the newly-minted Athenian navy, less than a decade old. The construction of that Athenian fleet was the vision of the hero of the Persian Wars, Themistocles, who desired to see Athens carve out an empire through naval strength. As Themistocles funded the construction of hundreds of triremes – a massive upgrade over the existing Greek navies which used the inferior two-levelled *pentekonters* – he cultivated the voting support of the *thetes* which proved integral to his and Athens' political and military success.

The Athenian aristocrat who bankrolled the provision and maintenance of one or more triremes was rewarded with the commanding role of *trierarch*, and this wealthy *trierarch* would command the ship, but with the decline of Athenian wealth and the surging cost of wages and maintenance, Athens found that they could not find enough individuals to finance triremes. By the start of the fourth century, the Athenians split the role of *trierarch* among two men, who worked out the command and subsidizing of a trireme.

In combat, the primary purpose of a trireme was to smash into their opponent using the bronze ram at the bow of the ship. Ideally, the trireme would smash their beak not into the centre of the enemy's hull, but at an angle with sustained damage along the length of the hull in order to maximize the breach's size. Accomplishing this took speed, above all else. By the end of the fifth century triremes had to be as fast and as light as possible, to the extent that construction of the ships was orientated around removing any unnecessary weight or personnel. Athenian triremes so prioritized speed that they eliminated the standard decks for each of the three levels of rowers, instead jamming them together in a single cramped deck. This was a far cry from the first phase of Athenian triremes which were relatively heavy and clunky compared to their Persian and Phoenician opponents. Yet Themistocles' heavier ships had benefited him in the Battle of Salamis where the Athenians decimated the Persian fleet in a small, congested area where the lighter Persian ships could not achieve sufficiently high speeds to effectively ram their enemies, but in open waters as at Cnidus, a sleek and fast ship was peerless.

A squadron of triremes aimed first to ram and then, if necessary, to board opposing ships. The two major manoeuvres were the *diekplous* or 'sail through' and the *periplous* or 'sail around'. In a *diekplous*, the triremes sailed between enemy ships, passing by them and immediately doubling back to strike the vulnerable sterns. A *periplous* movement instead saw faster ships sail far to the side of slower enemy ships, and again turn about to attack from the side or rear. These tactics were, however, predominantly Athenian given the Athenian bias in surviving sources. Yet at the height of the Athenian empire, only the Athenian triremes were disciplined and swift enough to accomplish such complex manoeuvres.[15] At the end of the Peloponnesian War, the Spartans and other Greeks were sufficiently capable of pulling off a *diekplous* or *periplous*, but they would often hire Athenian sailors to do the work if their coin purses allowed.

To combat these tactics, the most common defensive formation for a squadron was a crescent or circle with the ships' prows facing outwards. As the prow of the ship was the strongest and most durable given its bronze ram and additional wooden reinforcement, trireme commanders sought to avoid the weaker hull, particularly the sides. Another common method of neutralizing faster ships was to sail directly beside a ship after retracting their oars, thus slicing off the oars of their enemy and leaving them unable to steer effectively.

Marines were best utilized not necessarily as fighters but as throwers of grappling hooks which could then drag an enemy ship close enough to board. Fast ships remained ideal in these scenarios as they could better avoid the grappling hooks, but their light weight made them easier to tow if hooked. As such, most triremes in Greece since the Peloponnesian War eliminated all superfluous architecture on trireme decks to minimize footholds for the grappling hooks.

Although often built under rushed and imperfect circumstances, triremes of the early fourth century generally matched their Peloponnesian War predecessors in design and function. Other formidable navies of the Aegean and Mediterranean had counterbalanced Athenian naval dominance by constructing flatter prows and reinforced beams on the front of the trireme.[16] The Corinthian and later Syracusan navies did this in the Peloponnesian War to great effect in naval battles within confined quarters when the Athenian speed advantage was limited. Despite the Athens-centric historical knowledge of trireme warfare, any trireme rower or commander could easily adapt to a Phoenician, Egyptian, Syracusan or Peloponnesian trireme, as noted by Nicolle Hirschfeld.[17] Conon and his Athenian rowers would sail Ionian and Phoenician ships, but he wisely employed a mixture of Athenian tactics with cunning and unpredictable new schemes.

The Geographic and Historical Significance of Cnidus

Cnidus was a fascinating setting for a major battle. A beautiful city that jutted out into the Aegean Sea, its urban centre was on the Carian Chersonese peninsula and surrounded by the picturesque Ceramic Gulf. Cnidus may have claimed heritage from Sparta, making their longtime membership in the Delian League and therefore the Athenian empire ironic, but Cnidus abruptly left that league about a decade before the end of the Peloponnesian War and by 394 was a dependable member of the Persian Empire. Although not as culturally significant as its fellow Carian city-states Halicarnassus or Ceramus, Cnidus earned a reputation for the sciences. Many physicians hailed from their esteemed medical academy, and their observatory was among the most significant centres of astronomy in the Classical world.

Strategically, Cnidus was a prudent location for Conon's fleet. All ships travelling along the coast of Asia Minor essentially had to pass by Cnidus. Shielded from the worst of the treacherous weather of the Aegean by outlying islands, the cape on which Cnidus was nestled evenly split the journey between

Halicarnassus and Rhodes, the two major city-states in the region and necessary stopping-points along the coast. Turning north at the Carian Chersonese marked the entry point into the Aegean Sea from the Mediterranean and, at least in the Classical period, Cnidus was at the very point of the peninsula.[18]

From Conon's vantage point at Loryma, Cnidus was the logical funnel through which the Spartan navy had to traverse if they wished to go on the offensive. Conon waited for that bottleneck, for which there was significant precedent among Athenian admirals. At nearby Caunus, where Conon's fleet sheltered before besieging Rhodes, both Pericles and Alcibiades had blockaded the celebrated Phoenician navy from entering the Aegean Sea during the Peloponnesian War.[19] Conon himself had been trapped at Caunus by the *navarch* Pharax and the Spartan fleet before Pharnabazus arrived and forced a Spartan retreat.[20] Cnidus and its environs also provided sufficient space for beaching and bivouacking the many Persian triremes, a vital element for naval warfare as the hundreds of crewmen in each trireme had to come ashore for food and shelter each night since they were tightly crammed into the triremes. As such, trireme warfare almost always ended at nightfall. Cnidus was therefore a substantial tactical advantage for Conon and the Persians, and capable military strategists would identify this and account for it. Unfortunately for the Spartans, their new *navarch* Peisander was no such tactician.

It is not often that a historian has the opportunity to write themselves into their own narrative, but Ctesias of Cnidus accomplished that precise feat. While Xenophon and Thucydides were among many ancients who played a role in their own history-writing, Ctesias was the only historian to bridge the Persian and Greek worlds and serve as a primary source for many of the key events about which he wrote. Ctesias was one of the many esteemed physicians from Cnidus, but also harboured a passion for historical writing. His many travels in Asia Minor and Mesopotamia certainly qualified him for the post of historian. His vocation as a physician afforded him the opportunity to marry his two passions while serving as a court physician to many Persian leaders, culminating in the role of personal doctor to the King of Kings himself, Artaxerxes II.

Ctesias penned two major historical works: *Persica*, a history of Persia, and *Indica*, a history of India from Persia's perspective. *Persica* is a fascinating foil to the West's seminal text on the same material: Herodotus' *The Histories*. Herodotus was a fellow Carian historian from Halicarnassus, but Ctesias' history draws deeply on his travels and connections within the Persian Empire and diverges from the Greco-centric narrative of Herodotus, humanizing the Persians. As an eyewitness to many of his own historical accounts – Ctesias witnessed the Battle of Cunaxa in 401, for example – many modern historians are quick to give Ctesias accolades over his predecessor. The majority of Ctesias' works, however, have not survived the passage of time and are extant today mostly as quotes and summaries from other ancient writers.

By 397, Ctesias had concluded his service to the Persian king and returned home to Cnidus. He put the diplomatic skills learned in the Persian court to quick use, brokering the talks between Conon and the king to procure wages for the sailors of the Persian fleet. Ctesias even liaised with Evagoras of Cyprus and Artaxerxes II to improve Evagoras' ships with Persian gold. This tactic was a guardrail against Spartan aggression but also reinforced the Cypriot ships, whose malcontent sailors had led the brief revolt against Conon and the Persian naval leadership.

Indeed, Ctesias was an integral player in both raising and coordinating the entire Persian fleet during the Persian-Spartan War and the Corinthian War. At a minimum, Ctesias served as the intermediary between Conon and Artaxerxes II when Conon approached the Persians with the idea to lead their Aegean fleet and disrupt Sparta's invasion.[21] Ctesias claims this was entirely of the king's accord, but Plutarch believes that Ctesias downplayed his role for political reasons and even 'added to the suggestions which Conon made to the king'.[22] Ctesias further personally delivered Artaxerxes II's response letters to Conon and, amusingly, to the Spartans.[23]

It was in 394, though, that Ctesias personally witnessed another groundbreaking event that made its way into his *Persica*: Conon's naval battle against the Spartans.

The Battle of Cnidus

Diodorus, Polyaenus and Xenophon only dedicate a paragraph each to the Battle of Cnidus, while Ctesias' writings have not survived but are cited by Plutarch and others in their summaries. As such, reconstructing the battle remains difficult. It is clear that Conon established a defensive line that stretched south of Cnidus from Rhodes to Loryma to Caunus.[24] Conon's long wait at this defensive line stemmed not only from his concerns about securing wages for sailors, but also from Persia's anxiety about Spartan-Egyptian collusion and the Spartan ability to draw on the vast Egyptian resources to support their flagging invasion. The defensive line from Rhodes to Caunus stopped Spartan ships from travelling eastward to Egypt and Egyptian ships from travelling westward to link with Peisander. The Spartans, meanwhile, camped somewhere slightly north of Cnidus. The Battle of Cnidus therefore was probably not at the actual city of Cnidus, but in the bay off the Carian Chersonese; Stephen Ruzicka proposes the bay near the city of Bybassus.[25]

The *satrap* Pharnabazus joined the Persian fleet, which numbered more than ninety triremes.[26] Pharnabazus' arrival not only added to the defensive front, but also represented Conon's influence on the Persian king's military strategy. After two years of defensive standing, the Persian fleet was ready to go on the offensive. Conon had just shy of 200 triremes in his entire fleet, but the forces at Cnidus were likely just an offensive vanguard of 90 triremes.[27] Isocrates would later note that Evagoras of Cyprus was the main patron of this fleet, making Pharnabazus' Phoenician reinforcements minimal. Pharnabazus took command of the Phoenician ships in the fleet, while Conon continued his command of the Cypriot and Cilician triremes. They were officially co-commanders, though this was Pharnabazus' first known naval admiralship.

Meanwhile, the Spartan fleet numbered eighty-five triremes, although the manpower and maintenance plagues suffered by Sparta may have caused their triremes to be undermanned and in various states of seaworthiness. Though a novice, Peisander was not incompetent and he plotted an astute course of travel that began at Physcus, a city of uncertain modern location, and curved around Cnidus and the Carian Chersonese peninsula and south towards Rhodes and the defensive wall of Conon. Peisander had a challenging hand considering Conon had now spent two years tarrying at Loryma with no indication of any upcoming movements. However, Peisander figured that Pharnabazus' recent arrival at Loryma with Phoenician triremes signalled that the Persians would soon attack the Spartan fleet near Cnidus or depart across the Aegean to attack Spartan interests back in Greece.[28] Peisander chose to attack first and eliminate either opportunity for the Persians.

In early August 394, Peisander departed the Spartan camp, rounded Cnidus and headed to Conon's location at Loryma. Despite Conon's preparations to go on the offensive, Peisander caught the Persian fleet off guard. Conon was able to scramble his ships into action, although as a result, Peisander and the Spartans had a decisive advantage early in the battle. While the specific timing favoured Sparta, Conon nevertheless knew that an attack was coming. The Greek historian Polyaenus, writing in his second-century AD military history text *Strategems*, shares that Conon returned to his Athenian roots and employed a cunning ruse before the battle. A Spartan defector, likely motivated by a lack of wages, shared the news that Peisander's primary objective was to seize Conon's ship at all costs.[29] Conon responded by dressing a separate trireme as his own, including placing his uniform on its captain, and gave that trireme the command position on the right flank.[30] The Spartans fell for it completely.

As the triremes began to engage, the Persian fleet formed two lines: the first line consisted of Cypriot and Cilician ships led by Conon, and the second line was Phoenician ships led by Pharnabazus. This organization was born out of the rush to assemble the fleet and not necessarily a tactical manoeuvre, as it is probable that the early advantage enjoyed by the Spartans was due to the uneven waves of the Persian fleet. When the Spartans faced off against only Conon's line, they had numerical superiority and, despite Peisander's relative inexperience, began to sink or disable an impressive number of Persian ships, but when the Phoenician ships arrived and took formation, the Spartans were caught unawares. Having overcommitted to the first Persian assault, the Spartan navy was in no position to shield themselves from a *diekplous* or *periplous* attack and could not protect their sterns or sides. Compounding the Spartan situation was that they had prioritized attacking the right wing of the Persians, probably since they fell for Conon's trick and thought they had a chance of eliminating the Athenian admiral.

In a move that illustrated Peisander's tenuous command as *navarch*, the entire left flank of the Spartan fleet 'took to flight immediately' upon seeing Pharnabazus' ships.[31] This flank was the Spartan allies, leaving only the Spartans themselves to fight. In a desperate attempt to restore Spartan fortunes, Peisander channelled Sparta's famous military virtue of courage and charged the Phoenician ships. Under barrage from the Persian ships and their relentless rams, Peisander's ship and many other Spartan triremes ran aground on the beach. The Persian marines stormed the Spartan ships, and almost all the Spartans fled inland towards Cnidus and the remaining Spartan ships that hadn't come to the battle. Only one Spartan stayed onboard to fight. Peisander was killed on his flagship with his sword in hand.[32]

Conon and the Persians captured fifty triremes, with the remaining thirty-five escaping back to Cnidus and the Spartan camp.[33] These numbers from Diodorus suggest that the fifty triremes were the Spartans', while the remaining thirty-five were largely composed of their departed allies. The Persians further took about 500 prisoners, although most of the Spartan and allied sailors were able to escape by land or were lost overboard. The loss of fifty triremes was nigh insurmountable for the Spartan navy given its declining health over the past decade. Sparta's hegemony faced its clearest danger in decades.

The Implications of Cnidus

The dominoes fell quickly after Cnidus. In one afternoon, Sparta had lost her naval supremacy and with it her ability to maintain her overseas empire. Diodorus bluntly says that the Spartans 'lost the sovereignty of the sea',[34] but perhaps the most significant outcome was Sparta's failure to continue the Corinthian War on two fronts. With the retreat of Agesilaus and the loss at Cnidus, their expedition to Asia Minor was officially over. With Cnidus and Caria ceded to Persia, Agesilaus' remaining allies in Asia Minor saw no hope for his return with their many soldiers. Many acquiesced to Persian rule, ending almost all

Spartan *harmosts* and decarchies in Asia Minor and the Aegean islands. Many Spartan leaders were overthrown, and still more willingly joined Conon and the Persians. Conon wisely advised the Persians to reassert themselves with a light touch and avoid Tissaphernes' fatal mistake of antagonizing the Ionian Greeks. Taxation and tribute to the Persian King of Kings soon recommenced among Agesilaus' – and Lysander's – former admirers.

Most devastating was not the loss of Spartan naval superiority, but the loss of the entire Spartan navy. The forfeiture of their navy was so influential that several ancient historians label 394 as the end of Spartan hegemony in the Aegean. The Hellenistic-era historian Polybius numbered the length of Sparta's empire at just twelve years.[35] Given that the Peloponnesian War's end in 404 is the obvious start date, 394 and the Battle of Cnidus was clearly seen by Polybius as the end of Sparta's uncontested hegemony. One historian whose works do not survive, Theopompus of Chios, ended his book *Hellenistic History* with the Battle of Cnidus, perhaps finding it a fitting bookend to Sparta's empire.[36] Most damningly, Plutarch in his *Life of Artaxerxes* likewise named Cnidus as the impetus for the very end of the Corinthian War:

> But after Artaxerxes, by the sea-fight which Pharnabazus and Conon won for him off Cnidus, had stripped the Lacedaemonians of their power on the sea, he brought the whole of Greece into dependence upon him, so that he dictated to the Greeks the celebrated peace [treaty which ended the Corinthian War].[37]

Artaxerxes opted to exploit this rare opportunity to annihilate Sparta instead of moving on to his original target of Egypt. He sent Conon and his fleet across the Aegean with orders to establish new garrisons and pave the way for the overdue Persian conquest of Greece. Conon added many new territories to Artaxerxes' empire including Cos, Chios, Mytilene, Ephesus, the Cycladic Islands and Cythera.[38] His ambition unquenched, Conon sailed for Corinth to convene with the anti-Spartan confederacy and lend Persian aid to their cause. The Persian king may have hoped to cultivate more chaos in Greece, but Conon's goal was increasingly palpable: return to Athens and revive her empire. He was rapidly fulfilling that dream.

Sparta meanwhile realized that she could not take on both Persia and the allied Greeks, and pivoted to a divide-and-conquer strategy prioritizing the strongest of the allies: Thebes. Seeking retribution for the stinging naval defeat, Agesilaus would make his long-awaited entry into the war at the Battle of Coronea just days after the disaster at Cnidus.

Chapter Seven

A Costly Victory at Coronea

Agesilaus' Triumphant Return to Greece

On 14 August 394, the sun went dark as Agesilaus heard news of the disastrous defeat at Cnidus. A solar eclipse occurred that day, apparently just as messengers arrived with the ominous report that Agesilaus' appointed *navarch* Peisander was dead, along with virtually the entire Spartan navy.

Agesilaus figured that such news could not be shared immediately with his army. After all, many of his army were Ionian Greeks who, upon learning such news, might now be precariously loyal to Agesilaus given that their homeland was now under Persian control. His Spartan and *neodamode* soldiers would be enormously disheartened given the loss at Haliartus and the leadership changes with the losses of Lysander and Pausanias. Agesilaus was on the eve of the next battle of the Corinthian War, the Battle of Coronea, and decided that 'the moral quality of more than half his troops well entitled them to share in the sunshine of success.'[1] Agesilaus lied to his men and announced that they had won a great naval victory at Cnidus, although Peisander had heroically perished.

Continuing his pattern of re-enacting the path traversed by Xerxes the Great and the invading Persians, Agesilaus journeyed through the narrow pass of Thermopylae in the late summer of 394. During his travels southward, Agesilaus' army was harried by Thessalians and other northern Greeks. These Thessalians had a loose alliance with the Boeotians, and so were aiming to impair Agesilaus' army as much as possible before their return to Greece and formal entry into the Corinthian War.

Before reaching Boeotia, Agesilaus' army was composed of almost no Spartiates, fewer than 2,000 *neodamodes*, Ionian Greek soldiers who were new to Spartan command and, most critically, the veterans of the March of the Ten Thousand. He further had a few hundred cavalry that had been trained only recently in Asia Minor. To Agesilaus' credit, those cavalry were able to consistently defeat the prestigious Thessalian cavalry who were often judged to be the best of the ancients. Upon reaching Boeotia, Agesilaus first camped at Orchomenus, where Lysander's half-*mora* of Spartiates had garrisoned since before the Battle of Haliartus the year before. This half-*mora* of about 300 men joined Agesilaus' army, along with a full *mora* of about 600 men that had been dispatched from Sparta and crossed the Gulf of Corinth to join the war effort. In a show of desperation about their declining Spartiates and citizenship, the *ephors* also authorized lowering the fighting age, selecting fifty youths to join Agesilaus in an unprecedented move.[2] A contingent of Spartan-allied Phocian and Orchomenian hoplites further augmented Agesilaus' army.

No ancient sources give total numbers, but Lazenby suggests that Agesilaus had 15,000 hoplites with a few thousand light infantry and a few hundred cavalry.[3] In all, we can approximate the Spartan army at 18,000. While he makes no mention of the total count, Xenophon goes out of his way to note that the Spartans had many more light infantry than the Thebans, but about the same number of cavalry.[4]

The anti-Spartan confederacy had an army composed of Boeotians, Athenians, Argives, Corinthians, Aenianians, Euboeans and Locrians, although the exact proportions are unspecified.[5] Because the battle was in Boeotia, it was likely that the Thebans were better represented in the allied army than they had been at Nemea; conversely, the Corinthians and other Peloponnesians were less represented given the distance from their homeland. Lazenby reasonably suggests a total of 20,000 soldiers for the anti-Spartan coalition, giving them a slight edge over the Spartans.[6] The two armies met near the Boeotian city of Coronea in August 394.

The location of Boeotia was influential in the battle's flow. Even before he heard of the loss at Cnidus, Agesilaus had a singular mission to destroy the Thebans. Born of his failed sacrifice at Aulis and compounded through the events of the Corinthian War, Agesilaus' passionate hatred of the Thebans bordered on irrational. Defeating the Thebans at Coronea would not only bring Agesilaus vengeance against the enemy he blamed for his discontinued invasion of Asia Minor, but also strike down the resurgent anti-Spartan confederacy that was buoyed by their victory at Cnidus.

After departing from Orchomenus, Agesilaus hurriedly arrived at Coronea from the north and settled in the farmland and plains east of the city after crossing the Cephissus River. The city-state Coronea was situated not far from the southwestern banks of Lake Copais, and only about a dozen miles from Haliartus. Like Haliartus, Coronea was nestled in the foothills near Mount Helicon, not far from the mountain peak dedicated to the muse Leibethrides. Coronea was most well-known for its proximity to this place sacred to Leibethrides, who was also the namesake of a natural spring that had been dedicated to the muse by Thracian immigrants to Boeotia centuries earlier.

The anti-Spartan forces headquartered in the foothills near Mount Leibethrides prior to the fighting. The Thebans, encouraged by the relative lack of Spartans in this Spartan army, set out with similar alacrity north from Helicon towards the plains outside Coronea. Each side was brimming with optimism and sought out the battle with fervour.

The Battle of Coronea in 394 was not, in fact, the first Battle of Coronea. At the same location in 447, the Thebans had expelled the Athenian presence from Boeotia during a series of civil wars prior to the Peloponnesian War. That battle had been one of the first major resistance movements against the Delian League and dealt a major blow to the Athenian Empire. This second battle, if won by the Thebans and her allies, would do the same to the Spartan Empire.

The Battle of Coronea

Xenophon described the Battle of Coronea as 'different from all the battles of our day'.[7] For him, this was an intensely personal remark. While Coronea was certainly significant, as we shall soon see, it would have been dwarfed by the Battle of Leuctra in 371 which put an official end to the Spartan Empire. Xenophon was alive for both events and wrote after their occurrences, but it is likely that he placed greater value on the Battle of Coronea for the simple reason that he was present in the battle alongside the other veterans of the March of the Ten Thousand.[8]

As for troop arrangement, Xenophon and the scant other ancient sources give limited information. Agesilaus personally led the Spartan hoplites on the honourable right side, and he would fight on the front lines at Coronea in a blood thirst against the Thebans. The only other specifics we have are the placement of the Orchomenians on the left side. It is probable that Xenophon and the other distinguished warriors of the Ten Thousand fought alongside the Spartans on the centre-right. Directly meeting the Spartans on this flank were the Argives. Argos had long coveted the chance to diminish Sparta's grip on the Peloponnese, but the Argive hoplites at this battle were not the strongest offered by Argos, which most probably kept their strongest warriors home after Nemea to protect the Peloponnese, while the Thebans took the lead among the allied Greeks in this second Boeotian battle. The Thebans took the right flank, hoping to avoid the Spartan *mora* and a half in direct battle.

Xenophon took care to emphasize the deafening silence of both armies before battle. The forces assembled and marched towards each other in this silence until they were within a couple of hundred yards, when the Thebans began the battle with their war cry of 'Alalah!' and with this 'loud hurrah the Thebans, quickening to a run, rushed furiously'.[9] In response, the Ionian Greeks and others in the centre of the Spartan line burst forward. The battle had begun.

The *neodamodes* and Ionian Greeks in the centre had immediate success, piercing the front lines of the allied Greeks' phalanx and therefore breaking the enemy formation in two parts. The Spartans had similar success, of a sort, when the Argives they were to face simply turned and fled into the foothills near Mount Helicon. With two-thirds of the anti-Spartan coalition's army defeated, the Spartans thought the battle finished. Some Spartan soldiers even began to crown Agesilaus with a victory wreath.

However, the battle was far from over. As in their previous Boeotian battle at Haliartus, the Spartan army's failure to communicate was costly. On the left flank of the Spartan line, the Orchomenians had been overwhelmed by the Theban phalanx. The Thebans had advanced into the 'baggage train' of the Spartan formation.[10] If they were to pivot towards the unsuspecting Agesilaus, they would be able to encircle the Spartiates.

News of the battle's revival finally reached Agesilaus who, in a panic, ordered the Spartan army to turn to their right and directly engage the Thebans. This was an overcorrection, as each army had now seen their left flanks pushed back by the enemy, and to turn at a sharp right angle would mitigate any advantageous angle the Spartan phalanxes might have been able to exploit had they advanced more strategically towards the Theban flank or rear. The Thebans, who should have been on the defensive, were instead able to meet the Spartans head on, but by this point Agesilaus was possessed by a bloodlust akin to Achilles on the plains of Troy and his burning hatred of Thebes clouded his judgement. Plutarch describes him as 'carried away by passion and the ardour of battle...[and] wishing to bear [the Thebans] down by sheer force.'[11] Xenophon, meanwhile, offers a rare departure from his hagiography of Agesilaus, writing that 'no one will dispute the valour of Agesilaus, but he certainly did not choose the safest course.'[12]

Seeing the Spartan offensive manoeuvre, the Thebans 'formed in close order and tramped forward stoutly'.[13] The opaque description of 'in close order' from Xenophon might mean that the Thebans simply stood closer together than in a normal phalanx, expecting a fiercer fight than usual.[14] It is clear, however, that the sight of their anti-Spartan allies either cut off on the other side of the Spartan phalanx or in retreat towards Mount Helicon motivated them to fight for the honour of a Homeric-style final stand in battle. Xenophon, accordingly, draws on Homeric language in his detailed depiction of Coronea's second round: 'Thereupon, with close interlock of shield wedged in with shield, they shoved, they fought, they dealt death, they breathed out life, till at last a portion of the Thebans broke their way through towards Helicon, but paid for that departure by the loss of many lives.'[15]

The battle was a vigorous and violent meeting between the two strongest armies in Greece, even though the Spartiates were fewer in number. It was an even match, and neither phalanx could break the line of the enemy. Surrounded by fifty hoplites, Agesilaus saw the worst of the fighting. He was struck multiple times by Theban swords and spears and he fell to the ground wounded.[16] His bodyguards were able to drag him back to safety behind the front lines of the Spartan phalanx, although at the cost of many lives. Agesilaus would survive, but at Coronea his courage in battle was matched only by his tactical ineptitude.

The Spartans had, for once, met their match in hoplite warfare. They simply could not defeat the Thebans on equal ground. The Spartans pivoted towards trickery when their combat skill proved insufficient. Drawing on a tactic that 'at the outset they were loath to do', the Spartans intentionally opened the centre of their phalanx.[17] When the Thebans, thinking this was their hard-won moment of victory, funnelled into the opening and set off for Mount Helicon to rejoin their allies and depart the battle, the Spartans pounced as soon as sufficient Thebans had passed through and broke formation, attacking the unguarded Theban flanks and killing hundreds.[18]

Despite the bloodshed, many Thebans successfully retreated into the foothills. The battle was over, but Sparta's victory rang hollow without an obliterated Thebes and with an injured Agesilaus. Numbers on the first part of the battle are uncertain, although heavy losses among the Argives and Orchomenians were likely. Diodorus reports that the Thebans lost more than 600 soldiers while the Spartan coalition lost 350.[19]

Failing to achieve the decisive end to the Corinthian War, the Spartans were crestfallen. By contrast, the Thebans were elated. Plutarch describes the Thebans as 'greatly elated over the battle, in which, as they reasoned, their own contingent had been undefeated.'[20] The dubious nature of their 'undefeated' performance aside, the *Boeotarchs* surely saw the Battle of Coronea as a moral victory considering their army over-performed against the famously exceptional commander Agesilaus.

Despite his grievous wounds, Agesilaus had never relinquished command. The next morning, he ordered triumphant music and victory laurels to be handed out to his soldiers in an ostentatious display. His aim was not to celebrate the victory, but instead to tempt the Thebans into returning to battle and giving the Spartans the chance to truly eliminate the Theban army.[21] He was unsuccessful, and the Thebans instead asked permission to gather their dead. Meanwhile, eighty Thebans had been unable to retreat with their countrymen and sheltered underneath the Temple of Athena in nearby Coronea. When his lieutenants asked permission to put them to the spear, Agesilaus – his injuries giving some lucidity amid his hatred of Thebes – allowed them to journey home unscathed in a show of piety.[22] Immediately after the battle, Agesilaus evacuated to Delphi to take advantage of their famous healers. On arrival, he offered an astonishing

Battle of Coronea, 394 BC
Phase One

Phase Two

1. The Spartans break the Argive front.

2. After realising the battle is not over, the Spartans rush to meet the Boeotians.

Battle of Coronea, 394 BC
Phase Three

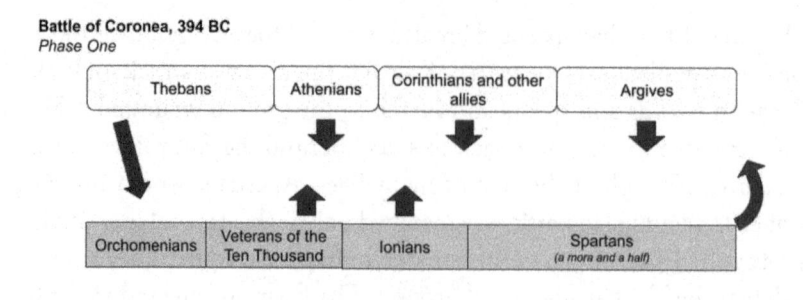

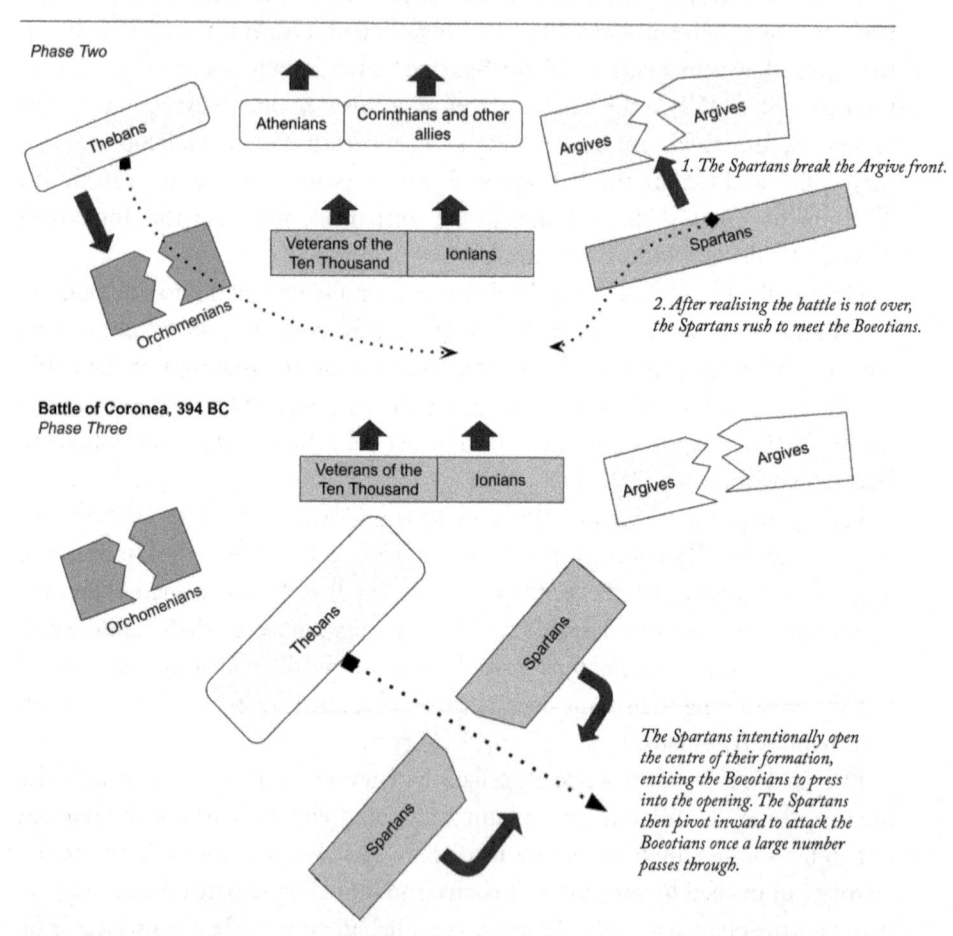

The Spartans intentionally open the centre of their formation, enticing the Boeotians to press into the opening. The Spartans then pivot inward to attack the Boeotians once a large number passes through.

A depiction of the Battle of Coronea's events.

show of the wealth and prosperity of his campaign in Asia Minor with a tithe of 100 talents.[23]

With Agesilaus in the infirmary, the *polemarch* Gylis was given command of the Spartan army. After giving the victory wreaths to the Spartan citizens, he withdrew to Spartan-allied Phocis and aimed to pillage city-states in nearby

Theban-allied Locris. The Spartans secured a day's worth of booty, but by nightfall the Locrians had tempted the Spartans into an uphill pursuit. Under cover of night, the Locrians massacred almost two dozen Spartiates including Gylis and his top commander.[24] It was yet another black eye for the vaunted Spartan army and an unnecessary continuation of Spartiate population decline.

Agesilaus' Wounded Return to Sparta

Even though Coronea was a victory for Sparta, it had a disastrous impact on their empire. In the wake of the loss at Cnidus, Sparta had needed an overwhelming victory to regain the upper hand against the allied Greeks or even to end the war, but Sparta delivered a hollow retribution for their loss at Cnidus. They remained without a navy and, with their withdrawal from Asia Minor, without foreign holdings. The majority of their Ionian allies at Coronea were disbanded from the army and sent home.[25] Meanwhile, the Theban army was inspired by their performance, while the Argive, Corinthian and Athenian armies remained relatively intact, having withheld their best fighters. None of the major anti-Spartans was knocked out of the war effort, and Agesilaus' quest for vengeance against Thebes remained unquenched.

For Agesilaus personally, Coronea was a costly victory. The most immediate consequence was not his dire health, but rather his dire political standing. While he had distinguished himself in battle, Coronea's limited victory could not overcome his political rivals in Sparta. Instead of bringing about Agesilaus' functional ascent to the role of emperor, Coronea threw oil on the fire that was the Spartan *stasis*. Lysander's political capital had not dissipated, and many supporters of his imperial vision still existed and sought to undermine Agesilaus.

His political rivals further took notice of his 100-talent donation at Delphi. While they supported the religious devotion, such an amount could have gone a long way towards rebuilding the lost navy from Cnidus, and Agesilaus already bore the brunt of the blame for Cnidus since he had appointed his inept brother-in-law Peisander as *navarch*. Lysander's supporters were quick to point out that without a navy, the Spartans could not engage the Persians in Asia Minor.[26] Worse, his bravery at Coronea was an inadequate substitute for eliminating the Theban military, and with the departure of his army after the battle, Agesilaus lost his faithful Ionian Greeks. With limited success and allies after his perceived failures at Cnidus and Coronea, Agesilaus languished in Sparta from 394 to 392 with few reports regarding his activities. Xenophon puts a romantic spin on this demotion: 'Agesilaus departed homewards, having chosen, in lieu of supreme greatness in Asia, to rule, and to be ruled, in obedience to the laws at home.'[27]

Despite his military and political troubles, the general population of Sparta still adored Agesilaus. Of particular note was his fidelity to the Spartan ideal and identity; his successes in Asia Minor had not only not changed him, but in fact reinforced the traditional Lycurgan reputation of Sparta and its kings:

> For, unlike most of their generals, he came back from foreign parts unchanged and unaffected by alien customs; he showed no dislike towards home fashions, nor was he restive under them, but honoured and loved what he found there just as much as those did who had never crossed the Eurotas; he made no change in his table, or his baths, or the attendance on his wife, or the decoration of his armour, or the furniture of his house.[28]

Instead of directly confronting his political rivals, Agesilaus busied himself with Spartan culture and civil society, laying the groundwork for a reemergence in foreign affairs. Apart from chariot races and cultivating a closer relationship with Xenophon by convincing him to raise his sons in the *agoge*, the only significant action we know embarked on by Agesilaus was a cover-up for, of all people, his old rival Lysander. Frustrated by the lingering influence of the deceased Lysander and his followers' ability to hinder Agesilaus' own career, Agesilaus 'set out to prove what manner of citizen Lysander had been while alive.'[29] Searching through Lysander's former home, Agesilaus obtained a copy of a speech Lysander had prepared proposing his passion project: the overturning of the Spartan monarchy and allowing sub-elites to become king.

Agesilaus felt that he had struck gold and immediately desired to publish the speech, thereby destroying Lysander's legacy and his political faction with it.[30] Agesilaus, however, was persuaded not to advertise Lysander's potential treason after speaking to a member of the *Gerousia* who warned, rightfully, that the Spartan civil strife may not survive a scandal of such magnitude. Agesilaus acquiesced.

He instead found a more diplomatic method of eliminating his rivals, by making them his allies:

> And as for those who were in opposition to him, he would do them no open injury, but would exert himself to send some of them away from time to time as generals and commanders, and would shew them up if they proved base and grasping in their exercise of authority; then, contrariwise, when they were brought to trial, he would come to their aid and exert himself in their behalf, and so would make them friends instead of enemies, and bring them over to his side, so that no one was left to oppose him.[31]

While Sparta licked its wounds after Coronea, Agesilaus maximized his demotion, patiently preparing for his inevitable return to Aegean geopolitics. Indeed, Agesilaus' pseudo-exile was akin to Conon's exile on Cyprus. Yet while Agesilaus had to wait until 391 to re-emerge as a leader, Conon's prophetic return to Athens came shortly after Cnidus and Coronea.

With the frantic array of battles in 394 now concluded, the Spartans needed to cast a new vision for their shrinking empire. The reformed Spartan strategy ignored the resilience of Thebes and the resurgence of Athens and instead focused on one enemy city-state: Corinth, which not only had the most strategic location, but the other allied Greeks had, by this point, made Corinth the headquarters of their alliance.

Yet they would not yet fight Corinth directly. Instead, the Spartan strategy from 394 to 391 was a deeply imperial one, inspired by the Athenian and Persian model of diplomacy. They would pour money into anti-democratic partisans in the Corinthian *stasis*, funding political discord and turmoil with the hopes of securing Spartan allies within Corinth or even the outbreak of a civil war. In this, Spartan subterfuge was farming fertile ground. Xenophon recounts how, given that Corinthian territory had seen the most devastation of the war thus far, 'the majority of [the Corinthians], including the better class, desired peace, and gathering into knots they indoctrinated one another with these views.'[32] Spartan spies, patrons and *proxenies* were sent to Corinth to lure at least some aristocrats back into the Peloponnesian League.

This would, of course, take time, and during these few years, with Spartan attention focused on cultivating chaos in Corinth, the Spartans neglected to address the rejuvenation of the Athenian empire.

Chapter Eight
The Reconstruction of Athens

The Return of Conon and the Reconstruction of the Athenian Walls

Much like their tradition of *medizing* politicians, Athens also had a penchant for the return of exiled politicians. The most notable was none other than Alcibiades who, after betraying Athens for Sparta and then Sparta for Persia during the Peloponnesian War, had returned to Athens to trumpet-calls and parades. Other Athenian politicians like Cleisthenes, Aristides the Just and Xanthippus had further set the precedent of the prodigal statesman restored not just to power but to a greater height than before.

The popularity of Conon's homecoming in 393 was second only to the fanfare enjoyed by Alcibiades in 407. Conon sailed into the Athenian harbour of Piraeus with eighty triremes, many of which were crewed by Athenian sailors. It was the largest navy Athens had seen since the Peloponnesian War and the glory days of their empire, but it was not technically their navy. Conon's fleet still belonged to Persia.

Conon, nevertheless, abdicated his Persian commitments upon the fulfilment of his long-awaited restoration to Athens. His first action was to refortify the walls of Piraeus. The protective walls of Piraeus had become a symbol of the health of the Athenian Empire itself. The first fortification of the walls had been paired with the construction of Piraeus as the main Athenian harbour, a strategic move by the statesmen Themistocles a century earlier. Themistocles' construction of the harbour was an integral part of his vision for Athens to become a naval empire and coincided with his later construction of almost 200 triremes. When Athens and all its structures were burned by the invaders during the Persian invasion of 480, Themistocles rebuilt the walls before the city itself, foreseeing the tension with Sparta that would grow into the Peloponnesian War. When the Athenian orator Andocides elucidated on the history of the Athenian golden days of empire, the first benefits he mentioned were the Long Walls and fortification of Piraeus.[1]

Pericles later expanded the Themistoclean Walls to encompass the entire port of Piraeus and link it to the urban centre of Athens 7 miles away. These Long Walls became the stalwart defensive structure of the Peloponnesian War and enabled them to survive the annual sieges by the Spartan hoplites. With such a reputation, it is clear why Lysander's ceremonial deconstruction of the Long Walls employed such theatrics as young dancers and musicians. As part of the peace treaty ending the Peloponnesian War, Sparta consequently restricted Athens from refortifying Piraeus and the Long Walls, although that mattered little now in the midst of the Corinthian War. Athenian panic after the loss at Nemea spurred interest in refortifying Athens lest the Spartans march on the unsecured city after their victory. In 394, the *archon* Diophantus attempted to rebuild parts of the city walls, although insufficient funds and manpower led to a failed initiative.[2]

In 393, it was Conon's turn to enter the hallowed halls of Athenian wall-builders. Upon his return, Conon was immediately given the proverbial keys to Athens. The voting assembly approved two statues of Conon, including one on the Acropolis, and one of his patron Evagoras of Cyprus. They also absolved him of taxation in a rare move, especially in a financially downtrodden democracy.[3]

There was, however, one major roadblock for the project: financing. With the decline of their empire and their paltry navy came economic hardship that prohibited funding the reconstruction of their city walls. Conon was on a strict financial leash, and his Persian patrons would have only a limited stake in re-equipping the Athenian military and virtually no interest in funding construction projects in Athens. Conon was determined to sell the Persians on the value of a strengthened Athens in their war against Sparta. The Persians might be persuaded of this, but they would never agree to the full extent of his plans for Athens. After the city walls were rebuilt, Conon's true strategy was to rebuild the Athenian navy, revitalizing Themistocles' vision of an Athenian naval empire and re-establishing Athenian prominence in the Aegean.

The circumstances of Conon's return to Athens are integral to understanding the formulation of his schemes for Athens. His return had in fact only been made possible through a vigorous negotiation with his Persian overseer Pharnabazus. After Cnidus, Conon and Pharnabazus resecured territories across Asia Minor and then island-hopped across the Aegean, liberating Spartan-colonized city-states, expelling Spartan *harmosts* and making golden promises of not building Persian garrisons or interfering with Greek autonomy.[4] This was wonderful news to the perennially oppressed Aegean islands who welcomed the Persians, but was less well received by those states in Asia Minor who remained sympathetic to Sparta, Agesilaus or both. Conon spent much of late 394 and early 393 occupying major Greek city-states in Asia Minor including Sestos on the Thracian Chersonese. Pharnabazus had left Conon in charge for some time, and his faithfulness both at Cnidus and in Asia Minor endeared him to the *satrap*. Pharnabazus found Conon a useful weapon in his fight against Sparta; a fight which by now had become his obsession. Xenophon describes the transformation of Pharnabazus' disposition to Sparta over the course of Agesilaus' invasion and the Corinthian War: 'his paramount object was to invade their territory and exact what vengeance he could.'[5] Conon opted to leverage his own reputation with Pharnabazus and Pharnabazus' bloodlust for Sparta into the end of his exile from Athens.

Conon established a new forward base on the island of Cythera off the coast of the Peloponnese in early 393. Cythera was a strategic choice to siege the Peloponnesian peninsula, but was also a sore spot for the Spartans. The traitorous Spartan king Demaratus, who had *medized* and joined Persia briefly before the Persian Wars, once advised Xerxes the Great to garrison Cythera and pressure Sparta.[6] His advice went unheeded by Xerxes, but the Athenians followed through a generation later and used Cythera to embargo the Peloponnese. Sparta and the Peloponnesian League were starved for the length of the war, and this symbolism was not lost on Conon's decision to reestablish a garrison on Cythera. From the Persian perspective, Cythera further served as a helpful bulwark against any Egyptian intervention, which was a lingering concern of the Persian king even after years of no further Egyptian aid to the Spartans. The local population was evicted and an Athenian crony of Conon was installed as governor. Sparta, with no navy, was powerless to stop the advance into their home territories.

Spurred on by his vision for the reconstruction of his home city, Conon made a formal request to Pharnabazus to take a portion of the Persian fleet and return to Athens, ostensibly to improve the Athenian military and therefore be a more useful pawn against Sparta. Conon laced his petition with Athenian eloquence: 'You will win the eternal gratitude of the Athenians and wreak consummate vengeance on the [Spartans], since at one stroke you will render null and void that on which they have bestowed their utmost labour.'[7]

Amid his wrath for Sparta, Pharnabazus agreed. There were, however, stipulations on how the Persian gold could be spent. The Persians gave permission for limited funds, but the diplomatic and military advantages of fortifying Athens were paramount. Conon also could not take the entire fleet, but instead just a portion. Yet Conon had so ingratiated himself with the Persians that Pharnabazus dispatched him 'with alacrity' to Athens.[8] Persian money covered the materials and labour, both through direct purchases and the reappropriation of Conon's trireme crews into temporary masons. Athens and Thebes, meanwhile, raised the remaining funds and manpower to complete the walls.[9] Within a year, Athens' harbour fortifications and Long Walls were once again standing and sending a clear message to the rest of Greece about Athens' intentions of remaking her empire.

Pharnabazus meanwhile travelled to Corinth, where he met with the anti-Spartan coalition amid the Persian strategy to finally end the Spartan threat. Pharnabazus travelled to the Isthmus of Corinth to speak at a second congress where he begged the allies 'to prosecute the war vigorously, and to show

Conon's reconstruction of the walls of Athens. (*Wikimedia Commons, 2022. Public domain*)

themselves faithful to the Great King.'[10] As Hyland notes, the clear implication of Pharnabazus' words was that the Persians would invest more capital in those Greek city-states who pivoted to a more aggressive campaign against the Peloponnesian League.[11] This squares with Conon's quick journey to Athens and the publicized reconstruction of the walls. Persia's involvement in Athenian refortification, then, was primarily an advertisement to the rest of Greece that if they put a quick end to the Corinthian War, Persia would finance their post-war recovery.

This endeavour was apparently successful, since Corinth was shortly rewarded with money for the new equipping and crewing of triremes. Xenophon goes so far as to describe this new Corinthian navy as the 'undisputed masters of the sea within the gulf [around] Achaea and Lechaeum.'[12] With Conon's ambitious plans for Athens' navy, Corinth and Athens were now in an arms race for naval supremacy in Greece, each jockeying for the forging of a new thalassocracy once the Persian fleet departed. This was, perhaps, a clever part of Persia's long-running plan to divide the Greek city-states and keep them at odds with each other.

With the reconstruction of Athens' walls, Sparta had to wrestle with the sobering facts that they would now never conquer Athens or stop the revival of their navy. If Sparta were to stop this Athenian resurrection, they would need to earn a decisive victory against the anti-Spartan confederacy, but this was an elusive goal in the aftermath of Coronea. Instead, it was Athenian infighting and civil conflict that would most effectively impede Athens from once again eclipsing Sparta. Altogether, Conon's reconstruction of the Athenian walls was also an attempt at the reconstruction and restoration of Athenian social order.

Philosophy, Theatre and Athenian Political Commentary in the 390s

The Athens that Conon had left in 404 was not the same one he returned to a decade later. Their political and military decline had precipitated major cultural and social trends that reshaped the Athenian worldview. With the end of their empire came the end of their optimism.

Even after the oppression of the Thirty Tyrants ended, Athens' participation in the Corinthian War was a major risk. As Strauss describes, the litany of trials that the 'thousands of Athenians who, in a generation of war and revolution, had gone from riches to rags (or at least from silk to homespun)'[13] had to endure from 404 to 393 was excruciatingly long. Population decline, poverty, a lack of city fortifications, the destruction of their navy, famine, class conflict, foreign-appointed oppressors and cultural turmoil only scratched the surface of the daily challenges endured by an Athenian.

The legacy of the Thirty Tyrants especially fomented civil strife. This was most obvious in 399 in the famous trial of the philosopher Socrates. Although it was four years after the end of the Thirty's reign, Socrates' guilty verdict was, in part, a result of his close friendship with Critias the tyrant. A former student of Socrates, Critias was utterly reviled by the remaining Athenian populace, as all supporters of the Thirty had emigrated to Eleusis after Thrasybulus restored democracy. Despite a strong base of aristocratic supporters, Socrates never overcame his affiliation with Critias.[14]

Athenian perception of Socrates is illustrated by the comedy *The Clouds* by Aristophanes. Although it was two decades old by the time of Socrates' trial, it had cemented public opinion about Socrates and the validity of intellectual pursuits. The plot centred on Socrates ruining the life of the protagonist with worthless philosophical pursuits such as measuring a flea's jump or determining why a gnat buzzes. Aristophanes was criticizing Athenian intellectualism and its increasing lack of practicality in a dying democracy. He did, however, likely have a special distaste for Socrates, who was infamous for public deconstructions of celebrated politicians, playwrights and artists in Athens. *The Clouds* was not successful at the Dionysia, the annual theatre competition in Athens, but was pivotal in shaping public thought about Socrates. In the opening lines of Socrates' *The Apology*, Plato remarks that the Athenian citizenship was surely aware of Aristophanes' play and acknowledged that it was responsible for the Athenian perception of Socrates and philosophers.[15]

The end of the Peloponnesian War and the reign of the Thirty Tyrants catalyzed such anti-intellectualism among the lower classes. As Athens grappled with prevailing poverty and a dismal outlook on the Corinthian War, particularly after Spartan victory at Nemea, this cultural unrest crescendoed. Like the waning days of the Peloponnesian War, the lower classes generally favoured consistent war as a means of economic opportunity, primarily from service as rowers on a trireme or as labourers in military projects such as Conon's wall-building. Conversely, the wealthy opposed the Corinthian War since it, like all wars, brought less financial predictability. While Thrasybulus' leadership deftly navigated diplomatic and political tensions and stabilized both Athenian democracy and military, he was unable to truly revive Athens as a cultural or economic power.

Given such social upheaval, theatre's lasting influence by and over political events was not confined to *The Clouds*. By the Corinthian War, no cultural artefacts represented the Athenian cultural milieu better than Aristophanes' two plays *Assemblywomen* and *Plutus*. In the history of Greek theatre, both works are awkwardly situated outside traditional categories and represent the transition from Old Comedy to Middle Comedy. Though it fits the chronology and structure of Middle Comedy, including a demotion of the chorus, *Assemblywomen* and *Plutus* are nevertheless predicated on one of the defining characteristics of Old Comedy: political commentary.

Assemblywomen was composed in 391 and is a manifestation of the economic and cultural angst experienced by Athens during the Corinthian War. The play imagines that women have seized control of the hapless Athenian government and instituted widespread class reforms to fix the problem. The protagonist Praxagora offers a radical solution to the Athenian problem of wealth inequality:

> I want all to have a share of everything and all property to be in common; there will no longer be either rich or poor; no longer shall we see one man harvesting vast tracts of land, while another has not ground enough to be buried in, nor one man surround himself with a whole army of slaves, while another has not a single attendant; I intend that there shall only be one and the same condition of life for all.[16]

That women would be so empowered was already an affront to the notoriously misogynistic Athenian mentality, but the proposal to eliminate property and wealth was downright astonishing to the Athenian audience. Even the prostitutes were not spared in Praxagora's government; they were all dismissed from the city or assigned new roles. Such a favourable presentation of communalism was more Lycurgan than the Athenians might care to admit. Aristophanes would have been keenly aware that praising Sparta during the war would be a sore subject for his Athenian audience. While managing to avoid *laconophilia*, Aristophanes was drawing on Sparta's historic – and overly romantic – reputation for being the 'most Greek' of the Greek city-states given their emphasis on virtue and sacrifice for the community. With Aristophanes' emphasis on political commentary, *Assemblywomen* served as a siren song calling the Athenians to return to their Greek – though not necessarily democratic – roots in order to address the overwhelming challenges of Athens in the 390s. Aristophanes reasserts this position when his character Praxagora essentially repackages part of the Lycurgan Reforms: 'I shall begin by making land, money, everything that is private property, common to all. Then we shall live on this common wealth, which we shall take care to administer with wise thrift.'[17]

Such communalism in Praxagora's new female-led government sought to amend Athens' economic recession and political corruption, which were themes that paralleled Plato's ideal government form in *The Republic* led by philosopher-kings. A citizen of Athens during the Peloponnesian and Corinthian Wars and a relative of Critias of the Thirty Tyrants, Plato was likewise disgusted by the sorry state of Athens in contrast to the Athens of a half-century earlier.

This striking pessimism was a major historical motivation for his rejection of democracy and embracing of a unique style of aristocracy (or technocracy) wherein those select few whose soul is most governed by reason marry political finesse with philosophical and ethical wisdom. The core Socratic question at the heart of *The Republic* – the definition of justice and the nature of the 'just state' – was indicative of the Athenian rejection of their current political situation, the lingering trauma over their subjugation to Sparta and their desperate cry for a revival of their empire.

Plato potentially delivered parts of *The Republic* in lectures in Athens, even though his Academy had also not yet been founded and *The Republic*'s publication would not be until the 370s. Plato likely travelled to Sicily between 390 and 388 under patronage of Dionysius I, the powerful and wealthy tyrant of Syracuse who had long-term plans to conquer parts of Greece, partly out of revenge for the ill-fated Athenian invasion of Sicily decades earlier. Plato would later be appointed to actually install his ideal government by Dionysius' successor, although it failed due to the tyrant's inability to embody the ideal Platonic ruler of the philosopher-king.

If *Assemblywomen* gave a biting criticism of political corruption and ineptitude in Athens, then Aristophanes' other work of the 390s, *Plutus*, targeted the other pressing issue of poverty and wealth inequality. Originally penned in 408, *Plutus* was heavily edited by 388 to encapsulate the crushing anxiety over Athens' crisis and its failure to financially recover. In *Plutus*, the protagonist strives for the elimination of poverty, arguing that wealth is given out at random both to the unjust and to the virtuous. Like Praxagora's elimination of property and wealth in *Assemblywomen*, the deity of poverty, Penia, summarizes this idea when she argues that the difference between poverty and beggary is as vast as the difference between the restored democracy of Thrasybulus and the corrupt tyranny of Dionysius I of Syracuse:

> Thrasybulus and Dionysius are one and the same according to you. No, my life is not like that and never will be. The beggar, whom you have depicted to us, never possesses anything. The poor man lives thriftily and attentive to his work; he has not got too much, but he does not lack what he really needs.[18]

Aristophanes' argument that poverty is not only not a vice but often a virtue illustrates Athenian self-justification of their economic predicament and their own culpability for their destiny. These late plays of Aristophanes were citizenship manifest: questioning, criticizing and making problematic the Athenian culture as a form of *agon*.

In such a hostile political environment, the public oratory of the day cast a similar message and created a constant turnover of rhetoricians, populists and orators who tried to capture the fickle will of the Athenian people. Lucia Cecchet described the extent to which civil discourse became both a minefield and a tool for public figures: 'accusations about the dishonest enrichment of public speakers and political leaders and the impoverishment of the [citizens] were powerful weapons in the political contests that played out before the [voting] Assembly.'[19]

Public Oration and Athenian Cultural Disillusionment in the 390s

The precarious economic and cultural context in 390s Athens also gave rise to a new era of rhetoricians, orators and logographers. The Athenian Golden Age of the fifth century saw famous orators like Pericles and the later fourth century would see similar oratory titans such as Demosthenes and Isocrates, but in the late fifth and early fourth centuries, few such public speakers have surviving speeches amid Athens' ruination. However, it is clear that two Athenian orators towered above the rest: Lysias and Andocides.

Lysias was a Sicilian immigrant to Athens; a rather awkward position following the Athenian invasion of Sicily in 415. From a wealthy family and a highly-trained rhetorician, Lysias was an influential social figure in the late Athenian Empire, but fled the city multiple times during his long career. He first departed after the Sicilian invasion, and later fled after the Thirty Tyrants placed him on an early blacklist of their political undesirables. After aiding the Phyle rebels, he earned Thrasybulus' favour and was even considered for citizenship, but by the restoration of Athenian democracy, Lysias flirted with poverty, his entire fortune spent on surviving a decayed Athens as a resident alien.

By the 390s, Lysias was a sort of elder statesman in Athenian politics, a relic of the Athenian glory days whose career had diminished alongside Athens' supremacy. His social prospects gone, Lysias employed his rhetorical skills as a logographer, a type of speechwriter-attorney hybrid in the Athenian judicial system who consulted plaintiffs or defendants and wrote their court speeches for a fee. In his speeches, Lysias drew deeply not just from Athenian patriotism and anti-Spartan sentiment, but also from the surging opposition to the Athenian political elites and the resultant economic anxiety.

It was in this context that he delivered his most famous speech, the Funeral Oration, in 392. Much like the famous Funeral Oration of Pericles several decades earlier, Lysias delivered a eulogy to commemorate the Athenian soldiers lost during the Corinthian War. His speech was an insightful snapshot of Athenian justification for the war and their conflicted opinion on the prospect of reviving their own contentious empire:

> Those who are now buried, aiding the Corinthians who were wronged by their old friends, became renewed allies, not sharing the ideas of the [Spartans], (for they envied their good fortunes, while the former pitied them when wronged, not remembering the previous hostility, but caring more for the present friendship) made evident to all men their own valour. For they dared, trying to make Greece great, not only to incur danger for their own safety but to die for the liberty of their enemies; for they fought with Sparta's allies for their freedom. And when victorious they thought them worthy of the same privileges which they enjoyed, and if unsuccessful they would have fastened slavery firmly on the Peloponnesians.
>
> As they so conducted themselves their life was pitiful, and their death desired; but these lived and died praised, being brought up in the virtues of their ancestors, and on becoming men they kept their fame untarnished and exhibited their own valour.[20]

Much like Aristophanes' comedies, the prevailing theme of Lysias' orations during the Corinthian War was poverty and wealth. Lucia Cecchet points to Lysias as indicative of how Athenian 'public speakers evoked poverty as a dangerous threat for ordinary citizens during acute economic crisis.'[21] Lysias spoke often of the plague of Athenian political corruption and channelled the voice of the lower classes against the elite. He ended one speech against a corrupt bureaucrat named Ergocles with a call for the Athenian people to fight back against the rising tide of political malfeasance:

> It is to be clearly known, fellow Athenians, whoever in such lack of resources on your side either betrays cities, or embezzles funds, or bribes (others), is the sort of man to betray the walls and fleet to the enemy, and changes our democracy to an oligarchy. It is not right for you to submit to their schemes, but to establish a precedent to all men, and let no considerations of gain, compassion, or anything else be of more importance to you than their punishment.[22]

Lysias' peer in Athenian oration of the 390s was Andocides, a volatile diplomat whose turbulent career likewise coincided with the declining arc of Athenian prosperity. Andocides was born into an influential aristocratic family in Athens at the height of her empire, and he was groomed from a young age for diplomatic service. His promising future was derailed multiple times, however, both due to poor fortune and his own impropriety.

His first challenge came in 415 when he helped to frame Alcibiades in order to sabotage the invasion of Sicily, for which he was imprisoned and eventually turned over four of his co-conspirators to earn his freedom. A cutthroat man, he was even alleged to have become an informant against his own father. Such infamy in Athens made him unable to shake free of traitorous accusations and he fled in exile.

Andocides attempted to return to Athens during the brief oligarchic coup of 411, but was arrested almost immediately. Upon his release with the restoration of democracy, Andocides took advantage of those foreign patrons who sought for Athenians. Atop this list was Evagoras of Cyprus. Evagoras funded Andocides to join him in Cyprus alongside Conon and other Athenians in pursuit of Cypriot independence, but Andocides soon fell into old habits and ran afoul of Evagoras, and he was yet again imprisoned.

Seizing advantage of the blanket pardons issued in Athens after the fall of the Thirty Tyrants, Andocides ingratiated himself enough to Thrasybulus to earn a pardon and an elevated bureaucratic position. With his third exile now under his belt, Andocides leaped right into the middle of the Athenian *stasis*. He entered straight into a rivalry with fellow leaders of Athenian civil society, making formal accusations against a number of aristocrats within a few weeks of his return. Lysias took umbrage at Andocides' audacity, and delivered a series of speeches eviscerating him. In Lysias' prosecution of Andocides a few years later, Lysias delivered a quip worthy of the laconic phrases of Sparta: '[Andocides is] the type of person who has the unique skill of avoiding harming his enemies but causing as much harm as possible to his friends.'[23]

Despite this notoriety, Andocides served as a diplomat in peace negotiations to Sparta in 392 following the anti-Spartan allies' victory at Cnidus. This expedition failed to broker a true peace, but succeeded in reviving Andocides' fragile career. It was nevertheless an important cultural illustration of Athenian excitement about the hope of their revived empire. This expedition was even the subject of political lampooning in a play by the comic playwright Plato.

In 393, Andocides delivered his most famous speech, 'On the Peace with the Spartans,' arguing that the Athenians would be justified in abandoning their ideals of liberty from Spartan tyranny and should instead pursue peace with Sparta to resolve the Corinthian War.

Despite his trademark overuse of rhetorical questions and a dense, information-laden style, Andocides verbalized the sentiment of many an Athenian regarding the reestablishment of their empire:

> Our defeat came at last. We lost not only our empire to Sparta, but they also took our navy and our city walls. They stole our fleet and destroyed our walls in order to stop us from using them as the pillars of a new era of Athenian power. Because of the hard work of our diplomats, Spartan

emissaries have arrived with the authority to restore our navy and our walls to us, and to acknowledge our rightful ownership over our islands.[24]

Although many Athenians decried the decay of their beloved *polis* in the 390s, the victory at Cnidus, which had loosened the Spartan yoke on the Aegean, so inspired the Athenians that many public figures began to look beyond their present struggle towards the hope of a restored empire. Conon had given the beleaguered Athenian population a taste of this hope, first at Cnidus and then with the rebuilding of the walls. Conon even addressed the concerns about class struggle; even though he was an aristocrat, his closest advisors and counsellors were predominantly selected from the underprivileged and working classes.[25] It was Conon's reconstruction of the vaunted Athenian navy, however, that would both cement him as a saviour of Athens and force his final departure from it.

Athens' New Navy

Conon's political activities in Athens after his return saw him mired in the richest tradition of Athenian democracy: factionalism and bickering. His primary antagonist was none other than his fellow hero of Athens, Thrasybulus.

The existence of the rivalry between Conon and Thrasybulus is undoubted, but the nature of their animus is disputed. Scholars have historically interpreted their conflict as tension either between the radical democracy of Conon and the conservative aristocracy of Thrasybulus, or conversely between the conflicted Persian loyalties of Conon versus the Hellenistic patriotism of Thrasybulus.[26] Neither argument was incorrect and, as Strauss compellingly argues, 'the likeliest explanation of their hostility is a combination of personal factors. A factional rivalry of nearly 20 years' standing and the extraordinary success of each man's earlier career left neither Thrasybulus nor Conon willing to subordinate himself to the other by 393.'[27]

Conon's support of the lower classes and *thetes* was a natural foil to the traditionalism of Thrasybulus, despite Thrasybulus' sterling reputation for restoring democracy. Conon's arrival with a fleet and rebuilding of the city walls assuaged the Athenian economic and political anxiety of the day. Thrasybulus was no match for Conon's influence. By capitalizing on the potent Athenian disillusionment of the 390s, he earned unparalleled loyalty from the Athenian voters. Subsequently, he was wildly successful in implementing his vision of a resurgent Athenian navy and empire.

Settling into his new role as the undisputed leader of Athens, Conon accomplished a long list of items: funding a new arts festival, meddling with internal politics in Chios, building a temple to Aphrodite of Cnidus, prosecuting surviving admirals of Aegospotami in order to exonerate his own name and dispatching an ambassador to Syracuse to peel their wealthy tyrant's support away from Sparta.[28] Conon then retook several islands near Athens including Lemnos, Imbros and Scyros, restoring the Athenian imperial and diplomatic presence across the Mediterranean.[29] These were the first steps in a second naval campaign, motivated not only by a reborn Athenian empire, but also by the pressing need to fund his navy through taxes and tribute. Pascual proposes that this was the start of an enterprising crusade that stretched all the way to 'Delos, the Thracian Chersonese and the coasts of Aeolis and Ionia',[30] and culminated in Athenian annexation of the coveted Hellespontine grain trade. With her empire, her navy and her commerce reestablished, Conon had succeeded in his mission to bring Athens back from the brink of death.

Five decades later, Conon retained his primacy among great leaders of Athenian culture. The orator Demosthenes, attempting to restore Athens to her former glory in the face of the growing Macedonian threat, eulogized Conon:

> Many of you who knew Conon can vouch for the fact that he, after the revival of democracy in our beloved city, returned to an Athens that had neither ships nor military strength. It was Conon who, in service to the Persians, crushed the Spartans at Cnidus and forced them to once again show respect and honour towards Athens. He removed the Spartan harmosts across the Aegean and rebuilt our Long Walls when he triumphantly returned to Athens. He alone was able to revive the competition between Athens and Sparta for supremacy in Greece. Accordingly, his gravestone inscription remarks, 'Conon liberated Athens and her allies....' Those who knew him therefore acquitted him from all crimes, and even immortalised him by creating a bronze statue. Conon earned this by breaking Sparta's oppressive empire...and he was the first Athenian given this honour in generations.

However, by essentially converting his Persian navy into a personal Athenian navy, Conon embarked on an arrogant wager that his Athenian support could withstand criticism from Persia. Communication with his Persian co-commander Pharnabazus had long since ceased, so no Persian gave permission to use their fleet in military campaigns. Further, Conon had functionally used Persian funds to rebuild the walls and the navy as it was technically the Persian-supplied salaries of his sailors, which he had fought so hard to secure, that paid for the labour and materials.

From both outside and inside Athens, it appeared as though Conon's command was reversing their fortunes since their defeat in the Peloponnesian War. The middle- and lower-class Athenians had unbridled optimism, but Athens' enemies and even new allies took notice. Persia was no exception. Across the Aegean, Conon's success appeared to be flirting with overstepping his role. Cornelius Nepos did not parse words: 'thinking that he had avenged his country's wrongs, [Conon] entertained ambitions beyond his powers.'[31]

Complicating matters, the Persians had appointed a new commander to replace Pharnabazus, who had accepted a promotion and even married the Great King's daughter. Conon and his fleet now reported to the new *satrap* of Lydia, Tiribazus. Tiribazus succeeded Tissaphernes and Tithraustes as *satrap*, and he was an experienced governor and commander who had earned distinction serving in Armenia. Tiribazus would prove to be less forgiving than Pharnabazus or his predecessors.

Conon's Downfall

Like Tiribazus, Sparta was not ignorant of Conon's reconstruction of Athens. Chagrined, Sparta took a more delicate and strategic approach instead of marching on Athens. The Spartan *ephors* sent messengers to Conon's new co-commander in the Persian regional capital of Sardis in 392. Their intentions were simple: either cut off the funding of Conon's pseudo-Persian, pseudo-Athenian fleet or recall Conon to Persian territory entirely. An outright peace treaty between Sparta and Persia was even feasible. According to Xenophon, 'The [Spartans] were well informed of the proceedings of Conon. They knew that he was not only restoring the fortifications of Athens by help of the king's gold, but maintaining a fleet at his expense besides, and conciliating the islands and seaboard cities towards Athens.'[32]

Sparta's chief emissary was one Antalcidas. A relative of Agesilaus, Antalcidas was a young Spartan politician who would eventually become the pre-eminent diplomat of the Corinthian War. Though he was a novice in foreign affairs at Sardis, his selection by the Spartan *ephors* exemplified his impressive skillset when it came to statecraft and diplomacy. After flattering Tiribazus, Antalcidas made the Spartan offer: Sparta would no longer claim any Greek cities in Asia Minor if Persia revoked support for Conon and laid down claims to the Aegean islands. In so doing, Antalcidas cleverly highlighted Conon's abuse of Persian patronage and his personal use of the fleet for reviving Athenian naval power. This framed perfectly with Hamilton's summary of Antalcidas' true mission: 'to relinquish the unprofitable war in Asia Minor and to establish an international order in which the sovereignty of every *polis* would be guaranteed.'[33] Antalcidas ended his overtures with an appeal to logic: 'The king is guaranteed against attack on the part of Hellas, since the

Athenians are powerless apart from our hegemony, and we are powerless so long as the separate states are independent.'[34]

Not to be outdone, Conon attended the summit at Sardis himself, accompanied by influential Athenian dignitaries Hermogenes, Dion, Callisthenes and Callimedon.[35] A contingent of Thebans, Argives and Corinthians also joined, making the negotiations a genuine opportunity to end the Corinthian War. Strauss explains Conon's audacious self-assurance in attending the conference:

> Conon had been sufficiently confident of his position to present himself to Tiribazus at Sardis: he would not have if he had been openly rebuilding the Athenian empire in 393/92 at Persia's expense. Rather, his foreign policy seems to have been to pursue the war against Sparta in a way that would help Athens without openly hurting Persia.[36]

The main result of the summit at Sardis in 392 was not, however, a peace treaty. Tiribazus was inclined to accept Antalcidas' proposal, but neither the Athenians, Corinthians, Argives nor Thebans were willing to accept the Spartan terms, fearing challenges to their own vassal city-states or imperial ambitions. Tiribazus, however, distinguished himself from his predecessors by defying the Persian king and sending Antalcidas back to Sparta with Persian gold.[37] His intent was to fund the construction of a new Spartan navy to challenge Athens, forcing the Athenians to desperately reconsider the peace terms and end the war.

This was the smaller of the olive branches offered by Tiribazus to Sparta. The more significant one, by far, was the imprisoning of Conon.[38] Intent on appeasing both Sparta and Artaxerxes II, Tiribazus was more than willing to sacrifice the rebellious Athenian admiral for his own purposes. Tiribazus travelled to the Persian heartland to gain Artaxerxes' approval of the Spartan treaty, potentially taking Conon with him. Although some sources say that Conon escaped or fled back to the safety of Evagoras' court in Cyprus, he vanished from the ancient sources after his arrest.

Both these talks and Sparta's entertainment of the allies' embassy led by Andocides of Athens proved that, as Hyland suggests, these peace talks should have led to the end of the Corinthian War.[39] Given Sparta's shrinking empire and supply lines, and their internal chaos after Lysander's death and especially after the decimation of their navy at Cnidus, Sparta was for the first time genuinely interested in ending the war if the allied Greeks could coalesce around a united mission and give up Corinthian and Argive power. However, it was not meant to be, either for the allies or for the Spartans. The Persian imprisonment of Conon tore apart the anti-Spartan confederacy, while Sparta's factionalism divided and confused her own peace terms.[40]

The peace terms failed, but Sparta succeeded in driving a wedge between the anti-Spartan coalition and Persia. Athenian defiance against Persian interventionism was showing in Athens, as Athens now rejected Persian autonomy over both the allied Greeks and the city-states of Asia Minor.[41] Worse, the Athenians could not look past the injustice of Conon's arrest and the renascent Athenian Empire along with it. Andocides' subsequent peace talks in Sparta in 392 were conducted without Persian involvement. With the best Athenian and Persian admiral now out of the picture, Sparta transitioned to a more aggressive strategy, fomenting civil conflict in Corinth with the aim of finally crushing the allied Greek armies in the decisive land battle of the Corinthian War.

Chapter Nine
Lechaeum: A Final Athenian Victory

Civil War in Corinth

In the spring of 393, the Persian *satrap* Pharnabazus arrived at the Isthmus of Corinth to meet with the anti-Spartan allies, intent on a triumphant reception that would lavish him with praise and thanksgiving. He did not receive it. The allied Greeks no longer had any magnanimity towards Persia.

Though grateful for their aid, the Greeks could no longer look past the cost of the war and the notion that Persia had sacrificed little in the war effort while the anti-Spartan confederacy had sacrificed so very much. After the Battle of Nemea in 394, Corinth's farmlands burned and her city proper was besieged by Sparta which made its base of operations in nearby Sicyon.[1] While the reconstruction of Athens was a welcome development for the allies, Sparta's land power remained unchallenged after Nemea and Coronea.

To assuage such fears, Pharnabazus had a singular goal: he implored the Greeks 'to prosecute the war vigorously, and to show themselves faithful to the Great King.'[2] The implicit promise, of course, was more Persian gold. Pharnabazus would keep his word too, and the Greeks' souring taste for the Persians was not so deeply held that it prohibited personal profit. On his departure, Pharnabazus left the Corinthians with funds to rebuild their navy.

One year later, Sparta grew concerned about the re-emergence of a Corinthian navy. It was almost as sore a point as the return of the Athenian navy. Certain pro-democracy Corinthian politicians favoured a *synoecism*, or formal unification of city-states, with Argos to centralize their resources and overcome the Spartan threat. It was a dramatic change from Corinth's long-held membership of the Peloponnesian League, and represented perhaps the most direct threat to the future of Sparta's hegemony and *symmachy* outside of the war itself. By combining their power, Corinth and Argos as the second and third most powerful *poleis* of the Peloponnese just may be able to topple the strongest one, Sparta. The Spartans were also concerned about Argive dominance of trade routes on both sides of the Peloponnese, given Corinth's strategic location on the isthmus.

The Spartan imperialists sought to take Corinth entirely, while the Spartan traditionalists wished to simply divorce Corinth and Argos once more. It is quite clear, however, that Spartan factionalism again confused Spartan policymaking.

Agesilaus disapproved of Antalcidas' vision for the Spartan Empire as laid out in the peace talks at Sardis. Antalcidas perhaps inherited the devout followers of Lysander in Spartan politics, while Agesilaus' diminished position after Cnidus and Coronea made it impossible for him to halt the peace negotiations of 392. While Agesilaus may have had noble intentions, it is more likely that he refused to consider the forfeiture of the Greek city-states of Asia Minor back to Persia. For now, he was unwilling to lose his prestigious position among the Ionian Greeks, although the long war would soon change that.[3]

Among such cascading dysfunction on both sides of the war, the new Corinthian fleet became the third Greek navy funded by Persia in just over a decade, following the Spartan fleet at Aegospotami and the Athenian fleet under Conon. The Corinthians capitalized on the opportunity and built or repaired dozens of triremes. Within months, Corinth seized naval control of the Gulf of Corinth, giving them breathing space in their blockaded city centre and a consistent supply of food and goods into their port at Lechaeum.

However, for the Corinthians, such a smashing success was regrettably hamstrung by deep-rooted domestic challenges. Much like Sparta, Athens and so many other *stasis* struggles among Greek city-states, the Corinthians faced dissension between a traditionalist, aristocratic faction and a democratic faction. The traditionalists of Corinth were pro-oligarchy, and notably held pro-Spartan viewpoints which were no doubt exacerbated by Spartan bribery. As Corinth was an aristocracy, these oligarchs held the levers of power for now, but recognized that growing social unrest threatened their position. As Hamilton remarks, 'extreme caution would be necessary to avoid losing the city through treason, and the allies were prepared to take action to just such an end in the late winter of 392.'[4]

The seeds of civil discord in Corinth stretched back most poignantly to the aftermath of the Battle of Nemea. After the battle, the Corinthians had initially refused to open the city gates to their own soldiers and allies. The 'fear produced by Nemea'[5] gripped Corinth and its citizens. The ensuing Spartan occupation of Sicyon, just 20 kilometres away, made matters worse. With their crops burned, they were fully reliant on their naval imports for survival, but they also knew that Pharnabazus and the Persian fleet were fickle masters at best, and Sparta may soon re-establish its naval presence.

The tendrils of Sparta's hegemony still extended into Corinth, and the oligarchs of the city decided that mistreatment under Spartan leadership was now preferable to death by the Spartan spear. Jealous of their allies in the anti-Spartan confederacy who were only slightly impacted by the war and concerned about the safety of their wealth, the Corinthian aristocrats raised their support for the war's end from whispers to shouts.

In an intriguing move, however, the democrats acted first. A coalition of pro-Athenian Corinthian citizens grew concerned that Spartan-friendly policies would end the war and saw only one solution: eliminating the oligarchs and establishing a democracy. Securing aid from Athens, Argos and Thebes, the Corinthian democrats hatched a plan to murder their fellow citizens. Xenophon painted a poetic picture: 'It seemed there was nothing for it but the remedy of the knife. There was a refinement of wickedness in the plan adopted.'[6]

As is so often the case in democratic revolutions, there was carnage. The democrats made a list of oligarchs and their sympathizers and blended into a crowd during a religious festival to Artemis. On cue, the democrats pulled out daggers and assassinated every person on their list. Blood ran through the streets. Wealthy citizens were killed while at the theatre, clinging to the temple's statues, judging a drama contest or shopping in the market. A group of younger men managed to fend off a small contingent of Argives sent to finish off the survivors.

A staunch supporter of Sparta and opponent of Athenian-style democracy, Xenophon held a dim view of the democrats and their massacre and his recounting of the conflict did not whitewash the tomb:

> Presented to their eyes was the spectacle of a tyranny in full exercise, and to their minds the consciousness of the obliteration of their city, seeing that boundaries were plucked up and the land of their fathers had come to be re-entitled by the name of Argos instead of Corinth; and furthermore, compulsion was put upon them to share in the constitution in vogue at Argos, for which they had little appetite, while in their own city they wielded less power than the resident aliens. So that a party sprang up among them whose creed was that life was not worth living on such terms: their endeavour must be to make their fatherland once more the Corinth of old days – to restore freedom to their city, purified from the murderer and his pollution and fairly rooted in good order and legality. It was a design worth the venture: if they succeeded they would become the saviours of their country; if not – why, in the effort to grasp the fairest flower of happiness, they would but overreach, and find instead a glorious termination to existence.[7]

Unhappy with democracy and with the union with Argos that forfeited centuries of Corinthian sovereignty, a small group of Corinthian aristocrats fled to Sicyon and joined forces with the Spartan occupiers. Not all the oligarchs' allies had left the city, however, and those who remained worked to unravel the new democracy. To do so, they turned to Sparta.

Under cover of night and hidden along a creek, two Corinthian aristocrats met with the Spartan *polemarch* Praxitas outside the city to strategize the city's conquest. The traitors pointed to an opening in the city walls where they just so happened to stand guard, near the harbour of Lechaeum.

Corinth had two harbours, one on each side of the isthmus. Some 7 miles south-east of the city centre was the harbour of Cenchreae. Opening into the Saronic Gulf, Cenchreae gave Corinth access to the eastern trade routes, especially with Athens, the Aegean islands, Persia and Egypt. Lechaeum served their commerce in the opposite direction. On the north shore of the Peloponnese, Lechaeum opened up into the calm waters of the Corinthian Gulf. From Lechaeum, Corinthian ships imported and exported to Delphi, Phocis and beyond into the Adriatic Sea and Italy. It was these trade routes that the newly-constructed Corinthian triremes were dutifully reestablishing thanks to their Persian investors. With fertile farmland and lucrative quarries nearby, there was no shortage of goods for the Corinthians to trade in each direction.

The harbour at Lechaeum, like Piraeus of Athens, was fortified by the city walls of Corinth. Again called the Long Walls, as in Athens, they linked the harbour and Corinth proper and had been built as a defensive measure first against Athens but later against Sparta. The western end of the Long Walls was at Lechaeum, while the eastern end incorporated the Acrocorinth. This towered almost 600 metres above the city, an acropolis that dwarfed even the mighty Acropolis of Athens and served as a beacon safeguarding the trade routes overland and overseas.

The Long Walls were impregnable to the overstretched Spartan army. As a result, the Spartan plan was to circumvent the Long Walls by waltzing through the gate. The *polemarch* Praxitas gathered his Spartan *mora* and the surviving Corinthian exiles who supported the oligarchy and marched on the city. After a brief hesitation, doubtful that the Corinthians would willingly betray their city, Praxitas walked into Lechaeum intent on taking the entire city.

However, the Argives, who now considered Corinth part of their own city after the 'unification', were eager to revisit their earlier skirmish with the oligarchs at the massacre by the democrats. Supported both by some democratic Corinthians and some Thebans, the Argives met the invaders in a brutal battle. Equipped with ladders, the Spartans scaled the walls and buildings, toppling fortifications and slaying unwitting workers and half-dressed soldiers alike. Bookending the earlier slaughter of the oligarchs, Xenophon illustrated the 'layers of human bodies'[8] that littered the battlefield, this time at the hands of the oligarchs and their Spartan allies.

Hamilton gave the *stasis* in Corinth during the late 390s a visceral description:

At Corinth the pressures of war brought on an internal crisis that resulted in a bloody and sacrilegious coup, shocking to the sensibilities of many Greeks, and inaugurated a domestic revolution that established democracy; a novel and intimate political alliance with Argos; and the final subjugation of Corinth to complete Argive control.[9]

While the Spartans were turned away from marching on to the city centre of Corinth, they firmly held the port of Lechaeum and the rich supply lines that came with it. They settled into almost a year of an uneasy peace, with the Spartans occupying Sicyon and Lechaeum and the anti-Spartan league holding Corinth and Cenchreae.

Such a ceasefire was unsatisfactory to the revived Athenian Empire, however, and they quickly sent masons and labourers to rebuild parts of the Long Walls destroyed in battle and construct new walls to protect Corinth. Sensing that the battle for the fate of Corinth, and indeed the entire Corinthian War, was soon at hand, the Athenians, Argives, Thebans and democratic Corinthians sent additional troops. The Athenian army was of special note as it was characterized by the substantial presence of a new type of Greek soldier with the potential to turn the tide of the war: the peltast.

The Rise of Iphicrates and the Peltast

The Athenian peltasts sent to aid the Corinthian democrats were led by a singularly impressive strategist named Iphicrates. Born to a lowly Athenian family, Iphicrates was already a grizzled veteran of the Corinthian War, despite being just 25 years of age. His prestige was due to gallantly boarding a Spartan trireme at Cnidus and capably leading a regiment at Coronea.[10] He was the first of a new generation of Athenian heroes that were earning their stripes in the Corinthian War instead of the Peloponnesian War.

Yet Iphicrates, like Xenophon, had loyalties outside of Athens. Unlike Xenophon, however, Iphicrates was not a *laconophile* but instead a *Thracophile*, a lover of Thrace. The northern neighbour of Greece, Thrace had long been considered the frontier of Greek civilization, and the Athenians often considered the Thracians to be a rather uncivilized yet traditional breed of pseudo-Greeks. Often the home of exiles and outcasts from Athens, Thrace held a special position as a kind of surviving legacy of Greece's heroic age. Matthew A. Sears captures the romantic allure that some Athenians like Iphicrates found in Thrace: 'Thrace was a forum for experimentation as it was a long way from the pitched hoplite battles that were the norm between mainland Greek *poleis*, and *Thracophiles* were frequently the sorts of leaders that were unconstrained by the hoplite ethos.'[11]

Composed almost entirely of Greek territory north of Thessaly and stretching over the northern coast of the Aegean Sea to Byzantium and Asia Minor, Thrace was home to bands of local tribes and fierce warriors who favoured light infantry, precision and mobility over the strength and power of a phalanx. Ironically, Thrace was a former Persian territory and had joined with the avowed Athenian enemies Darius the Great, Xerxes the Great and most recently Agesilaus of Sparta.

Iphicrates had wed a princess of Thrace and spent some formative years among the Thracians, fighting alongside them as a mercenary. While among the Thracians, Iphicrates was struck by their reliance not on the heavy infantry hoplites but instead on the lightly-armoured, javelin-throwing skirmishers, the peltasts. Indeed, many of his later army were peltasts and Thracian mercenaries.

The peltast was distinct from the hoplite primarily in armour and manoeuvrability. Whereas the hoplite was weighed down with 60lb to 90lb of equipment in order to maximize their performance in the cramped phalanx formation, the peltast shed such weight in pursuit of ranged assault. Their *pelte* shield, from which the name peltast is derived, was in the shape of a crescent and made of wicker. The shield weighed far less than the heavy, wooden and circular *aspis* of the hoplites.[12] The lighter shield still protected their body, especially from arrows and smaller javelins, but was light enough not to slow them. Their javelin was similarly shorter and lighter as its purpose was to be thrown at an enemy instead of stabbing an enemy phalanx. Peltasts carried a multitude of javelins to throw at the enemy, although they often had short swords for use at close quarters.

Peltasts were not new to Greece. They were a standard skirmisher unit sent out prior to the hoplite battle. By the fourth century, however, the non-Greek world had awakened to the versatility of peltasts, especially against cavalry and hoplites. At the Battle of Cunaxa in 401, Cyrus the Younger employed Thracian peltasts to great effect against Tissaphernes' Persian cavalry.[13] While peltasts had become more common in Greece, especially at the Battle of Sphacteria in 425, peltasts were an afterthought among the hoplite-loving Greeks. After disposing of a small contingent of peltasts before the Battle of Lechaeum, the Spartans remarked: 'Our allies…stand in as much awe of these peltasts as children of the bogies and hobgoblins of their nurses.'[14] After all, it was the hoplite and the trireme that had won Greek independence a century earlier against Persia.

In 393, Conon had established a small mercenary garrison at Corinth to bolster their defence against the Spartans in Sicyon. At some point after Coronea, Iphicrates, whose service under Conon at the Battle of Cnidus made him a trusted ally of both Conon and the Persians, took command of these mercenaries.[15] It was a wise decision that aggressively spearheaded the land component of Athens' re-established imperialism to complement their naval return. The ancient sources are unified about Iphicrates' renown as a commander and leader. According to Cornelius Nepos, 'He had, in addition to nobility of soul and great size of body, the aspect of one born to command, so that his appearance alone inspired admiration in all men.'[16]

It was clear that Iphicrates valued the Thracian worldview more than his own Athenian one, to the extent that his son, a renowned Athenian general in his own right, once remarked 'my father did everything in his power to make me a Thracian.'[17] His unorthodox style and interests were of no concern to the Athenians, who were desperate for a new military commander now that Conon was imprisoned. While Thrasybulus had reemerged via a fierce rejection of any peace treaties with Sparta, he was confined to policymaking and statecraft. It was now Iphicrates and his Thracian-influenced innovations that fuelled the Athenian military.

In 392, Iphicrates brought his Thracian-style peltasts from Athens to support the Corinthian democrats against the Spartan military machine. It was the first major employment of peltasts beyond their traditional Greek use as 'skirmishers, scouts and harassing troops'.[18] Iphicrates added to the traditional Thracian peltast by adding a heavier and longer javelin, which better pierced the shields of hoplites and phalanxes yet did not slow the peltasts considerably, and a new style of boot that was lighter, more manoeuvrable and easier to untie.[19] Iphicrates finally replaced the bulky bronze cuirasses of hoplites with linen ones that were again lighter but still provided a semblance of protection while allowing the range of motion necessary to throw javelins.[20] Iphicrates never intended to meet hoplites in direct battle, but instead to use ranged attacks on uneven terrain with hit-and-run tactics, frustrating the Spartans and delaying their organization and communication. In short, he planned to exploit the established Spartan weaknesses of the Corinthian War.

Iphicrates' 'reforms' were in fact more of a realignment of Athenian military strategy with Thracian ideals instead of Greek traditions. It was not meant to overthrow the hoplite system but instead to diversify and reinforce it, avoiding a stale overuse of heavy infantry and instead embracing a holistic mix of military arms. Plutarch would later remark that Iphicrates saw the army as a whole body, with 'the light-armed troops…like the hands, the cavalry like the feet, the line of men-at-arms itself like chest and breastplate, and the general like the head.'[21] This redesigned Athenian body, bolstered by its new peltasts, would soon test its mettle against the established strength of the Spartan hoplite.

Sparta's Renewed Imperialism and the Conflict in Rhodes

Iphicrates and his band of mercenaries arrived in Corinth in 392 amid the tenuous ceasefire between Spartan-occupied Lechaeum and Sicyon and the allied-held Corinth. For the next year, Iphicrates busied himself with raiding Spartan territory using guerrilla tactics, going as far as Arcadia.[22] The Arcadians refused to engage the Athenian peltasts out of fear. The Spartans meanwhile returned the favour, similarly raiding Corinthian farmland in an attempt to starve out the Corinthians who could no longer receive food shipments via the harbour at Lechaeum, but with Cenchreae firmly under Corinthian and Argive control, the Corinthians would not starve anytime soon.

After rebuilding the broken Long Walls, the anti-Spartan confederates waited inside the city for a prime opportunity to attack. Unfortunately, they waited too long. Agesilaus' brother Teleutias had been appointed *navarch* and, accompanied by Agesilaus' land army, attacked first Argos and then Corinth in an effort to destroy the allies' agriculture and trade. The brothers won back part of the Corinthian Long Walls, reinforcing their garrison at Lechaeum and destroying Corinthian naval supremacy in the Gulf of Corinth. Xenophon found himself downright giddy over the brothers' triumphs, noting how 'the mother of both was able to congratulate herself on the joint success of both her sons; one having captured the enemy's walls by land and the other his ships and naval arsenal by sea, on the same day.'[23]

Content with the reassertion of his supremacy in Sparta, Agesilaus disbanded his army and returned to Sparta. A year later in 390 they would return on a second expedition, but in the interim, Teleutias and the remnant of the Spartan navy sailed across the Aegean Sea to Rhodes. Like Corinth, Rhodes found itself overwhelmed by social upheaval and the unceasing *stasis* of Greek society.

In 391, Rhodian oligarchs who had been expelled from the island after the Athenians annexed it four years earlier pleaded with Sparta, whose post-Cnidus navy was slowly being rebuilt. The Spartans sensed good fortune. As Fornis notes, Sparta saw a chance 'to recover this important enclave and convert it into the spear-point of its counter-offensive in the Aegean.'[24] With newfound enmity in Athenian-Persian relations, Sparta could seize a key strategic Athenian ally and regain a foothold not just in Asia Minor but also in the naval arena of the war. Xenophon insightfully describes Spartan motivation: 'The [Spartans] were alive to the fact that the fate of Rhodes depended on which party in the state prevailed: if the democracy were to dominate, the whole island must fall into the hands of Athens; if the wealthier classes, into their own.'[25]

Sparta eventually sent Teleutias with a staggering twenty-seven triremes to retake the city.[26] It was a massive investment for Sparta and likely constituted almost all their available vessels. For the *ephors*, it was worth it. This is because Sparta's strike against Rhodes was in truth an assault on Evagoras of Cyprus. Sparta intended to win favour with Persia for attacking their insolent adversary in the hope that Persia would no longer intervene in Greek politics and the anti-Spartan allies would lose their financier.[27]

Sparta quickly retook Rhodes, although their control was fragile and the fighting would continue for several years. Along the way to Rhodes, Teleutias re-established Sparta's navy as he took Samos, Cnidus and then Rhodes. The pendulum of the Corinthian War now swung firmly in Sparta's favour. As Diodorus concludes, 'now that their affairs were prospering, [the Spartans] resolved to get control of the sea.'[28] The Spartan hope was that Agesilaus and his brother would finally end the war. While Agesilaus fulfilled the domestic Spartan strategy by pillaging Argolis and threatening the last stronghold of the anti-Spartan Greeks in Corinth, his brother Teleutias fulfilled the Spartan overseas imperial strategy. By 390, the Spartans decided it was time to march on Corinth and end the war once and for all.

The Battle of Lechaeum

Curiously, the final land battle of the Corinthian War occurred because of a few cows. The Spartan strategy of destroying enemy resources by burning farmland, cutting down trees and embargoing the harbours crescendoed when they learned that Corinthian livestock would be moved to Peiraeum, north of the city on the Isthmus of Corinth. Capturing the livestock was a cunning move, not only as it eliminated more allied resources but it also cut off the route that would be taken by Theban reinforcements to Corinth.[29] Most critically, though, taking Peiraeum would interrupt the Isthmian Games.

The Isthmian Games were Panhellenic athletic competitions held in honour of Poseidon, the patron deity of Corinth, and were among the sacred Olympian cycle of athletic contests with the Olympics, the Nemean Games and the Pythian Games. The Corinthians historically hosted the games, but this year for the first time the Corinthians were now also Argives due to their recent *synoecism*. Agesilaus led the Spartans' army to both seize the Corinthian cattle and belittle the Argive hosts, who quickly cancelled the games and then re-enacted them, some competitions even with different victors this time. Agesilaus relished in the Argive embarrassment. Plutarch describes how Agesilaus then 'declared that the Argives had brought down upon themselves the charge of great cowardice, since they regarded the conduct of the games as so great and august a privilege, and yet had not the courage to fight for it.'[30] With the Battle of Nemea, the Corinthian War had now interrupted two of the most important athletic contests in all of Greece.

Agesilaus moved on to besiege the small city-state of Peiraeum, capturing much gold and renown both in Peiraeum and neighbouring Heraion. While there, Agesilaus was approached by Theban ambassadors entreating him for peace. It was a stunning betrayal by the *Boeotarchs* and it would have unravelled the anti-Spartan coalition if word reached the Athenians, Corinthians, Persians or Argives, but the Thebans were unnerved by Sparta's resurgence in the war, the revival of the Athenian Empire and the union of Argos and Corinth. They wished to amend the fact that they were the only major city-state in Greece not to have gained an advantage in the past year.

Agesilaus' hatred for the Thebans, however, had not abated in the years since the failed sacrifice at Aulis before his invasion of Asia Minor. Agesilaus summarily dismissed the Thebans, ignoring a chance to end the war. What Agesilaus failed to realize was that the Spartan war effort had just faced perhaps its biggest setback yet.

When Agesilaus attacked Peiraeum, he wisely left more than a full Spartan *mora* behind to garrison the Corinthian harbour of Lechaeum. Unfortunately, among the Spartans he chose were those from Amyclae. The Amyclaeans were historic Spartan allies and respectable *perioeci* from a village just 2 miles south of Sparta on the Eurotas River, best known for their cult worship of the mythological hero Hyacinthus, the lover of Apollo and namesake of the hyacinth flower. The Amyclaeans also hosted the sacred Hyacinthia festival each year in the early summer for three days to commemorate Hyacinthus' untimely death, and nothing would stop them from attending their festival, not even the war.

The Spartan commander in Lechaeum therefore sent a full *mora* of 600 hoplites and accompanying cavalry to escort the Amyclaeans back to Spartan territory near Sicyon. The *mora* would then turn around and march back to Lechaeum with the cavalry not far behind. The Spartans knew that the fearsome Iphicrates and his mercenaries lurked nearby outside the Long Walls, but arrogantly assumed that their recent momentum in the war would bring them safety. The Athenians cleverly surveyed the troop movements and surmised the *mora*'s return to Lechaeum.

Safe inside the Long Walls of Corinth, the Athenians further took notice of the thin numbers of hoplites at Lechaeum and their lack of cavalry support. The Athenian general Callias, who led the Athenian hoplites, chose to seize the opportunity and coordinate an attack with Iphicrates' peltasts. Callias was no stranger to decisive Greek wars. His grandfather was the more famous Callias who had negotiated the formal end of the Persian Wars in 449 with the Peace of Callias, and his father was a formidable Athenian general during the

Peloponnesian War and one of the wealthiest Athenians. Callias claimed not only aristocratic wealth and a military pedigree, but even family relations to Pericles and Alcibiades. It is hard to find a foil more different to his fellow commander Iphicrates, the poor son of a shoemaker and a *Thracophile*. Nevertheless, Callias and Iphicrates synergized perfectly.

They determined that attacking the returning Spartan *mora* would put the enemy in a double bind: either the peltasts could flee from the Spartan hoplites or the peltasts would capitalize on the Spartan position on a high road to 'cut up by showers of javelins on [the Spartans'] exposed right flank'.[31] It was a brilliant plan. The *mora* would have to march east, exposing their right flank to the south. This right flank was the most vulnerable for the heavy infantry hoplites, and exploiting it properly would lead to butchery as in the Battle of Coronea.

Iphicrates and Callias led the Athenian soldiers outside the city, with Callias' hoplites serving as auxiliary forces while the peltasts advanced as the vanguard. The Spartan *mora* consisted exclusively of hoplites, weary from travelling about 14 miles in more than 70lb of armour. With no supporting peltasts, cavalry or skirmishers, the *mora* was a stubbornly limited fighting force.

The location of the battle is unusually specific, as Xenophon – not known for his historical precision – pinpointed it as 'two stades' from the Corinthian Gulf and 'twenty or thirty stades' from the harbour at Lechaeum.[32] Andreas Konecny notes that 'the only landform that meets these criteria is a noticeable elevation rising gently from south to north in the alluvium of the plain in the area of the modern village of Lechaio.'[33] After a rain shower the day before, it was a clear summer day and the location was well within the sightline from the top of the Long Walls.

From their southern position down this slight hill from the *mora*, Iphicrates and the Athenian peltasts prepared to throw javelins. Konecny argues that a series of fortifications extended past the Corinthian walls along a creek for about a few hundred metres.[34] These fortifications gave excellent coverage first from Spartan scouts and then as an escape route for when the Spartan hoplites inevitably pursued them. The fortifications and terrain were a considerable boon to the peltasts' hit-and-run tactics. They also augmented the Athenians' sizable statistical advantage: at least 1,500 peltasts and 1,000 hoplites outnumbered the 600 Spartan hoplites and various shield-bearers.[35]

When the Sparta *mora* was about 500 metres from Lechaeum, the Athenian peltasts sprinted out and began the battle with a volley of javelins.[36] According to Xenophon, the only contemporaneous source, the first moments of the battle were a bloodbath. Spartan hoplites fell in vast numbers, scattering their ranks and killing dozens. The shield-bearers, unarmoured servants or helots who nominally protected the right flank and helped carry hoplites' shields, were tasked with carrying wounded men back to Lechaeum. These fortunate few were the only Spartans to survive the slaughter.[37]

The Spartan *polemarch* opted to go on the offensive and ordered a wave of hoplites to charge the Athenians, despite the geographical complications. At this moment, the Spartans had to thin out their lines to reach the enemy. This allowed them to avoid making a large, congregated target for Athenian javelins, but caused them to depend on the speed and agility of heavy infantry, a poor strategy. It also played directly into the Athenians' plans.

The peltasts' primary directive from Iphicrates was to avoid close-quarter combat at all costs. As such, when the first Spartan hoplites to charge – those between the ages of 18 and 28 known as the 'ten years' – came close enough to attack, the peltasts retreated. Lazenby characterizes this as overconfidence on behalf of the unnamed Spartan *polemarch*: if the shield-bearers had time to reach Lechaeum, then no doubt the rest of the hoplites also had time.[38] However, the Spartan commander opted instead to assault the enemy by sending his first two ranks, about a third of the *mora* or about 200 men, out of formation. It was a predictable but long-proven Spartan tactic, although likely meant to disperse but not defeat the peltasts and keep them out of javelin range.[39]

Yet Xenophon describes how Iphicrates' manoeuvres ensured that the Spartan charges tantalizingly never reached the Athenians:

> Being heavy infantry opposed to light troops, before they could get to close quarters the enemy's word of command sounded 'Retire!' whilst as soon as their own ranks fell back, scattered as they were in consequence of a charge where each man's individual speed had told, Iphicrates and his men turned right about and renewed the javelin attack, while others, running alongside, harassed their exposed flank.[40]

The Spartans were shocked at the failed attack. At least twice before had Spartan hoplites charged peltasts in similar circumstances to great effect; first under the command of Brasidas against Thracian peltasts[41] and later under Pausanias at Piraeus.[42] Their temerity over these victories and in their impressive momentum in the Corinthian War was mistaken.

The Athenian hoplites under the command of Callias were positioned to hinder the inevitable Spartan offensive and discourage them from reforming their ranks.[43] In this they succeeded as the Spartan 'ten years' remained disorganized and thinned out under the barrage of javelins. The Spartan hoplites were unable to assemble in any meaningful formation or phalanx, and were evidently left alone to fight in haphazardly organized small groups spread out over at least 100 metres of battlefield under the constant barrage of the peltasts' javelins.[44] This Athenian strategy was likewise not a new one. A similar tactic had been used at the Battle of Sphacteria in 425, leading to a significant Athenian victory.[45]

After the failed attack of the 'ten years', the Spartan *polemarch*, who remained unidentified by Xenophon perhaps out of a fear of insulting his Spartan patrons, next sent in the 'fifteen years', those Spartans between the ages of 28 and 33. These hoplites numbered only about 100.[46] They fared worse than their younger counterparts. The Spartan hoplites could simply not reach the Athenian peltasts, who had thus far suffered virtually no casualties.

What remained of the Spartan *mora* was saved by the serendipitous return of the Spartan cavalry. The cavalry had finished their escort of the Amyclaeans to Sicyon and returned on the same road to Lechaeum, and at last gave the Spartan regiment the ability to diversify their tactics. They were quickly able to scatter the peltasts and keep them out of range for a moment.

The cavalry, however, did not prosecute the attack and instead remained conservative. They kept up a similar pace to the hoplites, making the *mora* one-dimensional in their speed and fumbling their one advantage. Instead of running down the peltasts and killing as many as they could before Callias' hoplites arrived for support, Xenophon says that the Spartan cavalry kept pace with their own hoplites in repeated charges out at the javelin-tossing peltasts, who always managed to retreat and regroup. The poor results never changed with each failed assault, but Spartan morale did: 'Again and again the monotonous tale of doing and suffering repeated itself, except that as their own ranks grew thinner and their courage ebbed, the courage of their assailants grew bolder and their numbers increased.'[47]

Sensing that victory was now impossible, the Spartan *polemarch* ordered one final assault meant not to pierce the enemy lines but instead to provide cover for retreat. There was only a single destination to which they could retreat: Lechaeum and the sea. However, the harbour was almost 3 kilometres away, and while their allies in Lechaeum had seen the battle and were sending out naval support to aid the retreat, it would be almost impossible to reach the safety of the walls without the peltasts' javelins bombarding them.[48]

The coast, however, was closer: less than half a kilometre away. The Spartan *mora* gathered on a small hill, intent on boarding the incoming ships from Lechaeum. It was a brief reprieve as the peltasts would lose their momentum had they charged up the hill. At this moment, Callias at long last ordered the Athenian hoplites forward. The surviving Spartans were now pinned between the sea and a fresh phalanx so far unsullied by the battle, with all their escape routes limited by the peltasts' range and alacrity.

Lechaeum: A Final Athenian Victory 115

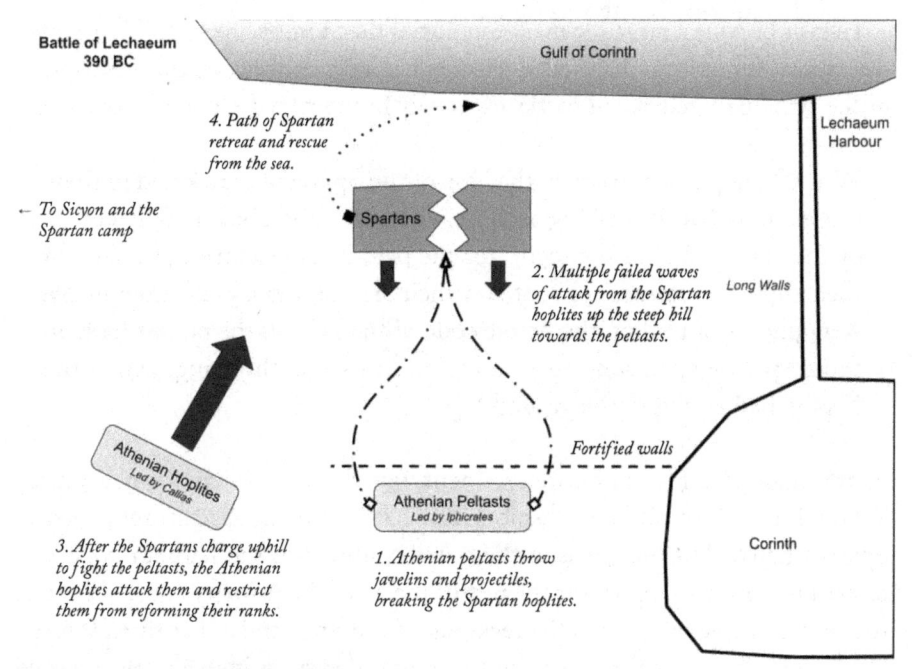

A depiction of the Battle of Lechaeum's events.

The Spartan lines broke. Xenophon describes the rare scene of Spartan battlefield panic, as 'some of them threw themselves into the sea; others – a mere handful – escaped with the cavalry into Lechaeum.'[49] While a handful escaped, this final phase of the battle was also the bloodiest as up to 150 Spartans were massacred by the Athenian hoplites.[50] The vast majority of the survivors were those able to make it to the boats.

The final tally of the battle was at least 250 Spartans dead with 100 or more wounded. The Athenian casualties were virtually non-existent. The anti-Spartan allies had, through cunning tactics and innovations, finally broken the Spartan war machine. Never before had Spartan hoplites faced such a devastating defeat in open battle.

From Battles to Skirmishes: The War's Final Mutation

The Battle of Lechaeum was a strategic win for the anti-Spartan confederates, but its main legacy was in the zeitgeist of Greek culture and military. It was the death knell for the legendary Greek hoplite. The wild success of the Iphicratean Reforms soon made peltasts the standard soldier in Greek militaries, even in Sparta which had all but abandoned the Classical hoplite by the Hellenistic era in favour of the peltast.

Peltasts became a romantic manifestation of the Homeric hero. As J.E. Lendon describes, Xenophon channelled Homer's poetic epithets in the description of the Athenian peltasts in battle, especially in their 'swift-footed' movement:

> When Xenophon notes that 'the best' of the Spartans were killed in these chases he is hardly striking a consciously epic note, but he is swept up by the epic quality of the scene, for the peltasts are victorious because of their supreme fleetness of foot and their skill at arms. Half-unknowing, Xenophon is unveiling the heroic code of the peltast: the peltast took up those epic competitions, in running and in spear-throwing, which the hoplite had let fall to the ground.[51]

Sparta may have lost an entire regiment, but the Corinthian War raged on, although now in a different fashion. The harbour of Lechaeum remained in Spartan hands, but the garrison there was confined to the harbour walls and offered no serious support for the rest of the war. The primary consequence of the Battle of Lechaeum was the recalling of the Spartan land army in Greece. Upon hearing news of the disaster at Lechaeum, Agesilaus immediately prepared his invasion force in Peiraeum to come and support. He himself led a small contingent and immediately travelled to Lechaeum, although he arrived far too late.[52]

He was forced to begrudgingly return to his army and simply retreat back to Sparta to await further command. The demeanour of Agesilaus' march back to Sparta revealed the Spartan king's disposition. He ordered his soldiers to break camp before dawn and march until the late hours of the day, minimizing their chance of hearing gossip about the lost *mora* or seeing the celebrations in occupied cities. Mantinea was even passed by in the dead of night, for Agesilaus thought that the sight of the Mantineans revelling at the Spartan tribulation 'would have been too severe an ordeal for his soldiers'.[53]

At this point, Agesilaus should have repented of his hatred for the Thebans and his discourteous rejection of the Theban envoys' offer of peace talks. The Theban ambassadors were summoned by Agesilaus and asked for their visit's purpose, but having seen the result of Lechaeum the ambassadors re-evaluated Sparta's position of strength. Instead of entering into peace negotiations, the Thebans remained silent.[54]

Hamilton argues that Agesilaus' vengeful and spiteful behaviour alienated the envoys and caused an opportunity for negotiating peace terms to be lost.[55] He further contends that it demoted him for the remainder of the war, as the boy king Agesipolis was given a more prestigious command in 388.[56] Xenophon, of course, takes a more sympathetic view of Agesilaus' leadership: 'as for the disasters which presently befell [Sparta], no one can maintain that they were brought about under the leadership of Agesilaus.'[57] Regardless of his position with the *ephors*, Agesilaus brought the entire occupying land army of Sparta back to Laconia. For the most part, they would remain there for the remainder of the Corinthian War.

The Athenians were a different story. Despite his Thracian favouritism, Iphicrates was nevertheless an Athenian imperialist. In the aftermath of Lechaeum, he desired to annex Corinth for the ascendant Athenian Empire. He began by retaking several Spartan garrisons surrounding Corinth at Oenoe in Peiraeum, Sidus and Crommyon, but he did not wish to stop there. Leveraging his popularity in Corinth after Lechaeum, Iphicrates wished to take Corinth for the Athenians. He was stopped only by the Athenian voters, who opted not to seize Corinth, presumably as such actions would surely rip apart the anti-Spartan coalition, losing both Corinthian and Argive support at a crucial moment in the war effort.[58] Instead, Iphicrates was relegated to a lowly return to Athens, far from becoming the next great Athenian empire-builder. By 389, he and his peltasts were available for overseas campaigns, indicating that the Athenian voting assembly restricted them from turning their victory at Lechaeum into a true imperial campaign.

Indeed, at this point the Corinthian War shifted away from land warfare altogether. After 390 and the Spartan defeat at Lechaeum, the Spartans were loath to engage in any major hoplite battles for perhaps the first time in their history. The war turned instead to naval skirmishes and diplomatic negotiations as each city-state recognized the war's devastation and wished to avoid rehashing the Peloponnesian War. The Battle of Lechaeum was a dazzling victory for Athens, but it would be their final victory in the Corinthian War.

Chapter Ten
Piraeus Burning

Agesilaus and Sparta's Peltast Scourge

After licking their wounds following the Battle of Lechaeum, Sparta briefly tried to reignite the land campaigns, although strategically avoiding direct engagement with Athenian peltasts and Iphicrates. In 389, Agesilaus was sent by the *ephors* on a campaign to retake the Athenian-allied Acarnanian city of Calydon for their Peloponnesian League allies Achaea. Agesilaus was sent with two *moras* and supporting forces from Achaea and other allies. Confident that the disaster at Lechaeum, like Haliartus, was not his fault, Agesilaus proudly waltzed into Acarnania. Yet even two *moras* under the command of the great Agesilaus were haunted by peltasts.

Agesilaus briefly showed Greece the traditional might of the Spartan land army as he ravaged Acarnanian territories, although it was a hollow sight after Lechaeum. Moving across the land at a snail's pace – only about 1 mile per day – Agesilaus enriched himself, and perhaps Sparta, by reselling Acarnanian livestock, slaves and horses during the summer of 389.[1] This fulfilled the Spartan threat to the Acarnanian League months earlier; if they renounced the anti-Spartan confederacy and instead allied with Sparta and Achaea, then this whole matter would have been avoided.[2]

It would have been an excellent show of force too, had Agesilaus not camped at the foot of a mountain. That evening at twilight, the Acarnanians sent a regiment of peltasts to throw their javelins from the mountainside, safe from the Spartan hoplites' spears and impossible for the hoplites to ascend the terrain quickly enough. Like Lechaeum, it exploited the very framework of the Classical Greek phalanx and the hoplite, and forced the Spartans to retreat to Achaea.[3] Agesilaus, however, chose one of the worst routes possible to return to Achaea when he selected a narrow mountain pass.

Their retreat was just the beginning of a tortuous journey back to the safety of Achaea. In a miniature recreation of the March of the Ten Thousand, the Spartans traversed the narrow path towards friendly territory while being harried and harassed by Acarnanian peltasts hiking the small trails above the pass. In his *Hellenica*, Xenophon gives a detailed account of the Acarnanian assault:

The Acarnanians, from the vantage-ground above, poured down a continuous pelt of stones and other missiles, or, creeping down to the fringes, dogged and annoyed them so much that the army was no longer able to proceed. If the heavy infantry or cavalry made sallies from the main line they did no harm to their assailants, for the Acarnanians had only to retire and they had quickly gained their strongholds.[4]

Xenophon goes on to recount how Agesilaus changed tactics and unexpectedly attacked the left flank of the Acarnanians, despite their superior numbers, and sent out the cavalry and the 'fifteen years' to charge forward and at last impede the peltast assault.[5] Later in his career, however, Xenophon whitewashed this battle account in his *Agesilaus*, perhaps at the behest of Spartan diplomats or in an attempt to rehabilitate his favourite commander. He instead presented a streamlined synthesis of Agesilaus' campaign, notably glossing over the agonizing Spartan trials with peltasts:

Storming the heights above his head with his light troops, he gave them battle, and slew many of them, and set up a trophy, nor stayed his hand until he had united the Acarnanians, the Aetolians, and the Argives, in friendship with the Achaeans and alliance with himself.[6]

In *Hellenica*, Xenophon curiously deconstructed the Battle of Lechaeum by having Agesilaus succeed precisely where the Spartan commander had failed: by simultaneously charging both the 'fifteen years' and the cavalry directly at peltasts. Yet no matter Xenophon's suspicious treatment of the campaign, it was clear that one year after Lechaeum, Sparta still had no answer for the peltast, a fact keenly observed by Athens and the rest of the allies.

To the Achaeans, however, this was a victory without a prize. No Acarnanian city had reverted to Achaean control. Agesilaus soon found his footing, however, and quickly turned the tide of the Acarnanian campaign. When he reached Achaea in the early autumn of 389, Agesilaus answered Achaean objections with impressive foresight: 'You forget…that I mean to invade your enemies again next summer; and therefore the larger their sowing now, the stronger will be their appetite for peace hereafter.'[7] The next spring, with the limited Acarnanian crops just starting to grow, Agesilaus made a pompous showing of preparing his army for the next invasion of Acarnania. Upon hearing this news, the Acarnanians, fearing famine should their farmlands again be burned by Agesilaus, surrendered.

The Acarnanian campaign was an uneven retaliation to the anti-Spartan confederates' present land advantage, but succeeded in reasserting Spartan military might. It was, however, the final contribution of Agesilaus in the Corinthian War. The estimable Spartan king faded.

Concurrent with Agesilaus' Acarnanian crusade, the boy king Agesipolis led the more prestigious campaign against the traditional Spartan rival of Argos. That Agesipolis would be given such a command accented the demotion of Agesilaus among the *ephors*, and perhaps influenced Agesilaus' showmanship in Acarnania. Argos was certainly the more strategic target; the Spartans rightly judged that the close proximity of Argos to Sparta made it impossible to make an expedition against Athens, Corinth or Thebes.[8]

So in 388, Agesipolis led a deeply traditional Spartan campaign against the Argives. As any good Spartan king must do, he made frequent religious sacrifices and scoured the remains for divine portents. After discerning the gods' approval at Olympia, Agesipolis marched with his army into Argive territory. The Argives, alarmed at a breach of a temporary truce, sent emissaries to negotiate a ceasefire, but Agesipolis brushed them aside and continued on towards Argos.

The gods were fickle, however, and that evening an earthquake rocked the Spartan camp. His men wished to retreat, recalling the actions of Agis against the Eleans, but Agesipolis held fast and proclaimed it a sign of divine favour for their invasion.[9] Determined to exceed Agesilaus' successful invasion of Argos a few years earlier, Agesipolis pressed on. He saw mild success, destroying farmland, bedevilling Theban cavalry and even reaching the city walls of Argos. Perhaps annoyed that Agesipolis failed to get their earlier message, the gods soon sent a clearer message as Agesipolis' camp was struck directly by a lightning bolt.[10] The pious Agesipolis disbanded his army and returned home to Sparta, content with the limited success of the campaign.

Agesipolis' expedition to Argos, minor though it was, marked the final Spartan land campaign of the Corinthian War. Though they generally won the Argive and Acarnanian invasions, the chief cost to the Spartans was a continued dissonance in their imperial and military vision. Hamilton traces these difficulties to the failed peace talks of 392, which had 'forced [Sparta] to renew the war on two fronts and to adopt a combination of two policies that had seemed mutually exclusive.'[11] Harangued by peltasts and natural disasters, Sparta finally opted to focus on a single dimension of the war: the seas.

The Second Renaissance of Thrasybulus

By 390, and now for the third time, Thrasybulus had clawed his way back to the top of Athenian democracy. Conon's brief ascendancy in Athens had reinvigorated their passion for empire, and he had dethroned Thrasybulus for the past few years since Cnidus, but now that Conon was imprisoned or executed by the Persians, Thrasybulus seized control of Athenian diplomacy and politics.

In contrast to the fervour for empire under Conon, Thrasybulus took a moderate position on Athenian imperialism. This was a wise approach. Persia's arrest of Conon in Sardis had crippled the revitalization of Athenian empire-building. After the victory at Cnidus and the early glory days of Conon's return to the city, Athens was restricted to rebuilding Piraeus and assisting in the allies' protection of Corinth. The Athenian voting assembly clearly had concerns about Persia's perception of their empire and the threat of coercive intervention if Persia sensed that Athens was rebuilding her Aegean thalassocracy. This renewed conservatism likely colourized Iphicrates' recall to Athens by the voting assembly, who feared that allowing him to take Corinthian territory from Sparta would invite Persian retribution.

Having experienced the cost of war, the middle-class voters of Athens were firmly under Thrasybulus' influence once again. Hamilton notes that their motivation was 'not merely a war of conquest for gross material gain, but rather a re-establishment of national power and sovereignty.'[12] Curiously, the middle class had not acquiesced to the peace talks of 392, which might have realized their goals as they had preserved their Aegean claims, but instead backed Thrasybulus' decorous resistance to Conon's more forthright diplomacy. Perturbed at Artaxerxes' claim to the Greek territories of Asia Minor, the Athenian voters had rejected the full peace terms of 392 and even exiled Andocides as retribution.[13]

In this volatile context, Thrasybulus found his most vibrant success in targeted naval campaigns from 389 to 388 in an attempt to hinder Spartan naval expansion under Teleutias, who had arrived in Rhodes the year before after his series of successful raids on Aegean islands and Greek city-states on the coast of Asia Minor. Thrasybulus judged this the proper time to challenge Sparta's renewed naval aggression and sailed with a fleet of forty triremes to Rhodes.[14] Upon arrival, however, Thrasybulus saw that the Spartans held the acropolis of Rhodes, an infamously formidable fortress, and that Teleutias' fleet lurked nearby.

On arrival, however, Thrasybulus saw that the pro-Athenian Rhodians were much larger in number and not at risk of defeat unless they were to attack the acropolis, which they steadfastly avoided. It was clear to him that the Rhodian democrats did not need immediate military aid, and his soldiers could not penetrate the fortress walls anyway, so intervention would be an unnecessary risk. Thrasybulus continued his policy of pragmatism and opted instead to sail to the Hellespont.

The chief problem with this approach was that there was no particular goal for Athenian diplomacy in the Hellespont and no pressing conflict in which they could mediate. Thrasybulus busied himself with reconciling two local kings and winning alliances for Athens. Leveraging the perception of Athens' alliance with Persia – and keeping the locals blissfully unaware of the many tensions between Athens and Persia – Thrasybulus revived the Athenian imperial tradition yet again. Enthused by such progress, he sailed to Byzantium and partnered with local pro-Athenian democrats to supplant its pro-Spartan oligarchy.[15]

Byzantium was truly the crown jewel for an Athenian Empire. Much fighting in the waning years of the Peloponnesian War had focused on Byzantium and the Hellespont in an endless pursuit of the coveted grain supply from the Black Sea which was shipped through the Byzantium ports. The city had paid an exorbitantly high tax to Athens as a result, illustrating its own prosperity but also its role as a linchpin to Athens' imperial vision. Thrasybulus, in a move motivated both by economics and symbolism, reinstated a similar tax on Byzantium and decreed it Athenian territory.[16]

Expanded alliances with other powerful city-states in the Black Sea, the Hellespont and even Chalcedon soon followed. Byzantium in hand, Thrasybulus set off to Lesbos and reconquered Mytilene, another emblematic addition to Athens' recreated empire in Asia Minor. With a force of 400 hoplites, Thrasybulus seized Mytilene for Athens. It was a contentious move, for in 428 the Mytileneans had infamously rebelled against the Athenian Empire and in response the Athenian voting assembly voted to massacre the entire city. With the clarity of the next morning's sobriety, the Athenians sent their fastest ship to cancel the orders and the damage was indeed limited, but Mytilene remained hateful of Athenian power, a fact strategically exploited by Thrasybulus.

It sent a powerful message: Thrasybulus soon moved to a land campaign in 389 and challenged both Spartan governors and Persian *satraps* for locations along the coast of Asia Minor. After taking the whole island of Lesbos, Thrasybulus and the Athenians worked their way southward down the coast with aspirations of forcing the Spartans at Rhodes to surrender. Thrasybulus, however, overextended the Athenian imperial model as they razed farmland and plundered territory. Cities from the Ionian coast to Lycia and from Clazomenae to Aspendos were looted and absorbed into the now twice-revived Athenian thalassocracy. Halicarnassus was so infuriated they formally complained of corruption and abuse of power.[17]

Much like Athens' own imperial demise or Sparta's current predicament, such maltreatment of subjects caused rebellion. Aspendos, which had been conquered by Cimon in the early days of the Athenian ascendancy, now finally got its retribution. Under cover of night, a band of nameless but vengeful Lycians murdered Thrasybulus in his tent as he camped outside the city of Aspendos. While the unknown, aggrieved parties may have had plenty of reasons to assassinate Thrasybulus, it is difficult to pardon both the Persians and Spartans. Hyland points the finger at Persian spycraft: 'No source mentions direct Persian involvement, but the Aspendians' reaction…served [Persian] imperial interests.'[18] If they were innocent, the Persians certainly did not mourn the loss of Thrasybulus and, with him, the encore of the destruction of Athenian naval power.

Thrasybulus, the venerated veteran of the Peloponnesian War and liberator of the Athenians in the struggle against the Thirty Tyrants, was now dead, and with him died the last great generation of Athenian empire-builders. In a panic, the Athenian forces retreated to Rhodes, while the voting assembly sent a commander named Agyrrhius to protect the new Athenian holdings.[19] He would need help against the Spartans. It was now time for a new generation of Athenians, one that had never truly known the prosperity of the Delian League or the Athenian Empire. Iphicrates was the first of this new era to make his mark.

Iphicrates, Anaxibius and another Wave of Imperial Conflict in Asia Minor

Sparta was not ignorant of Athens' territorial gains under Thrasybulus. Aiming to both stymie Athenian progress and entice Persia into peace talks, the *ephors* sent one Anaxibius to Asia Minor. Although it was not a formal expedition, Anaxibius was a competent general and given the title of *harmost* of Abydos. At Abydos he replaced Dercylidas, the commander who had campaigned in Asia Minor prior to Agesilaus' triumphant entry into the war. With limited diplomatic excursions, Dercylidas had long held Abydos which by now was one of the few remaining Spartan strongholds overseas. Dercylidas was also a close ally of the *ephors*, who recalled him either to keep him from danger or perhaps to spare him the shame of losing the remaining Spartan colonies to the resurgent Athenians.[20]

Anaxibius was an honourable commander most famous for his affiliation with the March of the Ten Thousand. Anaxibius had been the *harmost* of Byzantium, and had astonishingly refused to pay the Ten Thousand when they arrived in his territory after their arduous journey.[21] When they predictably mutinied, he even took to fleeing to the acropolis aboard a fisherman's vessel.[22] It was none other than Xenophon who helped mediate and de-escalate the tension, perhaps illuminating the poor depiction of Anaxibius in *Hellenica*.

Anaxibius had deep connections with Persian diplomats, especially Pharnabazus with whom he had brokered backroom alliances during Cyrus the Younger's rebellion and the Persian-Spartan War. As Pharnabazus was now supporting the Athenians, the Spartans clearly hoped to peel away a critical layer of Athenian patronage. He capitalized quickly on his experience and strengthened Abydos by capturing several nearby cities and increasing the size of its navy.[23]

Although previously sidelined by Sparta's refusal to directly engage Athenian peltasts, Iphicrates was sent by the voting assembly on a series of overseas conquests in 389 after the death of Thrasybulus. Their chief concern was the loss of Thrasybulus' new territories and, more crucially, the income from them in the form of taxes and grain. Iphicrates was given eight ships, 1,200 peltasts and a target of the Chersonese with Abydos to follow.

It was a new opportunity for Iphicrates to cement his standing in Athenian politics. Despite the glory won at Lechaeum, Iphicrates had not been able to leverage it for personal political gain as had been done by so many other triumphant Athenian military commanders. Perhaps due to his commoner origins, or more likely his suspicious ties to Thrace, the Athenian voters were so apprehensive about Iphicrates that they did not give him traditional honours and laurels for his victory at Lechaeum until 371, two full decades later.[24] He had resigned his Corinthian command in frustration just a year after his stunning accomplishment of destroying a Spartan *mora*. One boon to the Athenian strategy was the alliance not only with Evagoras of Cyprus but also to his greatest ally, the Egyptian pharaoh Hakor. By 388, the play *Plutus* mentioned a new alliance with Hakor and the Egyptians, which would have been fully developed by Iphicrates' campaign in a way that it perhaps was not for the prior conquests of Thrasybulus.[25]

With this support and a drive to prove himself, Iphicrates tested his peltasts in a new continent quite successfully, trading raids with Anaxibius for several weeks and garnering victories that contested the last Spartan stronghold in Asia. It was an audacious tactic, throwing caution to the wind in yet another attempt to revitalize their naval empire, all while Agesilaus burned the farmland of their allies in the anti-Spartan league and Agesipolis threatened to burn Argos. As Strauss judges it, 'the Athenians showed that they had lost none of their famous boldness of spirit. In fact, the next year saw them more reckless and aggressive than had the last.'[26] As on so many previous occasions, the Athenians' reckless pursuit of empire came at the cost of their allies.

Soon, Iphicrates heard news of Anaxibius' travels to Antandrus with a vanguard of 200 hoplites, which by this point had become a paltry number against the mighty peltast. Iphicrates deployed the trademark Athenian guile and sent a number of ships across the channel at the break of day, tricking the Spartans into thinking he had departed on a routine fund-raising trip, a standard Athenian practice in the resource-rich Hellespont.

Ignoring poor omens in the day's sacrifice, an unusual development for the pious Spartans, Anaxibius fell for the ruse and marched on Iphicrates' camp under the assumption that he was gone. The overland route from Antandrus to Abydos taken by Anaxibius, however, was a treacherous one with rocky elevation, thin trails and little infrastructure. Anaxibius' army, along with his Abydenian hoplites, was forced to travel the mountain paths in a long, thin column, the worst possible formation for a peltast ambush. As the Spartans were descending a hill and entering an open plain near the gold mines at Cremaste, Iphicrates sprang the trap. He cleverly timed his ambush for when the majority of the Spartans were already down the hill and into the plain, and he attacked the tail end of the formation. This hindered those hoplites at sea level from running up the steep hill under a barrage of peltast javelins and projectiles.

Deciphering that Iphicrates managed to steal a Lechaeum-style victory and not obliterate his Spartan adversaries, Anaxibius – who was stuck at the end of the formation and under the assault – gave his final orders to the Spartans: 'Sirs, it is good for me to die on this spot, where honour bids me; but for you, sirs, yonder your path lies, haste and save yourselves before the enemy can close with us.'[27]

Anaxibius died in the ensuing battle, along with 200 Spartans and 50 Abydenian hoplites.[28] More critically, with Anaxibius died the last of the Spartan imperial territories in Asia Minor and one of the final *harmosts*.

Meanwhile, Iphicrates returned to his campaigns in the Chersonese. The Athenians had not yet fulfilled their Rhodian ambitions. Now in late 388, with Iphicrates securing their Hellespontine holdings and their new allies the Egyptians supporting their old Cypriot allies, the Athenians were emboldened to retake Rhodes and end Sparta's imperial ambitions forever, but the Spartans had one last gasp in them and sent a new admiral named Hierax to take the reins of the naval campaign in Asia Minor. Consolidating their overseas fleets, several Spartan commanders amassed an astonishing twenty-five triremes that soon put in at Abydos and aimed to marshal an offensive to retake the Hellespont,[29] but Iphicrates outmanoeuvred them and found thirty-two Athenian and allied triremes to blockade them in the Abydenian harbour.

Sparta's primary ambition by late 388 was not to engage Athens in an imperial clash, but instead to beseech Persia into peace talks. In this fashion, Spartan diplomacy had been reduced to an audience of one – Artaxerxes II – and to get him to agree to negotiations, it would be the new champion of Spartan statecraft, Antalcidas, who would need to quell Spartan factionalism long enough to establish a coherent diplomatic vision. So by the end of 388, the Spartans gave Antalcidas the post of *navarch* with the express goal of ingratiating himself with Tiribazus, the reinstated *satrap* of Lydia, so that Persia would begin negotiations to end the Corinthian War.

For the Athenians, the ultimate result of this brash re-entry into Aegean naval imperialism was not the reasserted Delian League they had envisioned, but instead a disconcerted Persia and a diplomatic landscape much more conducive to peace talks than an endless war.[30]

Teleutias and the Burning of Athens' Harbour

While Iphicrates, Anaxibius and now Hierax squabbled in the Hellespont, Teleutias set his sights on a far more valuable target: Athens itself. Judging that a blow to Athens may convince the Persians to withdraw their support of the anti-Spartan confederates, Teleutias sailed to the island of Aegina. Just about 12 miles from the Athenian harbour of Piraeus, Aegina was an ancient rival of Athens that had endeavoured to oppose Athens in just about every conflict.

They first aligned with Persia in the Persian Wars and then with Sparta in the Peloponnesian War. At the onset of their war with Sparta in 431, the Athenians had enough and expelled the citizens of Aegina who moved to Spartan territory. Lysander repaid the favour at the start of the Corinthian War in 395 and repopulated the island, turning it into a Spartan naval base.[31] It remained a forward base for the Spartan fleet, although quite underused, for the duration of the war.

Teleutias first returned to Sparta, relinquishing his fleet in Asia Minor to Hierax, before sailing to Aegina. The Athenians had built a fortress on the coast of Aegina in response to raids on Attican farmlands. Bringing the war close to home for the first time, the Athenians and Spartans exchanged blows over the future of Aegina, including a stunning nighttime raid by the Spartan commander Gorgopas. However, after a brutal battle for the island in 388, Athens won back Aegina with such force that Xenophon remarked that, afterwards, 'the Athenians sailed the sea as freely as in the times of actual peace.'[32]

It was the Spartan survivors of this failed battle that inherited the renowned Teleutias as their new commander, an honour they were overjoyed to receive. Teleutias set straight to work, calling an assembly of the dispirited Spartan soldiers and announcing his new plans. Practising unusually sound historical methods, Xenophon records the entire speech:

> Soldiers, I am back again, but I bring with me no money. Yet if God be willing, and your zeal flag not, I will endeavour to supply you with provisions without stint. Be well assured, as often as I find myself in command of you, I have but one prayer – that your lives may be spared no less than mine…
>
> Soldiers, let [Sparta], our own mother-city, be to you an example. Her good fortune is reputed to stand high. That you know; and you know too,

that she purchased her glory and her greatness not by faint-heartedness, but by choosing to suffer pain and incur dangers in the day of need. 'Like city,' I say, 'like citizens.' You, too, as I can bear you witness, have been in times past brave; but to-day must we strive to be better than ourselves. So shall we share our pains without repining, and when fortune smiles, mingle our joys; for indeed the sweetest thing of all surely is to flatter no man, Hellene or Barbarian, for the sake of hire; we will suffice to ourselves, and from a source to which honour pre-eminently invites us; since, I need not remind you, abundance won from the enemy in war furnishes forth not bodily nutrition only, but a feast of glory the wide world over.

It was a magnificent heralding of Spartan imperialism, and a transparent alliance with Agesilaus, Lysander and their vision of a Spartan Empire on both sides of the Aegean. His men roused into a bloodlust, Teleutias quickly ordered the boarding of their triremes, after supper of course, and sailed the dozen miles into the Athenian harbour at Piraeus in the dead of night. It was a long journey and the men slept on the trireme during the night, but by dawn twelve Spartan triremes entered Athens.

Teleutias' timing was impeccable. The brazen move would have been dead on arrival had the Spartan ships arrived at any other time, but Teleutias knew that when Athenian triremes were anchored at their home port, the sailors would sleep at home or on the shore as opposed to overseas where they would sleep on the ship.[33] Teleutias was therefore 'under the firm persuasion that the Athenians were more careless than ever about their navy in the harbour since the death of Gorgopas.'[34]

As dawn came, the Spartans attacked. The orders were that no merchant vessel could be sunk, but any trireme or military ship was fair game. Larger merchant ships were ordered to be towed out to sea and looted. The top priority was not to conquer Athens, but instead to cripple her navy, inhibit her trade and, most crucially, strike fear into the heart of the Athenians. The plan worked beautifully.

The Athenians in the harbour were so panicked that many fled, even into the water. For one morning, the Spartans became little more than pirates, kidnapping merchants, overthrowing tables, robbing ships and causing pandemonium wherever they could. Piraeus, constructed by the visionary Athenian leader Themistocles a century earlier and the nerve centre of Athens' maritime empire, had never before been ransacked. Only Persia's burning of the city in 479 and Sparta's defeat of Athens and subsequent installation of the Thirty Tyrants could rival the burning of Piraeus in the histories of Athenian conflict.

The rest of the city finally awoke to the chaos in their precious harbour. Athenians grabbed armour, spears, swords and horses and raced to the harbour under the assumption that the Spartans were attacking outright, but once they had assembled their cavalry and phalanxes, the Athenians realized that their adversaries were simply buccaneers and not conquerors.

Content that he had caused the maximum amount of damage in just a few hours, Teleutias withdrew instead of facing the Athenians in outright combat. He ordered four triremes to escort the captured merchant ships straight back to Aegina, where the new funds would go directly towards Sparta's ceaseless shipbuilding. Teleutias sailed with his remaining eight triremes along the Attican coast, continuing to pillage those poor ships that were ignorantly sailing to the safety of Piraeus. At the southern tip of Attica's peninsula, Teleutias' marauders captured several more vessels' worth of grain heading to Athens from their holdings in the Hellespont and the Black Sea. This was the very same grain taxed through the ports of Byzantium and, in many ways, represented the revival of the Athenian imperial project. To make a statement, Teleutias took it back to Aegina and sold it to make his sailors an advance of a full month's pay.

Like his brother Agesilaus, Teleutias soon became wildly popular among the Spartan soldiers and citizens. This monumental victory solidified Sparta's previously tenuous grip on the Aegean and breathed life into their war effort, much needed after the disaster of Lechaeum. More importantly, however, it was the evidence that Artaxerxes needed to revisit peace negotiations. Seeing that Sparta was back in a position of strength and also desperate to end the war, the Persians made known their intentions to conduct diplomatic talks for the first time since the failed negotiations of 392. The Corinthian War, after eight long years, was ready to end, as long as Persia and Sparta could each unsnarl the Gordian Knots that comprised their internal political factionalism.

Chapter Eleven

The King's Peace or the Peace of Antalcidas?

Persia's Moribund Statecraft in Asia Minor

By 387, Persia's own imperial vision wrestled with instability and infighting, particularly with the maverick behaviour of the *satraps* of Asia Minor. Discord such as the rebellion of Cyrus the Younger and the rivalry of Tissaphernes and Pharnabazus merely scratched the surface of *satrapal* strife as each *satrap* constantly tried to climb the meritocratic ladder of the Persian political system. In the first two decades of the fourth century, the result was a fickle interventionism that diminished the Persian grip on Asia Minor and the Aegean, undermining the war effort and considerably deprioritizing the Corinthian War in the Persian courts.[1]

Hyland highlights the odd actions of Tiribazus in 392 and judges his alleged overreaction to the anti-Spartan confederacy's naval malaise. Tiribazus ended the peace conference in Sardis by funding a Spartan naval reconstruction; yet with the arrest of Conon and Corinth under siege, neither Athens nor Corinth could muster a serious naval threat. Hyland notes that this 'not only failed to equalize both sides but assisted Sparta in restoring an imbalance that might end the war.'[2]

From 392 to 387, the *satrap* of the influential Lydia was Struthas, an adamant ally of Athens who aggressively obstructed Spartan policy. He was a capable commander and performed admirably in fending off the Spartans in their new campaign in Asia Minor, but in late 388 or early 387 Struthas was replaced by his own predecessor Tiribazus. While Struthas' removal is not explained by the ancient sources, it was perhaps a demotion to the interior of the empire after he had slain the Spartan commander Thibron in battle. Ostensibly, eliminating a powerful enemy during a war would be laudable, but Struthas' reassignment illustrates Artaxerxes' increased desire for peace with Sparta, and for Tiribazus – 'a man who was pro-Spartan and anti-Athenian in sympathy'[3] – to broker the peace talks that would finally end the Corinthian War.

Struthas' replacement was both a rebuke to Athens and a diplomatic olive branch to Persia. Hyland argues that 'Thrasybulus' actions...convinced Artaxerxes that [Struthas'] diplomatic efforts had not restored Athenian respect for Persian authority.'[4] The combination of Athens' foolhardy attempt to abandon Iphicrates' steady conquests in the Greek mainland and instead pursue imperial projects in Asia Minor, together with her alliance with Egypt, placed them squarely in the targets of Persia, their alleged compatriot in the anti-Spartan alliance. However, this was a long time coming; as Hamilton argues, Athens' 'overt aid to Evagoras and to [Hakor] of Egypt, in 389, put her at war, indirectly, with Persia.'[5] Content with the admonishment of Athens, Sparta returned the favour to Persia. Their promotion of the pro-Persian Antalcidas to *navarch* coincided with the reascension of pro-Spartan Tiribazus in Lydia.

However, by vacillating between such extremes, the Persians sent unclear messaging to the Greeks about their imperial intentions. Much like Sparta at the height of her hegemony, the Persians had an unclear mission and vision for their empire. Still worse, after 392, Artaxerxes had now wasted multiple chances for peace with Greece. Further, Artaxerxes had not settled his budding conflict with Egypt. Indeed, Hakor had continued the Egyptian rebellion against Persian rule and his alliance with Evagoras of Cyprus was quickly becoming a much more significant threat to Persia's empire than the Greeks.

While Persia was not in such a difficult situation as Sparta, it was clear that Persia's primary interest in ending the Corinthian War was an admission that they would not accomplish all that they had set out to do. While they would likely maintain their holdings in Asia Minor, it was clear that their *satrapies* there were weaker than they had been before Sparta's invasion in 400. While Persia had successfully pitted Greeks against Greeks and sowed chaos for decades as a result, they had not yet leveraged that achievement into a stronger, more stable frontier for their empire. In fact, the Peloponnesian War and now the Corinthian War had fissured their crucial holdings in Asia Minor and provided a potential opening for a future rebellion or invasion into their empire, and a few decades later the Macedonians would exploit it.

Spartan Factionalism and an Unmoored Diplomacy

Sparta's sending of Antalcidas communicated desperation, which would surely bring a peace treaty but would limit Sparta's chances of gaining favourable terms in the negotiations. Sparta's ambition to liberate and annex the Greeks of Asia Minor while holding their grip on the mainland of Greece was simply not going to be possible in 387. Sparta's best hope was a pragmatic ceasefire and an affirmation of their claims to Athens, Corinth, Argos and Thebes.

In the peace talks of 392, Antalcidas advocated not for a personal empire akin to Lysander's, but instead for an end to hostilities without regard to Spartan claims on Greek territories anywhere north of Boeotia or east of the Peloponnese. The end of the war would almost certainly result in yet another Spartan abandonment of the Greeks of Asia Minor, and with that came some form of a temporary resolution to Sparta's factionalism.

The Lycurgan traditionalists led by Pausanias had dissipated by now. With his exile to Tegea in 395 after the loss at Haliartus, the traditionalists had been absorbed into their imperial rival groups, and Lysander's imperial faction had been swept away by the enthusiasm surrounding Agesilaus' wild successes. Now Agesilaus and his brother Teleutias represented the most powerful imperial faction among the Spartiates. They had refined their vision of empire to a centralized Spartan Empire in Greece, with a friendly relationship with the Greeks of Asia Minor. They would never accede to Persian control over the Ionian coast, but also saw little reason for the Spartans to waste precious resources and manpower controlling it.

Teleutias' speech on Aegina was a clear rejection of any Persian-friendly diplomacy, and his raiding of Piraeus was a call for a new, aggressive Spartan policy against Athens. For Agesilaus and Teleutias, this was the time to press their advantage on Athens and not acquiesce to Persian peace talks.

Straddling these partisan groups was the newcomer Antalcidas. Although purportedly a supporter of Agesilaus and the 'hegemons of Greece' faction, Antalcidas represented a new divide within this group. He was ultimately a pragmatist who saw little reason to die on the hill that was liberty for the Greeks of Asia Minor. He simply wanted the Corinthian War to end, and for Sparta to survive it. He therefore not only split from Agesilaus, with whom there is no recorded conflict prior to 387, but from the imperialist faction entirely. The pragmatist faction had now successfully splintered off from the imperialists and seized control of Spartan diplomacy and her empire with it.

Amid their fractured political situation, Antalcidas sailed to the Ionian coast and met with Tiribazus in late 388. Although it is curiously absent from Xenophon's account, Antalcidas likely travelled all the way to Susa, the capital of the Persian Empire, to negotiate directly with Artaxerxes. The time it took to travel to Susa, east of the Tigris River in the foothills of the Zagros Mountains, allowed for several months of inactivity during the winter of 388–387.

We know precious little of the talks in Sardis, but Antalcidas' diplomatic offerings in 387 were of little substantive difference from the talks in Sardis in 392. Both offered Persian control of Asia Minor, with limited exceptions. It appears that they reached an agreement on ending the Corinthian War, but only if Athens could be subdued, and that was a risk.

With Persia and Sparta now allied again, there was only one belligerent remaining: Athens, and Athens was refusing to back down. Thebes had functionally withdrawn from the war for the past few years, and Corinth was too busy dealing with their unification with Argos and stalemate with Sparta's garrison so near their city walls. Lastly, Argos was too threatened by Sparta and the almost successful attack by Agesipolis. Only Athens was hesitant to see the war's end, as with it would come the end of their hopes of a new empire.

It took a new navy to persuade Athens to the negotiating table. Antalcidas and Artaxerxes made it known that Sparta had not only secured the end of the war, but also military aid against Athens should they remain obstreperous. Antalcidas, keen to realize the terms he had set, quickly set to work fighting the remnant of the Athenian fleet in the Hellespont. He made quick work of it: besieging Abydos, encircling the Athenian fleet and stealing eight Athenian triremes sent as reinforcements. He then added a litany of impressive auxiliaries to his own fleet: twenty triremes from Sicily and several ships from Tiribazus' holdings in Asia Minor.[6] His iron-fisted grip on the Aegean was no illusion, and Xenophon grudgingly notes that it was a brief moment of a Spartan thalassocracy: 'Antalcidas ruled the seas, and was in a position not only to cut off the passage of vessels bound to Athens from the Euxine, but to convoy them into the harbours of Sparta's allies.'[7] Athens, recognizing their perilous predicament, sued for peace. Just as in the Peloponnesian War, it took a Spartan-Persian navy to bring about the end of Athens' empire.

Athens and representatives from the rest of the now-defunct anti-Spartan confederacy travelled to Sardis to complete the King's Peace. Overseeing the talks, the *satrap* Tiribazus read a scroll, complete with the king's royal seal, to the audience:

> The king, Artaxerxes, deems it just that the cities in Asia, with the islands of Clazomenae and Cyprus, should belong to himself; the rest of the Hellenic cities he thinks it just to leave independent, both small and great, with the exception of Lemnos, Imbros, and Scyros, which three are to belong to Athens as of yore. Should any of the parties concerned not accept this peace, I, Artaxerxes, will war against him or them with those who share my views. This will I do by land and by sea, with ships and with money.[8]

It was, of course, an overreach by the Persians. They hardly controlled Cyprus, which was in open rebellion and allied with Egypt, but the rest of the territories were firmly Persian, including the Greek cities of Asia Minor. Once the *ephors*, *Gerousia* and Spartan assembly heard of the terms, they would surely begin the frenzy, but for now Antalcidas had formally ended the Corinthian War.

The Peace's Reception in Sparta and across Greece

Laced with threats about any continued Greek opposition to Spartan supremacy or Persia's imperial border, the King's Peace was a decidedly selfish reversal of

Persia's diplomacy with Greece. Persia abandoned their patronage of the anti-Spartan coalition and reforged an alliance with Sparta in exchange for guaranteed peace and an uncontested claim to Asia Minor. Hyland synthesized Persia's goals in the accords: 'Its object was to offer the Spartans an overwhelming advantage over their rivals in exchange for their obedience…the peace is often interpreted as Artaxerxes' plan to secure the permanent possession of the Anatolian frontier.'

By empowering Sparta, Persia intended to keep a firm grasp on the Aegean without continuing to spend the resources and manpower needed to fund a war effort. The contents of those coffers would instead be directed to Egypt and Cyprus, while Persia trusted Sparta to keep Greece under their heel and away from meddling in the affairs of the Persian Empire. It was a deal that no other Spartan could have managed: Lysander's personal ambitions had disqualified him from Persian benefaction, while Agesilaus' campaigns against Persia did the same. Only the newcomer Antalcidas, successfully navigating pressure from Sparta's *ephors* and from Persia's *satraps*, was appeasing Artaxerxes.

Xenophon left out the details from Antalcidas' summit in Susa given his own allegiance to Agesilaus. Agesilaus' reaction to the treaty, however, was clear. He bitterly rejected Antalcidas' actions on the grounds that they abandoned the Greeks of Asia Minor: 'When the enemy, being desirous of peace, sent an embassy, it was Agesilaus who spoke against the peace, until he had forced the states of Corinth and of Thebes to welcome back those of them who, for Lacedaemon's sake, had suffered banishment.'[9]

Out of reverence for his Spartan patrons, Xenophon shares little more, but it is clear that little had changed by the time Plutarch was writing his *Parallel Lives* a few centuries later. Plutarch wrote:

[Antalcidas] in the most shameful and lawless fashion handed over to the King the Greeks resident in Asia, on whose behalf Agesilaus had waged war. Agesilaus, therefore, could have no part at all in this infamy. Antalcidas was his enemy, and put forth all his efforts to make the peace because he saw that the war enhanced to the utmost the reputation and power of Agesilaus.[10]

Plutarch's evisceration of Antalcidas did not stop there. He notes that the Persian king Artaxerxes 'showed great affection for Antalcidas when he came up to Persia',[11] going so far as to bestow Antalcidas with a wreath of flowers as one might honour a victor in war. The Persians thanked Antalcidas as a co-conspirator, not a diplomatic envoy from the enemy, and Sparta's political factions took notice.

Despite the blatant bias of Xenophon and Plutarch, it is clear that a victory in the Corinthian War would not sate Sparta's appetite for empire or bring resolution to its factionalism. Even Antalcidas' brief reign as naval emperor of the Aegean could not overcome the ire of Sparta's traditionalist and imperial partisans. For the imperialists, the most pressing point was the failure to annex any territory in Asia Minor. Consequently, Hyland proclaims the Corinthian War a tempered victory for Persia:

[The peace] marked a temporary settlement rather than a definitive solution of the problems of international politics in the eastern Mediterranean region...Persia clearly had gained the most through the settlement, for she emerged with undisputed possession of the Greek cities of Asia. Thus the object of Persian policy since 410 had been attained, and in this respect Sparta had lost the war she had begun against Persia in 400 on behalf of those Greeks.[12]

Athens, Thebes, Corinth and Argos had waged a spirited rebellion, but they had failed. With the Spartan-Persian treaty, their future was at the mercy of Sparta, and Persia would no longer serve as their patron or financier. Sparta was now the Persian-appointed guardian of the peace, and each state had to swear fealty in Sparta to both the Spartans and, by extension, the Persians. Worse, the anti-Spartan league had not gained anything other than a firmer position under the boot of Sparta. Hamilton aptly questions the King's Peace and the need for its very existence: 'Which elements of the settlement of 387/86 could not have been effected by diplomacy rather than by force?'[13]

Nevertheless, Xenophon catalogues the strategic successes of Sparta in the Corinthian War that were affirmed in the King's Peace of 387:

They had added Corinth to their alliance; they had obtained the independence of the states of Boeotia at the expense of Thebes, which meant the gratification of an old ambition; and lastly, by calling out the ban in case the Argives refused to evacuate Corinth, they had put a stop to the appropriation of that city by the Argives.[14]

Apart from life under the Spartan boot, the main impact of the war was the dissolution of any existing alliances or *symmachies,* apart from the Peloponnesian League of Sparta. Thebes relinquished their holdings in Boeotia, which functionally ended the Boeotian Confederacy for the time being. They did, however, survive the last few years of the war intact, although infighting and power-grabbing by their *polemarchs* would lead to turmoil in the coming years.

Argos and Corinth were forced to dissolve their unification and Corinth was forced back under Spartan leadership in the Peloponnesian League. In Athens, the peace was about survival; they managed to keep their traditional islands of Lemnos, Imbros and Scyros, but were forced to forfeit the rest of their new imperial gains. The resurgence of Athenian naval power led to a Second Athenian League, a spiritual successor to the Delian League, for a brief two decades beginning in 378.

Most members of the anti-Spartan league fell victim to their domestic *stasis*, except, of course, for Persia whose empire lumbered forward and focused on their more direct rivals in Egypt and Cyprus.

The First 'Common Peace'

The most challenging aspect for modern historians in evaluating the King's Peace is the absence of any meaningful extant sources. Xenophon's *laconophilia* is on full display as he avoids almost all details or content beyond an opportunity to elevate Agesilaus' reputation. Isocrates refers to a physical treaty inscribed on 'stone pillars'[15] in the public squares outside temples in Athens and across Greece, a humiliating display of subjugation to Persia. Persia certainly assumed suzerain status in the proclamation of peace. Diodorus Siculus records the clear threat from Persia against any Greek rebellion: 'upon those who refuse compliance and do not accept these terms I shall make war through the aid of those who consent to them.'[16]

The King's Peace holds a special place as the first of a new type of diplomacy for the fourth-century Greek world, the *Koine Eirene*. Translated as 'Common Peace', *Koine Eirene* was designed to be an end to the ceaseless wars that had ravaged Greece. It was an agreement that all Greek city-states were autonomous and legitimate, and while Sparta would retain its supremacy, she was to seek an equilibrium among all states. Xenophon proclaimed Sparta 'personal overseers and administrators of the autonomy of the states'.[17]

The term was first used by Andocides in the Sardis negotiations of 392, but it would become the precursor to the Theban hegemony and then the League of Corinth, the Macedonian domination over Greece and indeed much of the fourth century in Greece. Katrin Schmidt names the *Koine Eirene* as a movement for Panhellenic identity and political cooperation. She argues that the peace was 'to be valid for all Greeks and therefore indivisible in order to ensure that there was no choice but to live in peace…[it was] incited by the idealistic concept that everybody's autonomy could also induce equality as regards power and danger potential.'[18]

By 355, the notion of a common peace had become an institution across Greece. In Xenophon's *Ways and Means*, a treatise delivered to the Athenian voters encouraging them to make necessary reforms to revive their state and economy, he relies on *Koine Eirene* as the linchpin of a successful city-state:

> But now, if it is evident that, in order to get the full benefit of…revenue [from trade and commerce], peace is an indispensable condition – if that is plain, I say, the question suggests itself, would it not be worthwhile to appoint a board to act as guardians of peace? Since no doubt the election of such a magistracy would enhance the charm of this city in the eyes of the whole world, and add largely to the number of our visitors. But if any one is disposed to take the view that by adopting a persistent peace policy, this city will be shorn of her power, that her glory will dwindle and her good name be forgotten throughout the length and breadth of Hellas.[19]

Perhaps the most striking feature of the King's Peace of 387 was its multilateral status. Instead of being concerned with the two suzerains of Persia and Sparta, the treaty contained terms for all levels of the Greek hierarchy and not just the top city-states. Unlike the various Athenian-Spartan treaties of the fifth century, Antalcidas' peace integrated the vassal states of each city-state and designed terms around them, even if in broad strokes. Accordingly, the end of the Corinthian War restored an original vision for the Greek *polis*: a community of citizens in an urban centre and surrounding countryside who were organized around shared cultural, political and economic activity. The fifth century had warped this definition of the *polis* into a model of citizenship under a hegemonic power such as Athens or Sparta.

The King's Peace especially returned Greece to the original ideal of the *polis* and the city-state via its latter terms: the dissolving of all *symmachies* and alliances. This was supposed to ensure that no renegades would band together against Sparta, but in so doing it acknowledged, for the first time, the significance of the autonomy of each individual *polis*. The treaty of 387 protected and ensured the existence of each city-state as an independent entity. In this way, it fulfilled the earliest Spartan mission against Athens. Athenian empire-building had been the first Greek attempt at homogenizing Greek political and economic identity, and Sparta's initial rebellion against it in the Peloponnesian War had been proclaimed as a fight for liberty for the Greek city-states. Despite becoming the perpetrators themselves, one might say, quite generously, that Sparta finally realized that mission in 387 after failing to do so in 404.

Conclusion

The Repercussions of the Corinthian War

Sixteen years after the King's Peace, in 371, the Theban king Epaminondas defeated a Spartan force in a village outside Thebes named Leuctra. Although they outnumbered the enemy and were still effective warriors, the Spartan army at Leuctra was the compounded result of decades of Spartan population decline, overextension of their empire, internal factionalism and dysfunction in Sparta, Spartan maltreatment of allies and evolution in military strategy. The Spartan hoplites – primarily *neodamodes* given the lengthy decline of Spartiates – were outmanoeuvred and outstrategized. A new era of Greek hegemony had begun, with Thebes at its head. At long last, the Spartan Empire officially ended.

The Corinthian War had remade Greek diplomacy and military tactics. The Battle of Leuctra was little more than a distillation of Sparta's decayed empire and its consequences across Greece. In retrospect, the Corinthian War was the half-life of the Spartan hegemony. Despite the victory, Sparta lacked the imperial strength and political unity to hold its empire. In the year following the King's Peace, Sparta responded by bringing vengeance on the belligerents of the Corinthian War, especially against Mantinea in 386.[1] However, in their pursuit of retribution, Sparta relied on their historic hoplite strategies, peppered with some inclusion of skirmishers and peltasts. The Thebans meanwhile capitalized on new military developments such as the rise of peltasts, the companionship of their elite special force unit the Sacred Band, and uneven combat such Epaminondas' innovative oblique formation.

Notably, the most important Spartan military commander was absent from the Battle of Leuctra. In the years since the Corinthian War, Agesilaus had wisely perceived the decline of Sparta and her empire and, in an act of protest, refused to join the Spartan army at Leuctra. Although crippled by a serious illness later in his life, Agesilaus' protest against the battle was a cautious action following a dispute with the Theban king Epaminondas. This argument over justice and common peace was the pinnacle of the Theban hatred harboured by Agesilaus for so long. Even after the Corinthian War, Agesilaus – still despising the Thebans – wished to break apart the Boeotian Confederacy in addition to the Corinthian-Argive union.

The steady decline in population compounded with an amplified interventionist foreign policy following the King's Peace in 387, which mixed poorly with resurgent powers in Thebes and Athens. Sparta's revenge-seeking against Mantinea portended their treatment of the rest of the anti-Spartan allies as they tightened their grip militarily but lost control diplomatically. The other Greek city-states came to be defined as pro-Spartan or anti-Spartan. Most city-states continued their *stasis* with a cadre of democrats duelling for power against oligarchs. For better or worse, Sparta had made themselves the bellwether of the Greek world and tied their fate to Sparta's own internal malaise. Fornis uses Athens as a key example of the Greek response to the peace, arguing that all Athenian and Greek diplomatic policies in the years following the Corinthian War were 'now tethered to the King's Peace clause that dictated respect for the autonomy of the *poleis*…that would end up taking shape in the Second Athenian League.'[2]

As Sparta went, so did fourth-century Greece, and as the Spartan state declined, so did the rest of the Greek world.

The 'Twilight' of Sparta's Empire

Yet why proclaim, as this book's title has, that the Corinthian War was the 'twilight' of Sparta's empire when the years 395–387 fall firmly within the centre of Spartan ascendancy? It is because the Spartan 'victory' in the Corinthian War came at the deep cost of forfeiting her position as the standard-bearer of Greece. In their diplomatic aggression and appropriation of Athenian and Persian imperial practices, the Spartans won territories and holdings but lost the support of the other Greek city-states and created a litany of problems for Greece and for their own hegemony: the abandonment of the Greeks of Asia Minor, the permittance of Athens to revive their independence and naval presence, the sustained political factionalism in Sparta, the selfish and tortuous relationship with Persia and the facade of autonomy for the Greek city-states. Sparta's supremacy from 387 to 371 was a series of mixed results in their multitude of overzealous military and diplomatic actions.

The most enduring impact during those years was Sparta's stark departure from their Lycurgan roots. Despite Spartan decline, the Thebans could not successfully conquer Laconia following Leuctra. Plutarch credits Agesilaus for his singular ability to bind Sparta together under such circumstances. Plutarch ends his analysis, however, with a helpful theory on the fall of Sparta's empire: 'For to a civil polity best arranged for peace and virtue and unanimity they had attached empires and sovereignties won by force, not one of which Lycurgus thought needful for a city that was to live in happiness; and therefore they fell.'[3]

Such a position indicates the failure of the Lycurgan traditionalists in Sparta. With the passing of King Pausanias, this faction faded into obscurity before the Corinthian War even ended. While they enjoyed ostensible influence, Sparta changed dramatically as they more wholly embraced the concept of a Spartan Empire. The traditionalists' path was now impassable; as Hamilton notes, 'the decades between 405 and 386 had shown their effort to turn back to ancient paths a fruitless one.'[4] The imperialist factions, meanwhile, fused together after the King's Peace. Agesilaus and those who wanted a Spartan Empire – be it either just in Greece or across the Aegean world – laid aside their differences to confront their new rival: Antalcidas and the pragmatists. In the judgement of the imperialists, Antalcidas had forfeited Spartan leadership to Persia in the foolish name of peace. Knowing that undoing the peace would fracture Sparta even further, Agesilaus and the imperialists worked to maximize the now smaller Spartan Empire and strengthen their grip on Greece. Antalcidas remained influential and became an *ephor*, but he had spent all his capital. He was from 387 limited in his diplomatic and political range, and accomplished little more than laconic witticism in his remaining years.

However, Antalcidas still had some laconic phrases in him before fading into history. The internal partisanship continued to plague Spartan imperial health during the decades following the Corinthian War. Antalcidas specifically blamed Agesilaus and his anti-Theban sentiments. For years, the mutual hatred between Agesilaus and the Thebans had simmered, but Antalcidas went so far as to blame Agesilaus for empowering the Thebans by giving them a unifying goal:

> When Agesilaus was wounded in battle by the Thebans, Antalcidas said to his face, 'You have your just reward for the lessons in fighting you have given to that people who had no desire to fight and no knowledge even of fighting.' For it appeared that they had been made warlike by the continual campaigns of Agesilaus against them.[5]

Apart from the personal animosity between Agesilaus and Antalcidas, such a criticism conveys the deep divide between the new pragmatists of Sparta and the imperialists led by Agesilaus. Where they had once been under the same umbrella of imperialism, the split between their new partisan groups was now irreversible and influencing new policy. Antalcidas' words were likely also a critique of Sparta's inability to capitalize on Thebes' own *stasis*. A decade before Leuctra, Agesilaus campaigned in Boeotia and successfully occupied the Theban acropolis with the support of pro-Spartan oligarchs. A contingent of anti-Spartan Theban aristocrats fled the city to Athens, among them one Pelopidas. The statesman was the architect of Thebes' rise, and his years in Athens equipped him with the resources and networking needed to expel the oligarchs condoned by Sparta and replace Thebes' government with a democracy. For Antalcidas, this was a squandering of Sparta's diplomatic strength: they thrived on cultivating oligarchy-democracy civil strife in their rivals, and Agesilaus' short-sightedness directly led to failing to do so in their most critical rival.

However, factionalism was of course not the only hindrance to Spartan flourishing. In his post-mortem of the Spartan hegemony, Diodorus Siculus takes an intentional break from his intended objectivity to deliver a strongly-worded censure of the decline of Sparta:

> For who would not judge men to be deserving of accusation who had received from their ancestors a supremacy with such firm foundations and that too preserved by the high spirit of their ancestors for over five hundred years, and now beheld it, as the [Spartans] of that time did, overthrown by their own folly? And this is easy to understand. For the men who had lived before them won the glory they had by many labours and great struggles, treating their subjects the while fairly and humanely; but their successors used their allies roughly and harshly, stirring up, besides, unjust and insolent wars against the Greeks, and so it is quite to be understood that they lost their rule because of their own acts of folly. For the hatred of those they had wronged found in their disasters an opportunity to retaliate upon their aggressors, and they who had been unconquered from their ancestors' time were now attended by such contempt as, it stands to reason, must befall those who obliterate the virtues that characterized their ancestors. This explains why the Thebans, who for many generations had been subjects of their superiors, when they defeated them to everyone's surprise, became supreme among the Greeks, but the [Spartans], when once they had lost the supremacy, were never at any time able to recover the high position enjoyed by their ancestors.[6]

Diodorus' evaluation of Sparta's decline being primarily due to the abuse of their allies rings true. Roughly 2,500 years later, George Forrest came to the same conclusion, arguing that Sparta's 'grotesque abuse of the principle of autonomy'[7] among her allies after 387 was the deciding factor in her inability to recover at all from Leuctra. Sparta simply never intended to support the *Koine Eirene* of 387. For them, the peace that ended the war was instead a reset to the earlier centuries when Sparta's *symmachy* over the other Peloponnesian city-states was nigh unchallenged. In 382, the council of the Peloponnesian League, voting on whether to begin the First Olynthian War, acutely demonstrated this point. When Sparta made known their desires to wage war after open debate, the rest of the allies voted in favour simply to appease Sparta.[8] This tentative acquiescence by the Peloponnesian League was one of the final recordings of debate in Peloponnesian League policy; while the league would survive for another century it would no longer include the consensus of Sparta's allies.

Diodorus' secondary argument, however, is also worthy of consideration. He suggests that the Spartans of the fourth century had merely inherited their supremacy and had not won it through the grinding struggle of the previous few centuries. Over the years, that comfort – as far as a Spartan citizen could be labelled comfortable – corroded the Spartan grip on the helots and their foreign policy. With that comfort came internal division, the likes of which had not been seen since the turmoil of the butcher's knife that killed Lycurgus' father. Sparta's empire lasted only as long as they were under siege and at constant war with the helots and the Peloponnesus. The victory in the Peloponnesian War had caused the worst effect possible: a comfortable Spartan state.

This thesis frames with Paul Rahe's assessment of the 'one grave defect'[9] of the Spartan state: its system and order was predicated on an insular Peloponnesus. Until the middle of the sixth century, Sparta was able to dominate the Peloponnesus given their military strength, intricate social and political system and dominance of their neighbours in Messenia and beyond, but once the Peloponnesus became more involved with broader Greek and then Aegean and then the Mediterranean world, Sparta's system could not sustain the pressure.

Where Diodorus and Forrest depart from my argument is their overlooking of the importance of the Corinthian War and not the Theban-Spartan War as the nexus of Sparta's failed empire. If nothing else, the Corinthian War had two devastating impacts on Sparta's imperial ambitions: the accelerated attrition of Spartan manpower and the shift of Sparta's diplomatic attention away from the Aegean world and exclusively to the Greek mainland. Without the former, Sparta lacked the capacity to face innovative military threats and to keep their unhappy allies in line with garrisons or blockades. Without the latter, Sparta lost their financial patron in Persia and with it their ability to distract Athens, Thebes, Corinth and the other city-states with another antagonist.

By the time of Thebes' ascendancy, those disgruntled allies in the Peloponnesian League relished Sparta's decline. Perhaps the singular reason why Sparta had no ability to recover from their loss at Leuctra was their *oliganthropia*. As the decline of Spartan males continued in the latter fifth and early fourth centuries, Leuctra was the smashing prior to Leuctra; there were slightly fewer than 1,000 Spartiates remaining. After losing 400 Spartiates at Leuctra, the Spartan state counted only around 600 male citizens and fewer than 2,000 *perioeci*. It was a far cry from their armies of 8,000 or more strong hoplites at the height of their military power. The addition of new citizens in the *neodamodes* and freshly-liberated helots was unable to make even a dent in the rapid deterioration of Sparta's citizenship and hoplites.

After Leuctra, the Thebans accordingly marched straight into the Peloponnesian Peninsula almost unopposed and ravaged Laconia for the first time in Sparta's history. A foreign invader saw the Eurotas River for the first time in Spartan history. Within years, the major tenets of Spartan society broke down: the Peloponnesian League, the *agoge*, their subjugation of the helots, their barracks and dining halls and their Lycurgan identity at large. All that was distinctively Spartan soon became vaguely Greek, then Hellenistic and then Roman.

When, then, did the Spartan hegemony truly end? Polybius' dating of the Spartan hegemony's demise to their loss at Cnidus has merit, and at the least indicated a major turning-point in the Corinthian War.[10] The phase of the war after Cnidus and the failed peace talks of 392 could be seen as a second conflict entirely, and one that was predicated on Sparta's lessened imperial position. They no longer held Greece with an unchallenged and firm grip, and only through the benevolence of Persia did they regain any substantial naval presence or diplomatic grip on Asia Minor.

I propose a longer view of Spartan hegemony. Sparta's supremacy over Greece effectively emerged during the waning years of the Peloponnesian War between 411 and 404, and lasted until the challenge of Thebes in the mid-370s. The Corinthian War was not nestled chronologically in the middle of her hegemony, but instead the catalyst that brought about the end of the empire. By the time of the Battle of Leuctra, Thebes' supplanting of Sparta was a formality: the Spartans could still fight well, but had no means of actually holding their empire.

Sparta's expansionism was originally in the name of self-preservation against their Athenian foe, but gradually became necessary to continue their state. That expansionist policy gave them a taste of empire by 404, and they looked to overlay the Athenian imperial infrastructure onto a Lycurgan state that with its necessary agricultural, helot-fuelled system could not maintain an overseas empire. While the epitome of a Greek *polis* and hoplite army, Sparta became a befuddled mess of political factionalism and undeveloped imperial leadership from the moment that they stood alone atop of the Greek world.

Also the Spartans never recovered from their 'victory' in the Corinthian War. Despite the prevalence of Persian infighting, especially in their western *satrapies*, the Persians had effectively won the war. Sparta had lost far more than they gained in the Corinthian War. By the time of Philip of Macedon's conquest of Greece five decades later, they were a shell of their former selves. Philip's victory was important in its unprecedented diplomatic and military accomplishments, but the Spartans survived the Macedonians. They were sequestered away in Laconia, slowly shrinking back amid their population decline and crippled by the limitations of their agrarian structure that could no longer hold citizens or helots. The Romans eventually subdued the Spartans in the second century, but after two centuries of subjugation under Theban and Macedonian rule, the Spartans mustered a resistance far from their glory days. The trajectory of the fall of their empire was found from the hegemony's very beginning, but it was their overextended empire, oppression of Greek city-states and the results of the Corinthian War that accelerated their decline.

Character List

Agesilaus II – The renowned king of Sparta who invaded Persia and led many successful battles in the Corinthian War and the later Theban-Spartan War.

Agesipolis – A Spartan king who took the throne as a young boy shortly after the dawn of the Corinthian War.

Antalcidas – A Spartan diplomat who brokered the end of the Corinthian War.

Artaxerxes II – The king of the Achaemenid Persians during the Corinthian War. Endured a bloody civil war with his brother, Cyrus the Younger.

Cinadon – A Spartan reformer who tried to overthrow the Spartan government in 399.

Conon – An Athenian admiral who was exiled following failures during the Peloponnesian War. He sailed for the Persians before a resounding return to Athens during the Corinthian War.

Critias – An Athenian aristocrat and student of Socrates. He became a leading member of the Thirty Tyrants in Athens.

Cyrus the Younger – A prince of Persia who became close with Lysander and the Spartans at the end of the Peloponnesian War. He failed to win the throne after a war with his brother, Artaxerxes II.

Dercylidas – A Spartan general who fought in Asia Minor against the Persians.

Diodorus Siculus – A first century AD Roman historian of Greek heritage. Diodorus Siculus, meaning 'of Sicily', wrote a comprehensive history of the Greco-Roman world that compiled and quoted many sources now lost to history.

Evagoras of Cyprus – The king of Cyprus, he persistently aimed to destabilize Persian rule in the Aegean and over Cyprus. He sheltered Conon for many years, funded anti-Persian activity, and eventually rebelled against Persia.

Herodotus – The 'Father of History' who first wrote a detailed narrative of the world as he knew it. He was most famous for the history of the Persian Wars that he wrote after allegedly traveling to Persia, Babylon and Egypt, and interviewing witnesses from about 445 to 430 BC.

Iphicrates – An Athenian military commander who transformed Greek warfare with his *peltasts*, or light-armoured fighters. He won at the Battle of Lechaeum in resounding fashion, and became a leading political player in Athens.

Lycurgus – The mythical founder of Sparta, who instituted Sparta's military machine.

Lysander – A Spartan general and politician. The most influential Spartan at the end of the Peloponnesian War, he installed harmosts and decarchies across Greece, becoming perhaps the most powerful man in the Mediterranean world. His attempt at becoming king failed, however, and he was limited by a rivalry with Agesilaus until he was killed in battle at Haliartus.

Pausanias – A Spartan king who opposed Lysander and led the traditionalist faction of Spartan politics.

Peisander – A Spartan admiral who was defeated at the Battle of Cnidus in 394.

Pharnabazus – A Persian satrap in Asia Minor who fought Sparta in both the Peloponnesian and Corinthian Wars.

Plutarch – A second century AD Roman historian of Greek heritage. He wrote a famous set of biographies called *Parallel Lives* that chronicled the great figures of Greece and Rome. He included Agesilaus, Artaxerxes II, and Lysander among those biographies.

Teleutias – The Spartan admiral, and brother of Agesilaus, who burned the Athenian harbour in 389 BC.

Thrasybulus – An Athenian general and politician who lead the rebellion to restore democracy against the Spartan-installed Thirty Tyrants in Athens. Later served as a commander in the Corinthian War.

Thucydides – An Athenian general and historian, he wrote *The History of the Peloponnesian War* chronicling the narrative of the great war between Athens and Sparta, which Themistocles helped prepare the Athenians for. His history writing is more measured than Herodotus's, and he quotes many historians whose work has been destroyed.

Tirabazus – A Persian satrap in Asia Minor who worked with Antalcidas to negotiate the end of the Corinthian War, first in 392 and then successfully in 387.

Tissaphernes – A Persian satrap in Asia Minor during the Corinthian War. He fought against Agesilaus and the Spartans before being executed on the order of the Persian emperor for his shortcomings.

Xenophon – An Athenian citizen, educated by Socrates himself, who became a mercenary fighting for Sparta for much of his life. Xenophon went on to publish many influential writings, including *Hellenica* and *Agesilaus*, from which much of our information on the Corinthian War comes.

Notes

Introduction
1. Thucydides, *The History of the Peloponnesian War*, trans. Richard Crawley (Cambridge, Harvard University Press, 1874), 1.83.
2. Thucydides, *The History of the Peloponnesian War*, 1.23.
3. Gibbon, Edward, *The History of the Decline and Fall of the Roman Empire* (London, Penguin Classics, 2011), 16.4.
4. Xenophon, *Hellenica*, trans. H.G. Dakyns (London and New York, Macmillan and Co., 1891), 3.5.12.
5. Aristotle, *Politics*, trans. Benjamin Jowett (Oxford, Clarendon Press, 1885), 1271b.
6. Cawkwell, George, 'The King's Peace', *The Classical Quarterly* 31, no. 1 (1981), 79.
7. Plutarch, *Moralia*, 'On the Glory of the Athenians', trans. Frank Cole Babbitt (Cambridge, Harvard University Press, 1936), 1.
8. Plutarch, *Parallel Lives*, 'Life of Lycurgus', trans. Bernadotte Perrin (Cambridge, Harvard University Press, 1914), 2.2.
9. Plutarch, *Life of Lycurgus*, 2.2.
10. Herodotus, *The Histories*, trans. George Rawlinson (New York, Charles Scribner's Sons, 1897), 1.65.
11. Plutarch, *Moralia*, 'The Sayings of the Spartans', trans. Frank Cole Babbitt (Cambridge, Harvard University Press, 1931), *Antalcidas*, 7.
12. Aristotle, *Politics*, 1271b.
13. Thucydides, *The History of the Peloponnesian War*, 4.80.3.
14. Rahe, Paul A., *The Spartan Regime: Its Character, Origins, and Grand Strategy* (New Haven, Yale University Press, 2016), 7.
15. Thucydides, *The History of the Peloponnesian War*, 1.10.
16. Aristotle, *Politics*, 2.1265b.
17. Aristotle, *Politics*, 2.1265b.
18. Isocrates, *Nicocles or the Cyprians*, 3.24, trans. author's own, Greek text from the Perseus Digital Library Project, Tufts University.
19. Xenophon, *Polity of the Lacedaemonians*, 1.1, trans. author's own.
20. Hamilton, Charles D., *Sparta's Bitter Victories: Politics and Diplomacy in the Corinthian War* (Ithaca, NY, Cornell University Press, 1979), 41.
21. Thucydides, *The History of the Peloponnesian War*, 1.19.1.
22. Bolmarcich, Sarah, 'Thucydides 1.19.1 and the Peloponnesian League', *Greek, Roman and Byzantine Studies* 45 (2005), 7.
23. Xenophon, *Hellenica*, 2.2.20.
24. Herodotus, *The Histories*, 3.90–94. The precise figure of 15.8 per cent contains taxes from Cappadocia, Syria and beyond, regions not typically associated with Greece.
25. Herodotus, *The Histories*, 8.1 and 8.43.
26. Millender, Ellen, 'The Spartans "at Sea"', *Historika* 5 (2015), 299.
27. Thucydides, *The History of the Peloponnesian War*, 1.23.
28. Thucydides, *The History of the Peloponnesian War*, 1.80.3–1.81.4.

Chapter One

1. Xenophon, *Hellenica*, 2.2.23, trans. author's own.
2. Diodorus Siculus, *The Library of History: Volume VI: Books 14–15.19*, trans. C.H. Oldfather (Harvard University Press, 1954), 14.3.1 and 14.10.1. Diodorus Siculus credits Lysander with simply executing orders from the *ephors*, but it is clear that his personal involvement and profit exceed the *ephors'* directive to limit Athenian democratic influence.
3. Xenophon, *Hellenica*, 3.1.4.
4. Xenophon, *Hellenica*, 2.3.7.
5. Cartledge, Paul, *The Spartans: The World of the Warrior-Heroes of Ancient Greece* (New York, Vintage Books, 2004), 209.
6. Plutarch, *Parallel Lives*, 'Life of Lysander', trans. Bernadotte Perrin (Cambridge, Harvard University Press, 1914), 6.1–2.
7. Plutarch, *Life of Lysander*, 5.5.
8. Plutarch, *Life of Lysander*, 5.3.
9. Xenophon, *Polity of the Lacedaemonians*, trans. H.G. Dakyns (London and New York, Macmillan and Co., 1897), 14.
10. Thucydides, *The History of the Peloponnesian War*, 1.128–130.
11. Diodorus Siculus, *The Library of History*, 14.10.2.
12. Plutarch, *Life of Lysander*, 2.3.
13. Thucydides, *The History of the Peloponnesian War*, 8.5.
14. Thucydides, *The History of the Peloponnesian War*, 8.46.
15. Thucydides, *The History of the Peloponnesian War*, 8.46.
16. Xenophon, *Hellenica*, 1.1.26.
17. For an excellent analysis of the rivalry of Tissaphernes and Pharnabazus and the state of Persian politics and interventionism in the Greek world, see Hyland, John O., *Persian Interventions: The Achaemenid Empire, Athens & Sparta, 450–386 BCE* (Baltimore, Johns Hopkins University Press, 2018), Chapter 5, 'The King's Navy and the Failure of Satrapal Intervention', and Chapter 6, 'Cyrus the Younger and Spartan Victory'.
18. Xenophon, *Hellenica*, 1.4.3.
19. Xenophon, *Anabasis*, trans. H.G. Dakyns (London and New York, Macmillan and Co., 1891), 1.9.
20. Xenophon, *Hellenica*, 1.6.3–7.
21. Xenophon, *Hellenica*, 2.1.7.
22. Xenophon, *Hellenica*, 2.1.14.
23. Plutarch, *Life of Lysander*, 9.1–2.
24. Aristotle, *Politics*, 1270a.
25. Aristotle, *Politics*, 1269a, trans. author's own.
26. Xenophon, *Hellenica*, 3.3.6.
27. Diodorus Siculus, *The Library of History*, 11.63.1.
28. Thucydides, *The History of the Peloponnesian War*, 1.102.
29. Figueira, Thomas J., 'Population Patterns in Late Archaic and Classical Sparta', *Transactions of the American Philological Association (1974-)*, 116 (1986), 212–3.
30. Herodotus, *The Histories*, 9.10.2.
31. Herodotus, *The Histories*, 9.10.2.
32. Herodotus, *The Histories*, 9.10.2.
33. Herodotus, *The Histories*, 9.10.2.
34. It is probable that Brasidas intentionally freed only Laconian and not Messenian helots, the latter of whom were far more likely to revolt. For a closer examination see

Chambers, James T., 'On Messenian and Laconian Helots in the Fifth Century B.C.', *The Historian* 40, no. 2 (1978), 283.
35. Thucydides, *The History of the Peloponnesian War*, 5.34.
36. Doran, Timothy D., 'Demographic Fluctuation and Institutional Response in Sparta' (Berkeley, University of California at Berkeley, 2011), 4–11. Dissertation, retrieved from https://escholarship.org/uc/item/3pk467b6
37. Plutarch, *Life of Lysander*, 2.1.
38. Plutarch, *Life of Lysander*, 24.2.
39. Diodorus Siculus, *The Library of History*, 14.13.2.
40. Diodorus Siculus, *The Library of History*, 14.13.8.
41. Aristotle, *Politics*, 1306b.
42. Xenophon, *Hellenica*, 3.3.11.
43. Hamilton, *Sparta's Bitter Victories*, 326–7.
44. Hamilton, *Sparta's Bitter Victories*, 326. While Agesilaus campaigned and had many allies and friends in Asia Minor, his imperial vision more closely aligned with Agis than Lysander. He desired liberty for the Greeks of Asia, but not necessarily Spartan colonialism.
45. Hamilton, *Sparta's Bitter Victories*, 326.

Chapter Two
1. Plutarch, *Life of Lysander*, 13.2.
2. Xenophon, *Hellenica*, 2.2.2.
3. Strauss, Barry, *Athens after the Peloponnesian War: Class, Faction and Policy 403–386 B.C.*, Routledge Revivals edition (Ithaca, Cornell University Press, 2014), 73.
4. Xenophon, *Hellenica*, 1.5.18–20.
5. Hornblower, Simon, *The Greek World 479–323 BCE* (London, Routledge, 2011), 203. These statistics are similar to the proposal in Kagan, Donald, *The Fall of the Athenian Empire* (Ithaca, Cornell University Press, 1987).
6. Xenophon, *Ways and Means*, trans. H.G. Dakyns (London and New York, Macmillan and Co., 1897), 2.1–2.
7. Diogenes Laertius, 'Socrates' in *Lives of Eminent Philosophers*, trans. R.D. Hicks (Cambridge, Harvard University Press, 1925), 2.26.
8. Strauss, *Athens after the Peloponnesian War*, 122.
9. Strauss, *Athens after the Peloponnesian War*, 45.
10. Strauss, *Athens after the Peloponnesian War*, 12.
11. Pseudo-Xenophon, *Constitution of the Athenians*, 2.2.5, trans. author's own. Greek text from the Perseus Digital Library Project, Tufts University.
12. Aristophanes, *Ecclesiazusae* (or *The Assemblywomen*), trans. Eugene O'Neill (New York, Random House, 1938), 175–179.
13. Cornelius Nepos, *Lives of Eminent Commanders*, trans. John Selby Watson (London, Henry G. Bohn, 1853), Lysander 1.
14. Xenophon, *Hellenica*, 1.5.18–20.
15. Isocrates, *Evagoras*, 9.5, trans. author's own. Greek text from the Perseus Digital Library Project, Tufts University.
16. Plutarch, *Life of Lysander*, 13.2.
17. Xenophon, *Hellenica*, 2.2.2.
18. Xenophon, *Hellenica*, 2.2.5–6.
19. Xenophon, *Hellenica*, 2.2.8–10.

20. Plutarch, *Life of Lysander*, 15.2.
21. Xenophon, *Hellenica*, 2.2.19.
22. Plutarch, *Life of Lysander*, 15.3.
23. Xenophon, *Hellenica*, 2.2.20.
24. Xenophon, *Hellenica*, 2.2.20.
25. Xenophon, *Hellenica*, 2.2.21.
26. Plutarch, *Life of Lysander*, 16.1.
27. Xenophon, *Hellenica*, 2.2.20.
28. Diodorus Siculus, *The Library of History*, 14.3.7.
29. Aristotle, *The Constitution of Athens*, trans. Frederic G. Kenyon (London, G. Bell, 1891), 34.
30. Xenophon, *Hellenica*, 2.3.1.
31. Diodorus Siculus, *The Library of History*, 14.3.7.
32. Aristotle, *The Athenian Constitution*, 35.
33. Xenophon, *Hellenica*, 2.3.12–18 and Aristotle, *The Athenian Constitution*, 35.
34. Xenophon, *Hellenica*, 2.3.12.
35. Xenophon, *Hellenica*, 2.3.17.
36. Diodorus Siculus, *The Library of History*, 14.4.4.
37. Xenophon, *Hellenica*, 2.3.53.
38. Cornelius Nepos, *Lives of Eminent Commanders*, Thrasybulus 2.
39. Cornelius Nepos, *Lives of Eminent Commanders*, Thrasybulus 1.
40. Plutarch, *Life of Lysander*, 21.2.
41. Cornelius Nepos, *Lives of Eminent Commanders*, Thrasybulus 2.
42. Xenophon, *Hellenica*, 2.4.28.
43. Xenophon, *Hellenica*, 2.4.29.
44. Xenophon, *Hellenica*, 2.4.33.
45. Xenophon, *Hellenica*, 2.4.33.
46. Xenophon, *Hellenica*, 2.4.43.

Chapter Three
1. Diodorus Siculus, *The Library of History*, 14.6.1–3.
2. Xenophon, *Hellenica*, 2.4.30.
3. Pausanias, *Description of Greece*, trans. W.H.S. Jones and H.A. Ormerod (Cambridge, Harvard University Press and London, William Heinemann Ltd, 1918), 3.5.2.
4. Pausanias, *Description of Greece*, 3.5.2.
5. The date of the Elean War is unclear. Robert D. Strassler proposes 402 (Strassler, Robert D., *The Landmark Xenophon's Hellenica* (New York, Anchor Books, 2010), 92, while C.D. Hamilton proposes a later date of 400 (Hamilton, *Sparta's Bitter Victories*, 109). I have chosen 401 as the exact date is not as critical as the flow of events from 403 to 397.
6. Xenophon, *Hellenica*, 3.2.24.
7. Xenophon, *Hellenica*, 3.2.23.
8. Xenophon, *Hellenica*, 3.2.26.
9. Diodorus Siculus, *The Library of History*, 17.4.6.
10. Xenophon, *Anabasis*, 1.10.
11. Xenophon, *Hellenica*, 2.3.8–9.
12. Plutarch, *Life of Lysander*, 17.1.
13. Plutarch, *Life of Lysander*, 19.4.

14. Plutarch, *Life of Lysander*, 20.3 and Cornelius Nepos, *Lives of Eminent Commanders*, Lysander 4.
15. Plutarch, *Life of Lysander*, 19.1.
16. Plutarch, *Life of Lysander*, 19.1.
17. Xenophon, *Hellenica*, 3.3.3.
18. Plutarch, *Parallel Lives*, 'Life of Agesilaus', trans. Bernadotte Perrin (Cambridge, Harvard University Press, 1914), 2.2.
19. Plutarch, *Life of Lycurgus*, 22.6.
20. Plutarch, *Life of Lysander*, 22.3.
21. Xenophon, *Agesilaus*, trans. H.G. Dakyns (London and New York, Macmillan and Co., 1894), 1.1.
22. Xenophon, *Hellenica*, 3.3.6.
23. Plutarch, *Life of Agesilaus*, 5.3.
24. Xenophon, *Hellenica*, 3.1.3.
25. Hyland, John O., *Persian Interventions: The Achaemenid Empire, Athens & Sparta, 450–386 BCE* (Baltimore, Johns Hopkins University Press, 2018), 128–9.
26. Xenophon, *Hellenica*, 3.1.4.
27. Xenophon, *Hellenica*, 3.1.19–20.
28. Xenophon, *Hellenica*, 3.1.8.
29. Xenophon, *Agesilaus*, 1.8.
30. Xenophon, *Agesilaus*, 1.6–7.
31. Xenophon, *Agesilaus*, 1.6–7.
32. Xenophon, *Hellenica*, 3.4.4.
33. Plutarch, *Life of Agesilaus*, 6.6.
34. Pausanias, *Description of Greece*, 3.9.3. For an excellent analysis of these negotiations see Hamilton, *Sparta's Bitter Victories*, 152–153.
35. Plutarch, *Life of Agesilaus*, 7.1.
36. Plutarch, *Life of Lysander*, 23.5.
37. Plutarch, *Life of Lysander*, 23.8–9.
38. Xenophon, *Hellenica*, 3.4.12.
39. Xenophon, *Hellenica*, 3.4.16–19.
40. Xenophon, *Hellenica*, 3.4.17.
41. Xenophon and Plutarch both attribute Tissaphernes' death to Artaxerxes (Xenophon, *Hellenica*, 3.4.25 and Plutarch, *Life of Agesilaus*, 10.4) while Diodorus Siculus pinpoints the queen mother as the primary schemer in retaliation for the death of Cyrus the Younger (Diodorus Siculus, *The Library of History*, 14.80.6–8).
42. Xenophon, *Hellenica*, 3.5.1.
43. Xenophon, *Hellenica*, 3.5.1.
44. Xenophon, *Hellenica*, 3.5.3–4 and Diodorus Siculus, *The Library of History*, 14.81.1.
45. Xenophon, *Hellenica*, 3.5.5.
46. Forrest, W.G., *A History of Sparta: 950–192 BC* (London, W.W. Norton & Co., 1968), 123.

Chapter Four
1. Xenophon, *Hellenica*, 3.5.5.
2. Plutarch, *Life of Lysander*, 24.2.
3. Plutarch, *Parallel Lives*, 'Comparison of Lysander and Sulla', trans. Bernadotte Perrin (Harvard University Press, 1914), 1.1.
4. Xenophon, *Hellenica*, 3.5.6.

5. Hamilton, *Sparta's Bitter Victories*, 143.
6. Hamilton, *Sparta's Bitter Victories*, 143, referencing *Oxyrhynchus Hellenica*, 16.3.
7. Pascual, José, 'Theban Victory at Haliartos (395 BC)', *Gladius XXVII* (2007), 41.
8. Pascual, 'Theban Victory at Haliartos (395 BC)', 41.
9. Pascual, 'Theban Victory at Haliartos (395 BC)', 41.
10. Hamilton, *Sparta's Bitter Victories*, 143.
11. Pascual, 'Theban Victory at Haliartos (395 BC)', 41–42.
12. Plutarch, *Life of Lysander*, 28.1.
13. Pascual, 'Theban Victory at Haliartos (395 BC)', 42.
14. See Pascual, 'Theban Victory at Haliartos (395 BC)' 44 for a more detailed examination of the Boeotian battle strategy.
15. Xenophon, *Hellenica*, 3.5.8–10.
16. Xenophon, *Hellenica*, 3.5.10–11.
17. Xenophon, *Hellenica*, 3.5.12.
18. Beck, Hans, 'Thebes, the Boeotian League, and the Rise of Federalism' in P.A. Bernardini, ed. *Presenza e funzione della citta di Tebe nella cultura greca* (Pisa and Rome, Instituti Editoriali e Poligrafici Internazionali 2000, 1997), 332, citing Hornblower, *The Greek World 479–323 BC*, 168.
19. Pascual, 'Theban Victory at Haliartos (395 BC)', 62.
20. Pascual, 'Theban Victory at Haliartos (395 BC)', 62.
21. The historian Pausanias reports that the Athenians arrived in Haliartus prior to the battle (*Description of Greece*, 3.5.3), while Plutarch and Xenophon give later arrivals of one to three days (*Life of Lysander*, 29.1 and *Hellenica*, 3.5.22). Either way, the Haliartan army had substantial foreign aid of which Lysander was unaware.
22. Ray, Fred Eugene, *Greek and Macedonian Land Battles of the 4th Century B.C.* (Jefferson, NC, McFarland & Co., 2012), 21.
23. Pascual, 'Theban Victory at Haliartos (395 BC)', 50.
24. Diodorus Siculus, *The Library of History*, 14.82.1.
25. Pascual, 'Theban Victory at Haliartos (395 BC)', 50.
26. Pascual, 'Theban Victory at Haliartos (395 BC)', 50.
27. Xenophon, *Hellenica*, 3.5.19.
28. Plutarch, *Life of Lysander*, 28.5.
29. Plutarch, *Life of Lysander*, 28.3.
30. Plutarch, *Life of Lysander*, 28.4.
31. Plutarch, *Life of Lysander*, 29.6.
32. Pascual, 'Theban Victory at Haliartos (395 BC)', 62–3.
33. Xenophon, *Hellenica*, 3.5.20. Xenophon was reserved in discussing the battle proper, but offers plenty of details of the retreat into the hills, likely because his sources were Spartan survivors of the retreat.
34. Diodorus Siculus, *The Library of History*, 14.81.2.
35. Pascual, 'Theban Victory at Haliartos (395 BC)', 62.
36. Xenophon, *Hellenica*, 3.5.21.
37. Plutarch, *Comparison of Lysander and Sulla*, 4.2–3.
38. Xenophon, *Hellenica*, 3.5.23.
39. Xenophon, *Hellenica*, 3.5.24.
40. Xenophon, *Hellenica*, 3.5.25.
41. Xenophon, *Hellenica*, 3.5.16.
42. Diodorus Siculus, *The Library of History*, 14.79.4.

43. Diodorus Siculus, *The Library of History*, 14.79.6–7.
44. Cornelius Nepos, *Lives of Eminent Commanders*, Conon 2.
45. Diodorus Siculus, *The Library of History*, 14.39.3.
46. Cornelius Nepos, *Lives of Eminent Commanders*, Conon 2.
47. Hamilton, *Sparta's Bitter Victories*, 207.

Chapter Five
1. Plutarch, *Life of Agesilaus*, 15.6, paraphrased.
2. Plutarch, *Life of Agesilaus*, 14.2.
3. Xenophon, *Hellenica*, 3.4.29.
4. Xenophon, *Hellenica*, 4.1.32–33.
5. Plutarch, *Life of Agesilaus*, 14.1.
6. Xenophon, *Hellenica*, 4.2.1.
7. Plutarch, *Life of Agesilaus*, 15.4.
8. Xenophon, *Agesilaus*, 1.38.
9. Plutarch, *Life of Agesilaus*, 15.8.
10. Plutarch, *Life of Agesilaus*, 16.1.
11. Pausanias, *Description of Greece*, 3.9.8.
12. Xenophon, *Hellenica*, 4.2.12.
13. Xenophon, *Hellenica*, 4.2.12.
14. Lazenby, J.F., *The Spartan Army* (Barnsley, Pen & Sword Military, 2012), 132–133.
15. Fornis, César, 'MAXH KPATEIN en la guerra de Corinto: Las Batallas Hopliticas de Nemea y Coronea (394 A.C.)', *Gladius XXIII* (2003), 144. Lazenby agrees with this positioning (Lazenby, *The Spartan Army*, 133).
16. Xenophon, *Hellenica*, 4.2.16.
17. Diodorus Siculus, *The Library of History*, 14.83.1.
18. Hamilton, *Sparta's Bitter Victories*, 221.
19. Hamilton, *Sparta's Bitter Victories*, 221.
20. Xenophon, *Hellenica*, 4.2.17.
21. Xenophon, *Hellenica*, 4.2.17.
22. Xenophon, *Hellenica*, 4.2.15.
23. Hamilton, *Sparta's Bitter Victories*, 221.
24. Xenophon, *Hellenica*, 4.2.18.
25. Lazenby, *The Spartan Army*, 135.
26. Xenophon, *Hellenica*, 4.2.19.
27. Xenophon, *Hellenica*, 4.2.20.
28. Xenophon, *Hellenica*, 4.2.21.
29. Xenophon, *Hellenica*, 4.2.21.
30. Xenophon, *Hellenica*, 4.2.22.
31. Thucydides, *History of the Peloponnesian War*, 5.71.3.
32. Lazenby, *The Spartan Army*, 136–137.
33. Xenophon, *Hellenica*, 4.2.23.
34. Xenophon, *Hellenica*, 4.3.1 and Diodorus Siculus, *The Library of History*, 14.83.2.
35. Diodorus Siculus, *The Library of History*, 14.83.2.

Chapter Six
1. Hyland, John O., 'The Aftermath of Aigospotamoi and the Decline of Spartan Naval Power', *Ancient History Bulletin*, Vol. 33, no. 1–2 (2019), 19.

2. Diodorus Siculus, *The Library of History*, 14.83.4–5 and Hyland, 'The Aftermath of Aigospotamoi and the Decline of Spartan Naval Power', 19.
3. Hyland, 'The Aftermath of Aigospotamoi and the Decline of Spartan Naval Power', 19.
4. Hyland, 'The Aftermath of Aigospotamoi and the Decline of Spartan Naval Power', 20.
5. Xenophon, *Hellenica*, 3.4.1.
6. Diodorus Siculus, *The Library of History*, 14.79.6–7 and Hyland, 'The Aftermath of Aigospotamoi and the Decline of Spartan Naval Power', 27.
7. Xenophon, *Hellenica*, 3.4.27–29 and Hyland, 'The Aftermath of Aigospotamoi and the Decline of Spartan Naval Power', 27.
8. Hyland, *Persian Interventions*, 146.
9. Diodorus Siculus, *The Library of History*, 14.83.4–5 and Hyland, 'The Aftermath of Aigospotamoi and the Decline of Spartan Naval Power', 27.
10. Rop, Jeffrey, *Greek Military Service in the Ancient Near East, 401–330 BCE* (Cambridge, Cambridge University Press, 2019), 94.
11. *Hellenica Oxyrhynchia*, 19.2.
12. *Hellenica Oxyrhynchia*, 19.2.
13. Rees, Owen, *Great Naval Battles of the Ancient Greek World* (Yorkshire, Pen & Sword Maritime, 2018), 165.
14. Hirschfeld, Nicolle E., 'Appendix G: Trireme warfare in Thucydides' in *The Landmark Thucydides: A Comprehensive Guide to the Peloponnesian War* ed. by Robert B. Strassler (New York, Free Press, 1996), 608–613.
15. Hirschfeld, Nicolle E., 'Appendix G: Trireme warfare in Thucydides', 612.
16. Thucydides, *The History of the Peloponnesian War*, 7.34–36 and Hirschfeld, Nicolle E., 'Appendix G: Trireme warfare in Thucydides', 613.
17. Hirschfeld, Nicolle E., 'Appendix G: Trireme warfare in Thucydides', 612.
18. The Hellenistic and Roman city of Cnidus, which constitutes the majority of the archaeological remains, was possibly not in the same location as the Classical city of Cnidus. At the end of the Classical period, the growing city-state likely relocated towards the interior of the Carian Chersonese peninsula to accommodate their growing population. See Bresson, Alain, 'Knidos: topography for a battle' in *Hellenistic Karia*, ed. by Riet van Bremen & Carbon, Jan-Mathieu (Pessac, Ausonius Editions, 2010), 435–451.
19. Thucydides, *The History of the Peloponnesian War*, 1.8.88, 1.108.1, 116.1–3.
20. Diodorus Siculus, *The Library of History*, 14.79.5.
21. Plutarch, *Parallel Lives*, 'Life of Artaxerxes', trans. Bernadotte Perrin (Cambridge, Harvard University Press, 1914), 21.1–3.
22. Plutarch, *Life of Artaxerxes*, 21.3.
23. Photius, *Bibliotheca*, Library 72, Fragment 30.
24. Owen Rees' discussion of this defensive line (Rees, *Great Naval Battles of the Ancient Greek World*, 167) is drawn from Ruzicka, Stephen, *Trouble in the West: Egypt and the Persian Empire, 525–332 BC* (Oxford, Oxford University Press, 2012), 51.
25. Ruzicka, *Trouble in the West*, 56.
26. Diodorus Siculus, *The Library of History*, 14.83.4.
27. Diodorus Siculus, *The Library of History*, 14.83.5.
28. Rees, *Great Naval Battles of the Ancient Greek World*, 167.
29. Polyaenus, *Stratagems*, 1.48.5.
30. Polyaenus, *Stratagems*, 1.48.5.
31. Xenophon, *Hellenica*, 4.3.12.
32. Xenophon, *Hellenica*, 4.3.12.

33. Diodorus Siculus, *The Library of History*, 14.83.7.
34. Diodorus Siculus, *The Library of History*, 14.84.4.
35. Polybius, *The Histories*, 1.2.3.
36. Diodorus Siculus, *The Library of History*, 14.84.7.
37. Plutarch, *Life of Artaxerxes*, 21.4.
38. Diodorus Siculus, *The Library of History*, 14.84.3–4.

Chapter Seven
1. Xenophon, *Hellenica*, 4.3.13.
2. Plutarch, *Life of Agesilaus*, 17.2.
3. Lazenby, *The Spartan Army*, 141.
4. Xenophon, *Hellenica*, 4.3.15.
5. Xenophon, *Hellenica*, 4.3.15.
6. Lazenby, *The Spartan Army*, 141.
7. Xenophon, *Agesilaus*, 2.9.
8. Hamilton, Charles D., *Agesilaus and the Failure of Spartan Hegemony* (Ithaca, NY, Cornell University Press, 1991), 106.
9. Xenophon, *Hellenica*, 4.3.17.
10. Xenophon, *Hellenica*, 4.3.18.
11. Plutarch, *Life of Agesilaus*, 18.2. This movement was potentially the standard Spartan counter-march, essentially a reversal of marching order and rearrangement of the phalanx's file leaders to move in the opposite direction. See Lazenby, *The Spartan Army*, 141.
12. Xenophon, *Hellenica*, 4.3.19.
13. Xenophon, *Hellenica*, 4.3.18.
14. Lazenby, *The Spartan Army*, 141.
15. Xenophon, *Hellenica*, 4.3.19.
16. Plutarch, *Life of Agesilaus*, 18.3.
17. Plutarch, *Life of Agesilaus*, 18.4.
18. Plutarch, *Life of Agesilaus*, 18.4.
19. Diodorus Siculus, *The Library of History*, 14.84.2.
20. Plutarch, *Life of Agesilaus*, 18.4.
21. Plutarch, *Life of Agesilaus*, 19.2.
22. Xenophon, *Hellenica*, 4.3.18.
23. Xenophon, *Hellenica*, 4.3.21.
24. Xenophon, *Hellenica*, 4.3.21–23.
25. Xenophon, *Hellenica*, 4.4.1.
26. Hamilton, *Agesilaus and the Failure of Spartan Hegemony*, 109.
27. Xenophon, *Agesilaus*, 2.17.
28. Plutarch, *Life of Agesilaus*, 19.4.
29. Plutarch, *Life of Agesilaus*, 20.2.
30. Plutarch, *Life of Agesilaus*, 20.3.
31. Plutarch, *Life of Agesilaus*, 20.4.
32. Xenophon, *Hellenica*, 4.4.1.

Chapter Eight
1. Andocides, *On the Peace*, 3.25.
2. Hamilton, *Sparta's Bitter Victories*, 223.
3. Strauss, *Athens after the Peloponnesian War*, 128.

4. Xenophon, *Hellenica*, 4.8.1.
5. Xenophon, *Hellenica*, 4.8.6.
6. Herodotus, *The Histories*, 7.235 and Hyland, *Persian Interventions*, 152.
7. Xenophon, *Hellenica*, 4.8.9.
8. Xenophon, *Hellenica*, 4.8.9.
9. Xenophon, *Hellenica*, 4.8.10.
10. Xenophon, *Hellenica*, 4.8.8.
11. Hyland, *Persian Interventions*, 152.
12. Xenophon, *Hellenica*, 4.8.10.
13. Strauss, *Athens after the Peloponnesian War*, 1.
14. Fascinatingly, Xenophon was also a former student of Socrates. Xenophon's recount of *The Apology* overlaps with Plato's in its core narrative, but presents a less glamorized and idealized version of the philosopher. Xenophon was by this point more concerned with his Spartan military service and admiration for Agesilaus, Cyrus and other commanders.
15. Plato, *The Apology*, 19c.
16. Aristophanes, *Ecclesiazusae*, 591–4.
17. Aristophanes, *Ecclesiazusae*, 598–600.
18. Aristophanes, *Plutus* (London, The Athenian Society, 1912), 550–554.
19. Cecchet, Lucia, 'The Use and Abuse of Poverty: Aristophanes, Plutus 415–610 and the Public Speeches of the Corinthian War', *Hormos: Ricerche di Storia Antica*, 9 (2017), 106.
20. Lysias, 'Funeral Oration', *The Orations of Lysias*, trans. Handy Literal Translations (Project Gutenberg, 2004), 67–69.
21. Cecchet, 'The Use and Abuse of Poverty', 108.
22. Lysias, 'Against Ergocles', *The Orations of Lysias*, trans. Handy Literal Translations (Project Gutenberg, 2004), 10–11.
23. Lysias, *Against Andocides*, 3.39, trans. author's own, Greek text from the Perseus Digital Library Project, Tufts University.
24. Andocides, *On the Peace*, 3.39, trans. author's own.
25. Strauss, *Athens after the Peloponnesian War*, 133.
26. Strauss, Barry, 'Thrasybulus and Conon: A Rivalry in Athens in the 390s B.C.', *The American Journal of Philology* 105, no. 1 (1984), 37 and Strauss, *Athens after the Peloponnesian War*, 130.
27. Strauss, 'Thrasybulus and Conon: A Rivalry in Athens in the 390s B.C.', 37.
28. Strauss, *Athens after the Peloponnesian War*, 129 and Lysias, *On the Property of Aristophanes*, 19.19.
29. Aeschines, *On the Embassy*, 2.76 as referenced in Pascual, José, 'Conon, the Persian Fleet and a Second Naval Campaign in 393 BC', *Historia: Zeitschrift für Alte Geschichte* 65, no. 1 (2016), 18.
30. Pascual, 'Conon, the Persian Fleet and a Second Naval Campaign in 393 BC', 29.
31. Cornelius Nepos, *The Lives of Eminent Commanders*, Conon 5.1.
32. Xenophon, *Hellenica*, 4.8.12.
33. Hamilton, *Agesilaus and the Failure of Spartan Hegemony*, 112.
34. Xenophon, *Hellenica*, 4.8.14.
35. Xenophon, *Hellenica*, 4.8.13.
36. Strauss, *Athens after the Peloponnesian War*, 128.
37. Xenophon, *Hellenica*, 4.8.16.
38. Xenophon, *Hellenica*, 4.8.16 and Cornelius Nepos, *The Lives of Eminent Commanders*, Conon 5.3.
39. Hyland, *Persian Interventions*, 156.

40. Hamilton, Charles D., 'The Politics of Revolution in Corinth, 395–386 BC', *Historia: Zeitschrift für Alte Geschichte* 21, no. 1 (1972), 34.
41. Hyland, *Persian Interventions*, 156.

Chapter Nine
1. Xenophon, *Hellenica*, 4.4.1.
2. Xenophon, *Hellenica*, 4.8.8.
3. Hamilton, *Agesilaus and the Failure of Spartan Hegemony*, 113.
4. Hamilton, *Sparta's Bitter Victories*, 223.
5. Hamilton, *Sparta's Bitter Victories*, 223.
6. Xenophon, *Hellenica*, 4.4.2.
7. Xenophon, *Hellenica*, 4.4.6–7.
8. Xenophon, *Hellenica*, 4.4.12.
9. Hamilton, *Sparta's Bitter Victories*, 260.
10. Justin, *History of the World*, 6.5.
11. Sears, Matthew A., *Thrace and the Athenian Elite, ca. 550–338 BCE* (Unpublished doctoral dissertation, Ithaca, New York, Cornell University, 2011), 4.
12. Hamilton, *Sparta's Bitter Victories*, 281.
13. Xenophon, *Anabasis*, 1.10.7.
14. Xenophon, *Hellenica*, 4.4.17.
15. Sears, Matthew A., *Athens, Thrace and the Shaping of Athenian Leadership* (Cambridge, Cambridge University Press, 2013), 199.
16. Cornelius Nepos, *Lives of Eminent Commanders*, Iphicrates 3.1.
17. Cornelius Nepos, *Lives of Eminent Commanders*, Iphicrates 3.4.
18. Hamilton, *Sparta's Bitter Victories*, 281.
19. Diodorus Siculus, *The Library of History*, 15.44.3.
20. Cornelius Nepos, *Lives of Eminent Commanders*, Iphicrates 1.4.
21. Plutarch, *Parallel Lives*, 'Life of Pelopidas', trans. Bernadotte Perrin (Cambridge, Harvard University Press, 1914), 2.1.
22. Xenophon, *Hellenica*, 4.4.16.
23. Xenophon, *Hellenica*, 4.4.19.
24. Fornis, César, 'Rhodes during the Corinthian War: from strategic naval base to endemic stasis', *Historika: Studi di storia greca e romana V* (2015), 434.
25. Xenophon, *Hellenica*, 4.8.20.
26. Fornis, 'Rhodes during the Corinthian War: from strategic naval base to endemic stasis', 436.
27. Xenophon, *Hellenica*, 4.8.23–24.
28. Diodorus Siculus, *The Library of History*, 14.97.4.
29. Xenophon, *Agesilaus*, 2.29.
30. Plutarch, *Life of Agesilaus*, 21.3.
31. Xenophon, *Hellenica*, 4.5.13.
32. Xenophon, *Hellenica*, 4.5.17.
33. Konecny, Andreas, 'The Battle of Lechaeum, Early Summer 390 BC' in *Iphicrates, Peltasts and Lechaeum*, ed. by Nicholas Victor Secunda and Bogdan Burliga (Gdansk, Akanthina, 2014), 15.
34. Konecny, 'The Battle of Lechaeum, Early Summer 390 BC', 16.
35. Konecny, 'The Battle of Lechaeum, Early Summer 390 BC', 19–20.
36. Konecny, 'The Battle of Lechaeum, Early Summer 390 BC', 18.
37. Xenophon, *Hellenica*, 4.5.14.

38. Lazenby, *The Spartan Army*, 143.
39. Konecny, 'The Battle of Lechaeum, Early Summer 390 BC', 23.
40. Xenophon, *Hellenica*, 4.5.15.
41. Thucydides, *The History of the Peloponnesian War*, 4.128.1–3 and Konecny, 'The Battle of Lechaeum, Early Summer 390 BC', 23.
42. Xenophon, *Hellenica*, 2.4.31–34 and Konecny (2014), 23.
43. Lazenby, *The Spartan Army*, 143.
44. Konecny, 'The Battle of Lechaeum, Early Summer 390 BC', 24.
45. Lazenby, *The Spartan Army*, 143.
46. Konecny, 'The Battle of Lechaeum, Early Summer 390 BC', 24.
47. Xenophon, *Hellenica*, 4.5.16.
48. Konecny, 'The Battle of Lechaeum, Early Summer 390 BC', 27.
49. Xenophon, *Hellenica*, 4.5.17.
50. Konecny, 'The Battle of Lechaeum, Early Summer 390 BC', 29.
51. Lendon, J.E., *Soldiers and Ghosts: A History of Battle in Classical Antiquity* (New Haven, Yale University Press, 2005), 97–98.
52. Xenophon, *Hellenica*, 4.5.8.
53. Xenophon, *Hellenica*, 4.5.18.
54. Xenophon, *Hellenica*, 4.5.9.
55. Hamilton, *Agesilaus and the Failure of Spartan Hegemony*, 116.
56. Hamilton, *Agesilaus and the Failure of Spartan Hegemony*, 116.
57. Xenophon, *Agesilaus*, 2.33.
58. Diodorus Siculus, *The Library of History*, 14.92.2.

Chapter Ten
1. Xenophon, *Hellenica*, 4.6.6.
2. Xenophon, *Hellenica*, 4.6.4.
3. Xenophon, *Hellenica*, 4.6.6.
4. Xenophon, *Hellenica*, 4.6.8–9.
5. Xenophon, *Hellenica*, 4.6.10.
6. Xenophon, *Agesilaus*, 2.20.
7. Xenophon, *Hellenica*, 4.6.13.
8. Xenophon, *Hellenica*, 4.7.2.
9. Xenophon, *Hellenica*, 4.7.5.
10. Xenophon, *Hellenica*, 4.7.7.
11. Hamilton, *Sparta's Bitter Victories*, 292–293.
12. Hamilton, *Sparta's Bitter Victories*, 291.
13. Hyland, *Persian Interventions*, 159.
14. Xenophon, *Hellenica*, 4.8.25.
15. Xenophon, *Hellenica*, 4.8.27 and Hyland, *Persian Interventions*, 163.
16. Xenophon, *Hellenica*, 4.8.31.
17. Lysias, *Against Ergocles*, 28.12 and Hyland, *Persian Interventions*, 164.
18. Hyland, *Persian Interventions*, 164.
19. Diodorus Siculus, *The Library of History*, 14.99.4.
20. Xenophon, *Hellenica*, 4.8.32.
21. Xenophon, *Anabasis*, 6.1.16.
22. Xenophon, *Anabasis*, 7.1.20.
23. Xenophon, *Hellenica*, 4.8.33.
24. Strauss, *Athens after the Peloponnesian War*, 156.

25. Aristophanes, *Plutus*, 179.
26. Strauss, *Athens after the Peloponnesian War*, 158.
27. Xenophon, *Hellenica*, 4.8.38.
28. Xenophon, *Hellenica*, 4.8.39.
29. Xenophon, *Hellenica*, 5.1.6–7.
30. Hamilton, *Agesilaus and the Failure of Spartan Hegemony*, 116.
31. Xenophon, *Hellenica*, 2.2.9.
32. Xenophon, *Hellenica*, 5.1.13.
33. Xenophon, *Hellenica*, 5.1.20.
34. Xenophon, *Hellenica*, 5.1.20.

Chapter Eleven
1. Hyland, *Persian Interventions*, 161.
2. Hyland, *Persian Interventions*, 158.
3. Hamilton, *Sparta's Bitter Victories*, 298.
4. Hyland, *Persian Interventions*, 164.
5. Hamilton, *Sparta's Bitter Victories*, 298.
6. Xenophon, *Hellenica*, 5.1.25–28.
7. Xenophon, *Hellenica*, 5.1.28.
8. Xenophon, *Hellenica*, 5.1.31.
9. Xenophon, *Agesilaus*, 2.21.
10. Plutarch, *Life of Agesilaus*, 23.1–2.
11. Plutarch, *Life of Artaxerxes*, 22.1–2.
12. Hyland, *Persian Interventions*, 323–324.
13. Hamilton, *Sparta's Bitter Victories*, 325.
14. Xenophon, *Hellenica*, 5.1.36.
15. Isocrates, *Panegyric*, 4.180, trans. author's own. Greek text from the Perseus Digital Library Project, Tufts University.
16. Diodorus Siculus, *The Library of History*, 14.110.3.
17. Xenophon, *Hellenica*, 5.1.36, trans. author's own.
18. Schmidt, Katrin, 'The Peace of Antalcidas and the Idea of the *Koine Eirene*: A Panhellenic Peace Movement', *Revue internationale des droits de l'antiquité 46* (1999), 82.
19. Xenophon, *Ways and Means*, trans. H.G. Dakyns (London and New York, Macmillan and Co., 1897), 5.1–2.

Conclusion
1. Xenophon, *Hellenica*, 5.2.1–2.
2. Fornis, César and Domingo Plácido Suárez, 'De la guerra del Peloponeso a la Paz del Rey (I): *Prosopografía política ateniense*', *Rivista storica dell'antichità* 38 (2008), 78, trans. author's own.
3. Plutarch, *Life of Agesilaus*, 33.2.
4. Hamilton, *Sparta's Bitter Victories*, 329.
5. Plutarch, *Sayings of the Spartans*, Antalcidas 6.
6. Diodorus Siculus, *The Library of History*, 15.1.3–5.
7. Forrest, *A History of Sparta, 950–192 B.C.*, 127.
8. Xenophon, *Hellenica*, 5.2.20–24 and Forrest, *A History of Sparta, 950–192 B.C.*, 127.
9. Rahe, *The Spartan Regime*, 123.
10. Polybius, *The Histories*, 1.2.3.

Bibliography

Primary Sources
Aeschylus, *The Persians in Four Plays of Aeschylus*, trans. G.M. Cookson (Blackwell Publishing, Oxford, 1922)
Andocides, 'On the Peace' in *Minor Attic Orators*, Vol. I, trans. K.J. Maidment (Cambridge, Harvard University Press and London, William Heinemann Ltd, 1968)
Aristophanes, *Ecclesiazusae (or The Assemblywomen) in The Complete Greek Drama*, vol. 2, trans. Eugene O'Neill (New York, Random House, 1938)
Aristophanes, *Plutus* (London, The Athenian Society, 1912)
Aristotle, *The Constitution of Athens*, trans. Sir Frederic G. Kenyon (London, G. Bell, 1891)
Aristotle, *Politics*, trans. Benjamin Jowett (Oxford, Clarendon Press, 1885)
Cornelius Nepos, 'Lives of Eminent Commanders', trans. Rev. John Selby Watson, in *Justin, Cornelius Nepos, and Eutropius: Literally Translated, with Notes and a General Index* (London, Henry G. Bohn, 1853)
Diodorus Siculus, *The Library of History*, Volume VI: Books 14–15.19, trans. C.H. Oldfather (Loeb Classical Library, Cambridge, Harvard University Press, 1954)
Diogenes Laertius, *Lives of Eminent Philosophers*, trans. R.D. Hicks (Cambridge, Harvard University Press, 1925)
Herodotus, *The Histories*, trans. George Rawlinson (New York, Charles Scribner's Sons, 1897)
Isocrates, *Evagoras*, Greek text from the Perseus Digital Library Project (Tufts University, accessed 15 March 2022)
Isocrates, *Nicocles or the Cyprians*, Greek text from the Perseus Digital Library Project (Tufts University, accessed 18 March 2022)
Isocrates, *Panegyricus*, Greek text from the Perseus Digital Library Project (Tufts University, accessed 19 May 2022)
Lysias, *Against Andocides*, Greek text from the Perseus Digital Library Project (Tufts University, accessed 18 April 2022)
Lysias, 'Against Ergocles' in *The Orations of Lysias*, trans. Handy Literal Translations (Project Gutenberg, 2004, accessed 7 April 2022)
Lysias, 'Funeral Oration' in *The Orations of Lysias*, trans. Handy Literal Translations (Project Gutenberg, 2004, accessed 9 April 2022)
Pausanias, *Description of Greece*, trans. W.H.S. Jones and H.A. Ormerod (Cambridge, Harvard University Press and London, William Heinemann Ltd, 1918)
Plato, *The Republic*, trans. Benjamin Jowett (Oxford, Oxford University Press, 1888)
Plutarch, *Moralia*, Vol. III, 'Sayings of the Spartans', trans. Frank Cole Babbitt (Loeb Classical Library, Cambridge, Harvard University Press, 1931)
Plutarch, *Moralia*, Vol. IV, 'On the Glory of the Athenians', trans. by Frank Cole Babbitt (Loeb Classical Library, Cambridge, Harvard University Press, 1936)
Plutarch, *Parallel Lives*, 'Comparison of Lysander and Sulla', trans. Bernadotte Perrin (Loeb Classical Library, Cambridge, Harvard University Press, 1914)
Plutarch, *Parallel Lives*, 'Life of Agesilaus', trans. Bernadotte Perrin (Loeb Classical Library, Cambridge, Harvard University Press, 1914)

Plutarch, *Parallel Lives*, 'Life of Artaxerxes', trans. Bernadotte Perrin (Loeb Classical Library, Cambridge, Harvard University Press, 1914)
Plutarch, *Parallel Lives*, 'Life of Lysander', trans. Bernadotte Perrin (Loeb Classical Library, Cambridge, Harvard University Press, 1914)
Plutarch, *Parallel Lives*, 'Life of Lycurgus', trans. Bernadotte Perrin (Loeb Classical Library, Cambridge, Harvard University Press, 1914)
Plutarch, *Parallel Lives*, 'Life of Pelopidas', trans. Bernadotte Perrin (Loeb Classical Library, Cambridge, Harvard University Press, 1914)
Pseudo-Xenophon, *Constitution of the Athenians*, Greek text from the Perseus Digital Library Project (Tufts University, accessed 1 March 2022)
Thucydides, *The History of the Peloponnesian War*, trans. Richard Crawley (Cambridge, Harvard University Press, 1874)
Xenophon, *Agesilaus*, trans. H.G. Dakyns (London and New York, Macmillan and Co., 1894)
Xenophon, *Anabasis*, trans. H.G. Dakyns (London and New York, Macmillan and Co., 1891)
Xenophon, *Hellenica*, trans. H.G. Dakyns (London and New York, Macmillan and Co., 1891)
Xenophon, *Polity of the Athenians and the Lacedaemonians*, trans. H.G. Dakyns (London and New York, Macmillan and Co., 1897)
Xenophon, *Ways and Means*, trans. H.G. Dakyns (London and New York, Macmillan and Co., 1897)

Secondary Sources

Asmanti, Luca, *Conon the Athenian: Warfare and Politics in the Aegean, 414–386 B.C.* (Stuttgart, Franz Steiner Verlag, 2015)
Beck, Hans, 'Thebes, the Boeotian League and the Rise of Federalism' in *Presenza e funzione della citta di Tebe nella cultura greca*, edited by Paola A. Bernardini, 331–344 (Pisa and Rome, Instituti Editoriali e Poligrafici Internazionali, 2000, 1997)
Bolmarcich, Sarah, 'Thucydides 1.19.1 and the Peloponnesian League', *Greek, Roman and Byzantine Studies* 45 (2005), 5–34.
Bresson, Alain, 'Knidos: topography for a battle' in *Hellenistic Karia*, edited by Riet van Bremen & Carbon Jan-Mathieu, 435–451 (Pessac, Ausonius Editions, 2010)
Cartledge, Paul, *The Spartans: The World of the Warrior-Heroes of Ancient Greece* (New York, Vintage Books, 2004)
Cartledge, Paul, *Thebes: The Forgotten City of Ancient Greece* (London, Picador, 2020)
Cawkwell, G.L., 'The King's Peace', *The Classical Quarterly* 31, no. 1 (1981), 69–83.
Cecchet, Lucia, 'The Use and Abuse of Poverty: Aristophanes, Plutus 415–610 and the Public Speeches of the Corinthian War', *Hormos: Ricerche di Storia Antica* 9 (2017), 100–125.
Chambers, James T., 'On Messenian and Laconian Helots in the Fifth Century B.C.', *The Historian* 40, no. 2 (1978), 271–285.
Doran, Timothy, 'Demographic Fluctuation and Institutional Response in Sparta' (Berkeley, University of California at Berkeley, 2011)
Doran, Timothy, *Spartan Oliganthropia* (Leiden, Brill, 2018)
Figuera, Thomas J., 'Population Patterns in Late Archaic and Classical Sparta', *Transactions of the American Philological Association (1974-)*, 116 (1986), 165–213.
Fornis, César, '*MAXH KPATEIN en la guerra de Corinto: Las Batallas Hopliticas de Nemea y Coronea (394 A.C.)*', *Gladius* XXIII (2003), 141–160.
Fornis, César, 'Rhodes during the Corinthian War: from strategic naval base to endemic stasis', *Historika: Studi di storia greca e romana* V (2015), 433–441.
Fornis, César and Domingo Plácido Suárez, '*De la guerra del Peloponeso a la Paz del Rey* (I): Prosopografía política ateniense', Rivista storica dell'antichità 38 (2008), 45–88.

Forrest, W.G., *A History of Sparta, 950–192 B.C.* (New York, W.W. Norton & Co., 1968)
Gibbon, Edward, *The History of the Decline and Fall of the Roman Empire*, edited by David Womersley (London, Penguin Classics, 2001)
Hamilton, Charles D., *Agesilaus and the Failure of Spartan Hegemony* (Ithaca, NY, Cornell University Press, 1991)
Hamilton, Charles D., *Sparta's Bitter Victories: Politics and Diplomacy in the Corinthian War* (Ithaca, NY, Cornell University Press, 1979)
Hamilton, Charles D., 'The Politics of Revolution in Corinth, 395-386 BC', *Historia: Zeitschrift für Alte Geschichte* 21, no. 1 (1972), 21–37.
Hirschfeld, Nicolle E., 'Appendix G: Trireme warfare in Thucydides' in *The Landmark Thucydides: A Comprehensive Guide to the Peloponnesian War*, edited by Robert B. Strassler, 608–613 (New York, Free Press, 1996)
Hornblower, Simon, *The Greek World 479–323 BC* (London, Routledge, 2011)
Hyland, John O., *Persian Interventions: The Achaemenid Empire, Athens & Sparta, 450–386 BCE* (Baltimore, Johns Hopkins University Press, 2018)
Hyland, John O., 'The Aftermath of Aigospotamoi and the Decline of Spartan Naval Power', *Ancient History Bulletin* 33, no. 1–2 (2019), 19–37.
Kagan, Donald, *The Fall of the Athenian Empire* (Ithaca, NY, Cornell University Press, 1987)
Konecny, Andreas, 'The Battle of Lechaeum, Early Summer 390 BC' in *Iphicrates, Peltasts and Lechaeum*, edited by Nicholas Victor Secunda & Bogdan Burliga, 7–48 (Gdansk, Akanthina, 2014)
Lazenby, J.F., *The Spartan Army* (Barnsley, Pen & Sword Military, 2012)
Lendon, J.E., *Soldiers and Ghosts: A History of Battle in Classical Antiquity* (New Haven, Yale University Press, 2005)
Millender, Ellen, 'The Spartans at Sea', *Historika* 5, no. 5 (2015), 299–312.
Pascual, José, 'Conon, the Persian Fleet and a Second Naval Campaign in 393 BC', *Historia: Zeitschrift für Alte Geschichte* 65, no. 1 (2016), 14–30.
Pascual, José, 'Theban Victory at Haliartos (395 BC)', *Gladius* XXVII (2007), 39–66.
Rahe, Paul A., *The Spartan Regime: Its Character, Origins and Grand Strategy* (New Haven, CT, Yale University Press, 2016)
Ray, Fred Eugene, *Greek and Macedonian Land Battles of the 4th Century B.C.* (Jefferson, NC, McFarland & Co., 2012)
Rees, Owen, *Great Naval Battles of the Ancient Greek World* (Yorkshire, Pen & Sword Maritime, 2018)
Rop, Jeffrey, *Greek Military Service in the Ancient Near East, 401–330 BCE* (Cambridge, Cambridge University Press, 2019)
Ruzicka, Stephen, *Trouble in the West: Egypt and the Persian Empire, 525–332 BC* (Oxford, Oxford University Press, 2012)
Schmidt, Katrin, 'The Peace of Antalcidas and the Idea of the *Koine Eirene*: A Panhellenic Peace Movement', *Revue internationale des droits de l'antiquité* 46 (1999), 81–98.
Sears, Matthew A., *Athens, Thrace and the Shaping of Athenian Leadership* (Cambridge, Cambridge University Press, 2013)
Sears, Matthew A., *Thrace and the Athenian Elite, ca. 550–338 BCE* (Unpublished doctoral dissertation, Ithaca, New York, Cornell University, 2011)
Strassler, Robert D., *The Landmark Xenophon's Hellenika* (New York, Anchor Books, 2010)
Strauss, Barry S., *Athens after the Peloponnesian War: Class, Faction and Policy, 403–386 B.C.* (New York, Routledge, 2014)
Strauss, Barry, 'Thrasybulus and Conon: A Rivalry in Athens in the 390s B.C.', *The American Journal of Philology* (Johns Hopkins University Press) 105, no. 1 (1984), 37–48.

Index

Abydos, 5, 123–5, 132
Acarnaria, 118–20
Achaea, 62, 90, 118–19
Acrocorinth, 105
Aegina, 22, 126, 128, 131
Aegospotami, xxxii, 3, 9, 15–21, 54, 67, 98, 103
Agesilaus:
  ascent to power, 34–40
  campaigns in Asia Minor, 39–42, 53–9, 67–8, 75–6, 87–8
  diplomacy with Thebes, 38–9, 111, 116–17, 139
  see also Aulis
  factional leadership, 13–15, 131
  leadership in Corinthian War, xx–xxiii, xxvi, 60–1, 66, 77–88, 109–11, 116–28, 131, 133, 135, 138–40
  at Coronea, 77–86
  at Lechaeum, 17–21, 116–17
  in diplomacy, 131, 133, 135, 138–40
  relationship with Lysander, 40–1, 43, 45
Agesipolis, 60, 116, 120, 124, 132
Agis II, xx, xxvi, 14, 21–2, 30–1, 34–5, 55, 65, 120
Agoge, xxiv–xxv, 10–11, 35, 84, 142
Anaxibius, 123–6
Andocides, 86, 94–6, 100–101, 121, 135
Antalcidas, 15, 99–100, 103, 125, 130–4, 136, 139–40
  see also King's Peace
Argos, xviii, xxviii, xxx, 11, 31, 41–2, 59–61, 79, 82–3, 102, 104, 106, 109, 111, 120, 124, 130–5, 137
  alliance with Corinth, 102–105, 110
  diplomacy with Sparta, 11, 59–61, 120, 124, 130–1
  in the Corinthian War, 41–2, 79, 82–3, 102, 104, 106, 109, 111, 120, 130–5, 137

Aristodemus, 60–1, 64–5
Aristophanes, xxiii, 19, 91–3, 95, 124
Artaxerxes II, xix, xxiii, 8, 32, 40–1, 53–4, 56, 68–9, 72–3, 76, 100, 121, 125, 128–33
Assemblywomen, see Aristophanes
Athens:
  conquest of, 1–4, 16–24
  democracy, xvi–xvii, xxix–xxxi, 1–3, 10, 13, 16–30
  empire, xvi–xvii, xix–xx, xxx–xxxiii, 1–3, 12, 14, 16–20, 40, 70–1, 79, 85–6, 94, 98, 100–101, 106, 111, 117, 121–3, 136
  diplomacy with Greek states, 1–4, 29–34, 120–6, 129–36
  diplomacy with Sparta, *see* Peloponnesian War, Corinthian War *and* Thirty Tyrants
  military, xxiv, 16–19, 49, 106–26
  see also Peltast
  navy, xxx, 16–18, 20, 53–4, 69–71, 73–5, 86, 88, 90, 97–99, 132
  society, xvi–xvii, 16–20, 90–7, 106–109
Aulis, 38, 41, 58, 78, 111

Boeotarch, 39, 44–7, 81, 111
  see also Thebes
Boeotia, xxiii, 38–9, 44–5, 48–9, 51, 58, 77–9, 130, 134, 139
Boeotian Confederacy, 44, 47–8, 134
Byzantium, 4–5, 122–3, 128

Callias, 111–14
Caria, xxix, 7, 37, 40, 68, 71–5
Caunus, 72–3
Cenchreae, 105–106, 109
Chersonese, 71–4, 87, 124–5
Cilicia, xxix, 9, 53–4, 74
Cinadon, *see* Conspiracy of Cinadon

Cnidus:
  Battle of, 58, 66–78, 83, 85, 87,
    96–8, 100, 103, 106–107, 109–10,
    120–1, 142
  city of, 71–3
Conon:
  downfall, 99–101
  exile to Cyprus, 53–7, 68–9, 85
  relationship with Persia, 53–5, 59,
    68–76, 107–108
  return to Athens, 86–90, 120–1
  naval campaigns, xxiii, 20–3, 53–7,
    68–76, 86–90, 97–9
Conspiracy of Cinadon, xx, 13–5, 36
Corinth:
  alliance with Argos, 102–105, 110
  civil conflict, 101–106, 109
  Congress at, 59–61
  geography, 85, 89–90, 105–106, 110–15
  diplomacy with Persia, 89–90, 120–1,
    129–35, 141
  diplomacy with Sparta, xvi–xxix, 22,
    29–30, 76, 85, 89, 116–17,
    129–35, 141
  military, 62–6, 85
  navy, 41–2, 88–90, 102–103, 105
Corinthian War:
  conclusion of, *see* King's Peace
  course of, *see* Battle of Haliartus, Battle
    of Cnidus, Battle of Coronea, Battle
    of Nemea *or* Battle of Lechaeum
  outbreak of, 41–4
  significance of, xvii–xxi, 135–43
Coronea:
  Battle of, 76–85, 90, 102–103,
    106–107, 112
  city of, 78
Critias, 26–7, 91–2
Ctesias, 72–3
Cyprus, xxx, 20, 53–4, 68, 73–4, 85, 87, 96,
  100, 110, 124–5, 130, 132–5
Cyrus the Younger, xix, xxii, xxxii, 4–9,
  32–7, 41, 68, 107, 123, 129

Decarchy, 2–3, 12, 21, 24–5, 34, 38, 43,
  76
  see also Lysander
Decelea, 18, 21, 41, 48
Dercylidas, 37, 66, 123

Elean War, 31–5, 39
Eleusis, 18, 27–30, 91
  see also Thirty Tyrants
Elis, xxviii, 30–5, 39
Evagoras of Cyprus, 20–1, 53–4, 68, 73–4,
  87, 96, 100, 110, 124, 130

Hakor, 124, 130
Haliartus:
  Battle of, 41–52, 55, 57–8, 66, 77–8, 80,
    118, 131
    course of, 49–52
    prelude, 42–6
  city of, 41–8, 52
Halicarnassus, 71–2, 122
Harmost, 2–3, 8, 12, 21, 24–7, 33–4, 37, 45,
  76, 87, 98, 123, 125
Hellespont, xxxii, 16, 40, 58, 121–8, 132
Helot, xxv, xxviii, xxxii, 4, 10–15, 35–8, 55,
  61–2, 112, 141–3
Hierax, 125–6

Ionia, xxix, 2, 5–7, 37–8, 40–3, 58, 62, 66,
  71, 76–80, 83, 98, 103, 122, 131
Iphicrates:
  at Battle of Lechaeum, xxiii, 106–17
  background, 106–107
  Iphicratean Reforms, 106–109, 115
  Post-Lechaeum, 121, 123–6
  see also Peltast
Isthmus of Corinth, 89, 102, 105, 110

King's Peace, 129–39
Koine Eirene, *see* King's Peace

Lechaeum:
  Battle of, 102–19, 124–5, 128
  harbour, 61–2, 90, 102–104
Locris, 41, 48, 78, 83
Loryma, 68, 72–4
Lycurgan Reforms, xx, xxiv–xxviii, 3–4,
  9–14, 22, 28, 40, 84, 92, 131, 138–42
Lydia, xxix, 5, 7, 99, 125, 129–30
Lysander, viii, xiv, xx, xxiii, xxvi, xxxii, 1–5,
  8–10, 12–16, 19–28, 30, 32–40, 43–5,
  49–52, 55–8, 60, 67, 76–7, 83–4, 87, 103,
  126–7, 130–1, 133, 144–5
  Death at Haliartus, 100
  Personal empire, *see* Decarchy
Lysias, 94–6

Index

Mantinea, xvi, 31, 60, 62, 65, 116, 137–8
March of the Ten Thousand, xxii, 32, 77–9, 118, 123
Megara, 3, 26
Messenia, *see* Helots
Mora, 49, 77–9, 105, 111–16, 124

Navarch, xxxii, 1–2, 5, 8, 13, 27, 56, 58, 72, 75, 77, 83, 109, 125, 130
Nemea:
  Battle of, 11, 61–6, 78–9, 87, 91, 102–103, 111
  city, 61–3, 110
Neodamodes, 12, 37–8, 77, 80, 137, 142
  see also Oliganthropia

Oliganthropia, 9–15, 131
Orchomenus, 44, 49–50, 77
Oxyrhynchian Historian, xxiii, 48, 68

Pausanias (Spartan king), xxiii, 3, 8–9, 14, 21–2, 28–31, 34, 43–5, 49–52, 55, 60, 77, 113, 131, 139
Pausanias the Regent, 3–4, 11
Peace of Antalcidas, *see* King's Peace
Peiraeum, 110–11, 116–17
Peisander, 56–8, 66, 68, 72–7, 83
Persia:
  civil war, xix, xxii, xxxii, 4–9, 32–7, 41, 68, 107, 123, 129
  diplomacy with Sparta, 4–9, 34–41, 53–5, 56–9, 77–88, 99–101, 103, 125, 130–4, 136, 138–40
  empire, xviii–xxi, xx, xxvi–xxxiii, 4–6, 10–11, 27, 34, 39, 47, 55, 69, 88, 111, 126, 136, 138–40
Persian Wars, xxvi, xxix–xxxiii, 4, 6, 10–2, 27, 47, 55, 69, 88, 111, 126
Peloponnesian League, xvi, xxvi–xxxi, xxxiii, 6, 11, 14, 22, 28–32, 37, 39, 41–2, 44, 48, 60–2, 67, 85, 88, 90, 102, 118, 134–5, 140–2
  see also Symmachy
Peloponnesian War, xvi–xviii, xx–xxiii, xxix–xxxii, 1, 3–6, 9–12, 14, 17–18, 20, 26, 28–34, 41, 45, 48–9, 53, 57, 60, 67, 69–72, 76, 79, 86–7, 91, 98, 106, 112, 117, 122–3, 126, 130, 132, 136, 141–2

Peltast, 106–19, 124–5, 137
  Thracian origins, 106–107
  see also Iphicrates
Perioeci, 11–12, 45, 62, 111, 141
Pharax, 54, 72
Pharnabazus, 5–7, 33–7, 53–5, 57, 59, 72–6, 87–90, 98–9, 102–103, 123, 129
Phocis, 41–4, 49, 58, 82, 105
Phrygia, xxix, 5, 56–7
Phyle Campaign, 27–31, 41, 52–5, 94
  see also Thrasybulus
Piraeus, xxxi, 1, 22, 25, 27–8, 52, 86–7, 105, 113, 118–23, 127–8, 131
Plutarch, xxii–xxiii, 2, 5, 8, 16, 22, 35–9, 43, 51, 58, 73, 76, 80–1, 108–10, 133–4, 138
Plutus, *see* Aristophanes
Praxitas, 105

Rhodes, 41, 48, 53–6, 60, 67–9, 72–4, 109–10, 121–5

Sardis, xxix, 9, 41, 56, 99–100, 103, 121, 129, 131–2, 135
Sicyon, 61–2, 102–14
Sparta:
  class structure, xix–xxi, xxiv, 9–15, 35–6, 38
  decline in citizenship, *see Oliganthropia*
  diplomacy with Athens, *see* Peloponnesian War, Corinthian War *and* Thirty Tyrants
  diplomacy with Persia, 4–9, 34–41, 53–5, 56–9, 77–9, 83–5, 99–101, 103, 125, 130–4, 136, 139–40
  hegemony, xvi, xxvi–xxxi, xxxiii, 6, 11, 14, 22, 28–32, 37, 39, 41–2, 44, 48, 60–2, 67, 85, 88, 90, 102, 118, 134–5, 140–2
  military, xxiv–xxvi, xxix–xxxi, 1–4, 9–15, 17, 20–4, 26, 30–2, 34–46, 49–55, 62–6, 77–83, 109–20, 123–8
  military education, *see Agoge*
  navy, 4, 6, 54, 67–71, 73–7, 109, 171, 125–8, 138–43
  war with Persia, 4–9, 34–41, 77–88, 109–11, 116–28, 131, 133, 135, 138–40
Spartiate, xx, xxv, xxvii, xxxii, 10–13, 35, 38, 55, 60, 62, 77–8, 80, 83, 131, 137, 141

Stasis, xxvii, xxxiii, 10–13, 15, 19, 26, 34, 36, 38, 47–8, 61, 83, 85, 96, 103, 105, 109, 135, 138–9
Struthas, 129
Symmachy, xxviii–xxxi, 6, 14, 29, 37, 41, 44, 46–7, 61, 102, 140
  see also Peloponnesian League

Tegea, xxviii, 45, 49, 52, 61–4, 131
Teleutias, 109–10, 121, 126–8, 131
Thebes:
  diplomacy with Sparta, xvi–xviii, xxix, 14, 22, 26, 29–30, 38, 43–6, 49–52, 58, 62–6, 78–83, 100, 105–106, 110–11, 116, 120, 132–43
  history of, xxiii, xxix–xxx, 39, 46–8
  politics, xxiii, 39, 44–7, 68, 81, 111, 120, 132–43
  see also Boeotia *and* Boeotian Confederacy
Theramenes, 22–6
Thirty Tyrants, 24–30, 34, 37, 45, 55, 90–6, 123, 127

Thrace, 21, 58, 106–107, 124
Thrasybulus, xix, xiii, 26–31, 45, 53, 91, 93–7, 108, 120–4, 129
Thucydides, xvii, xxii, xxvi, xxx, 11, 47, 72
Timocrates of Rhodes, 41, 48, 53, 60
Timolaus, 60
Tiribazus, 99–100, 125, 129–32
Tissaphernes, 5–8, 21, 32, 34–7, 40–1, 54–7, 76, 99, 107, 129
Tithraustes, 41, 54, 68, 99

Xenophon:
  historical writing, xix, xxi–xxiii, xxviii, 10–11, 17, 22–6, 28, 33, 35–7, 40–1, 50–1, 58–9, 62–4, 67, 72–3, 78–80, 83–5, 90, 99, 109, 112–19
  life of, xxi–xxiii, 35–6, 104–106, 109, 123, 126, 131, 133–5
  relationship with Sparta, xix, xxi–xxiii, 3, 13, 35–7, 50, 58, 62, 78–80, 104–106, 131, 135–6